Opposing Viewpoints®

TERRORISM

Other Books of Related Interest in the Opposing Viewpoints Series:

Opposing Viewpoints®

TERRORISM

David L. Bender & Bruno Leone, *Series Editors*

Bonnie Szumski, *Book Editor*

OPPOSING VIEWPOINTS SERIES ®

Greenhaven Press   577 Shoreview Park Road   St. Paul, Minnesota 55126

Library of Congress Cataloging-in-Publication Data

Terrorism: opposing viewpoints.

(Opposing viewpoints series)
Bibliography: p.
Includes index.
1. Terrorism. I. Szumski, Bonnie. II. Series.
HV6431.T485 1986   303.6'25   86-18360
ISBN 0-89908-389-7 (lib. bdg.)
ISBN 0-89908-364-1 (pbk.)

"Congress shall make no law...
abridging the freedom of speech,
or of the press."

First Amendment to the US Constitution

The basic foundation of our democracy is the first amendment guarantee of freedom of expression. The *Opposing Viewpoints Series* is dedicated to the concept of this basic freedom and the idea that it is more important to practice it than to enshrine it.

Contents

        Page

Why Consider Opposing Viewpoints?   9

Introduction   13

Chapter 1: What Is Terrorism?

1. All Political Violence Is Terrorism   16
   Vice President's Task Force on
   Combatting Terrorism

2. All Political Violence Is Not Terrorism   22
   Charles William Maynes

3. Terrorism Is Criminal Activity   26
   David G. Hubbard

4. Terrorism Is International Warfare   33
   Robert H. Kupperman

5. Terrorism Is Murder   39
   Charles Krauthammer

A Critical Thinking Skill: Distinguishing Primary
from Secondary Sources   43

Periodical Bibliography   45

Chapter 2: What Are the Causes of Terrorism?

1. Terrorists Act to Achieve Freedom   47
   Robin Wright

2. Terrorists' Causes Are Lies   51
   Benzion Netanyahu

3. Terrorists Struggle Against Oppressive Governments   58
   Eqbal Ahmad

4. Economics—Not Oppression—Motivates Terrorists   62
   Bill Anderson

5. Media Publicity Causes Terrorism   69
   John O'Sullivan

6. The Media Must Report Terrorism   75
   Katharine Graham

A Critical Thinking Skill: Distinguishing
Bias from Reason   82

Periodical Bibliography   84

Chapter 3: Is Terrorism Justified?

1. Terrorism Is Sometimes Justified   86
   Martin Oppenheimer

2. Terrorism Is Never Justified   90
   William McGurn
3. IRA Terrorism Is Justified   96
   John M. Feehan
4. IRA Terrorism Is Not Justified   105
   Ian Paisley, Nora Bradford, and John Taylor
5. The Palestinian Goal Justifies Terrorism   113
   Abu Nidal
6. Terrorist Goals Do Not Justify Terrorism   119
   Jeane J. Kirkpatrick
A Critical Thinking Skill: Can Terrorist
Acts Be Justified?   123
Periodical Bibliography   126

Chapter 4: Do the Superpowers Sponsor Terrorism?

1. US Support of Terrorists Is Immoral   128
   The Progressive
2. US Support of Terrorists Is Necessary   133
   Geoffrey Kemp
3. US-Sponsored Contras Are Terrorists   137
   Edgar Chamorro
4. US-Sponsored Contras Are Freedom Fighters   142
   *Adolfo Calero, Arturo José Cruz, and
   Alfonso Robelo Callejas*
5. The Soviet Union Sponsors Terrorism   145
   Samuel T. Francis
6. Soviet-Backed Terrorism Is US Propaganda   152
   Edward S. Herman
7. Afghan Rebels Are Freedom Fighters   159
   Jack Wheeler
8. Afghan Rebels Are Terrorists   167
   G. Ustinov
9. Both Superpowers Encourage Terrorism   175
   Henry Steele Commager
A Critical Thinking Skill: Recognizing Statements
That Are Provable   178
Periodical Bibliography   180

Chapter 5: Can Terrorism Be Eliminated?

1. Terrorism Can Be Eliminated   183
   Benjamin Netanyahu
2. Terrorism Cannot Be Eliminated   191
   Brian Michael Jenkins

3. The US Must Retaliate Against Terrorist States 197
      George P. Shultz
4. Retaliatory Attacks Will Not Eliminate Terrorism 204
      George Ball
5. Terrorists Should Be Given Stricter Penalties 209
      Elliot Rothenberg
6. Stricter Penalties Will Not Eliminate Terrorism 215
      William O. Beeman
7. Covert Operations Can Fight Terrorism 218
      Michael Ledeen
8. Covert Operations Are Terrorism 223
      Revolutionary Worker
A Critical Thinking Skill: Distinguishing Between
   Fact and Opinion 229
Periodical Bibliography 231

Book Bibliography 233
Index 236

Why Consider Opposing Viewpoints?

The Importance of Examining Opposing Viewpoints

The purpose of the Opposing Viewpoints Series, and this book in particular, is to present balanced, and often difficult to find, opposing points of view on complex and sensitive issues.

Probably the best way to become informed is to analyze the positions of those who are regarded as experts and well studied on issues. It is important to consider every variety of opinion in an attempt to determine the truth. Opinions from the mainstream of society should be examined. But also important are opinions that are considered radical, reactionary, or minority as well as those stigmatized by some other uncomplimentary label. An important lesson of history is the eventual acceptance of many unpopular and even despised opinions. The ideas of Socrates, Jesus, and Galileo are good examples of this.

Readers will approach this book with their own opinions on the issues debated within it. However, to have a good grasp of one's own viewpoint, it is necessary to understand the arguments of those with whom one disagrees. It can be said that those who do not completely understand their adversary's point of view do not fully understand their own.

A persuasive case for considering opposing viewpoints has been presented by John Stuart Mill in his work *On Liberty*. When examining controversial issues it may be helpful to reflect on this suggestion:

> The only way in which a human being can make some approach to knowing the whole of a subject, is by hearing what can be said about it by persons of every variety of opinion, and studying all modes in which it can be looked at by every character of mind. No wise man ever acquired his wisdom in any mode but this.

Analyzing Sources of Information

The Opposing Viewpoints Series includes diverse materials taken from magazines, journals, books, and newspapers, as well as statements and position papers from a wide range of individuals, organizations and governments. This broad spectrum of sources helps to develop patterns of thinking which are open to the consideration of a variety of opinions.

Pitfalls to Avoid

A pitfall to avoid in considering opposing points of view is that of regarding one's own opinion as being common sense and the most rational stance and the point of view of others as being only opinion and naturally wrong. It may be that another's opinion is correct and one's own is in error.

Another pitfall to avoid is that of closing one's mind to the opinions of those with whom one disagrees. The best way to approach a dialogue is to make one's primary purpose that of understanding the mind and arguments of the other person and not that of enlightening him or her with one's own solutions. More can be learned by listening than speaking.

It is my hope that after reading this book the reader will have a deeper understanding of the issues debated and will appreciate the complexity of even seemingly simple issues on which good and honest people disagree. This awareness is particularly important in a democratic society such as ours where people enter into public debate to determine the common good. Those with whom one disagrees should not necessarily be regarded as enemies, but perhaps simply as people who suggest different paths to a common goal.

Developing Basic Reading and Thinking Skills

In this book, carefully edited opposing viewpoints are purposely placed back to back to create a running debate; each viewpoint is preceded by a short quotation that best expresses the author's main argument. This format instantly plunges the reader into the midst of a controversial issue and greatly aids that reader in mastering the basic skill of recognizing an author's point of view.

A number of basic skills for critical thinking are practiced in the activities that appear throughout the books in the series. Some of the skills are:

Evaluating Sources of Information The ability to choose from among alternative sources the most reliable and accurate source in relation to a given subject.

Separating Fact from Opinion The ability to make the basic distinction between factual statements (those that can be demonstrated or verified empirically) and statements of opinion (those that are beliefs or attitudes that cannot be proved).

Identifying Stereotypes The ability to identify oversimplified, exaggerated descriptions (favorable or unfavorable) about people and insulting statements about racial, religious or national groups, based upon misinformation or lack of information.

Recognizing Ethnocentrism The ability to recognize attitudes or opinions that express the view that one's own race, culture, or group is inherently superior, or those attitudes that judge another culture or group in terms of one's own.

It is important to consider opposing viewpoints and equally important to be able to critically analyze those viewpoints. The activities in this book are designed to help the reader master these thinking skills. Statements are taken from the book's viewpoints and the reader is asked to analyze them. This technique aids the reader in developing skills that not only can be applied to the viewpoints in this book, but also to situations where opinionated spokespersons comment on controversial issues. Although the activities are helpful to the solitary reader, they are most useful when the reader can benefit from the interaction of group discussion.

Using this book and others in the series should help readers develop basic reading and thinking skills. These skills should improve the reader's ability to understand what they read. Readers should be better able to separate fact from opinion, substance from rhetoric and become better consumers of information in our media-centered culture.

This volume of the Opposing Viewpoints Series does not advocate a particular point of view. Quite the contrary! The very nature of the book leaves it to the reader to formulate the opinions he or she finds most suitable. My purpose as publisher is to see that this is made possible by offering a wide range of viewpoints which are fairly presented.

David L. Bender
Publisher

Introduction

"There will always be disaffected, alienated and highly aggressive people claiming that the present state of affairs is intolerable and that only violence will bring about a change."

Walter Laqueur
The Terrorism Reader

While terrorism has occurred throughout history, today it is experiencing a global resurgence. No longer does terrorism affect only small, isolated populations of third world nations. Relatively free and open societies in Western Europe and elsewhere are regularly the victims of terrorist violence. As these seemingly irrational acts reverberate through the international media, and once completely unfamiliar Arab, Greek, and Muslim names and sects become part of everyday vocabulary, several relevant questions arise. What causes these desperate acts? What do they accomplish? Do terrorists act with justification? Are terrorists forced into the role of freedom fighter against intolerable situations, as claimed by members of the Palestine Liberation Organization and the Irish Republican Army? Or are they cowardly, immature, or even crazy, and is their cause empty rhetoric used to disguise a search for power, influence, and public attention?

This debate lies at the center of the terrorism controversy. If terrorist motivations are base ones, or even lunatic, then deterring terrorism by denying terrorists the goals they seek or by exacting retribution against them may be possible. This remains the philosophy of the Israeli government, whose members argue that its policy of swift retaliation against terrorism leaves Israel itself relatively free of it. Israel's controversial method makes no distinction between civilians and terrorists, and confronts the issue of terrorist elusiveness by randomly attacking cities thought to be Palestinian strongholds. President Reagan claimed Israel as his model when he ordered the bombing of terrorist Abu Nidal's headquarters in Libya. Whether or not these methods work remains a matter of opinion.

If, on the other hand, it is more noble motives that inspire the terrorist, then it can be argued that to eliminate terrorism, attention must be paid to its cause. The list of terrorist grievances is large and includes human rights violations such as lack of free speech and religion, enforced imprisonment, torture, and even death. Some, as in the case of the Irish Republican Army, protest foreign intervention. Thus, terrorists believe their actions are directly linked to the possibility of freeing the population they represent. As Stepan, a character from Albert Camus' play *The Just Assassins* explains, "when we kill, we're killing so as to build up a world in which there will be no more killing." This logic probably guided the suicide commandos who, in 1982, drove an explosive-laden truck into the US Marine barracks in Beirut to protest America's involvement in Lebanon.

Whether or not it is possible to respond to all terrorist grievances remains questionable. And whether such responses would eliminate terrorism is also debatable. For example, it seems unlikely that an Israeli agreement to create a Palestinian homeland would erase decades of hatred and political unrest between these two groups. Expert Brian Michael Jenkins even goes so far as to suggest that terrorism may be rooted in the human condition: "We cannot expect to eradicate terrorism, any more than we can expect to end murder."

The debate continues, too, as to terrorism's seriousness. Some individuals believe that the effort that is spent by major governments on the issue is wasted, arguing that terrorism is too insignificant a matter for concern: "Terrorism creates tremendous noise. It will continue to cause destruction and the loss of human life. It will always attract publicity, but politically, it tends to be ineffective. Compared with other dangers out there, it is almost irrelevant," states scholar Walter Laqueur. Yet Secretary of State George Shultz spoke for many others when he announced that terrorism is a "monumental challenge to civilized society."

The broad range of views that are anthologized in *Terrorism: Opposing Viewpoints*, debate many issues. But central to all of them is the question of whether or not terrorist acts are justified. The five topics debated are: What Is Terrorism? What Are the Causes of Terrorism? Is Terrorism Justified? Do the Superpowers Sponsor Terrorism? Can Terrorism Be Eliminated? And while readers examine the conflict over the terrorist's claims and society's needs, the historical persistance of terrorism warns us all that an easy solution will not be found.

What Is
Terrorism?

"Terrorism is. . . . the unlawful use or threat of violence against persons or property to further political or social objectives."

All Political Violence Is Terrorism

The Vice President's Task Force on Combatting Terrorism

The Vice President's Task Force on Combatting Terrorism was comprised of 14 government officials appointed by Vice President George Bush in July 1985. In February 1986 the group issued its final report recommending policies and approaches to counteract terrorism. In the following excerpt, the task force defines terrorism as a serious political threat to the US and emphasizes that all illegal political violence must be actively opposed.

As you read, consider the following questions:

1. What are some common characteristics of terrorists, according to the report?
2. According to the report, what are some of the reasons for state-sponsored terrorism?
3. What do the authors believe to be the purpose of terrorism?

Public Report of the Vice President's Task Force on Combatting Terrorism, released in February 1986.

The basic principles of freedom, justice and concern for human life on which our nation was founded have survived major threats during the course of America's history. Today, we face a unique and pervasive challenge to these ideals in the form of terrorism, an increasingly serious threat to the United States and its friends and allies around the world.

The Nature of Terrorism

Terrorism is a phenomenon that is easier to describe than define. It is the unlawful use or threat of violence against persons or property to further political or social objectives. It is generally intended to intimidate or coerce a government, individuals or groups to modify their behavior or policies.

The terrorist's methods may include hostage-taking, aircraft piracy or sabotage, assassination, threats, hoaxes, indiscriminate bombings or shootings. Yet, most victims of terrorism seldom have a role in either causing or affecting the terrorist's grievances.

Some experts see terrorism as the lower end of the warfare spectrum, a form of low-intensity, unconventional aggression. Others, however, believe that referring to it as war rather than criminal activity lends dignity to terrorists and places their acts in the context of accepted international behavior.

While neither the United States nor the United Nations has adopted official definitions of terrorism, Americans readily recognize the bombing of an embassy, political hostage-taking and most hijackings of an aircraft as terrorist acts. They realize that terrorism needs an audience; that it is propaganda designed to shock and stun them; that it is behavior that is uncivilized and lacks respect for human life. They also believe that terrorism constitutes a growing danger to our system, beliefs and policies worldwide.

Profile of a Terrorist

The motivations of those who engage in terrorism are many and varied, with activities spanning industrial societies to underdeveloped regions. Fully 60 percent of the Third World population is under 20 years of age; half are 15 years or less. These population pressures create a volatile mixture of youthful aspirations that when coupled with economic and political frustrations help form a large pool of potential terrorists. Many terrorists have a deep belief in the justice of their cause. They are tough and vicious and may have little regard for their own lives or those of their victims in attempting to achieve their goals. Others may even be hired assassins.

Terrorists generally get their weapons from a largely unregulated international arms market but also resort at times to illegal methods. They acquire timely information on targets and countermeasures. Lately, they have resorted to unprecedented

17

violent attacks and, when government security efforts against them become more effective, they simply shift to easier targets.

While there are several ways to categorize terrorists, for purposes of this report three main categories are used: self-supported, state-sponsored or aided, and those individuals who may engage in terrorism for limited tactical purposes.

Self-supported terrorists primarily rely on their own initiatives, such as extortion, kidnapping, bank robberies and narcotics trafficking to support their activities.

Defining Terrorism

Terrorism is a tactic, whether used by an established government, a revolutionary group, or an individual. The characterization of an action as "terrorism" depends on *what* is done, not on *who* does it. Terrorism includes threats or acts of violence, ranging from deprivation of basic human rights, to property destruction, physical violence, torture and murder. Terrorist acts are consciously chosen and committed for purposes that go beyond the violence itself. Terrorist acts are usually undertaken for an identifiable political goal, as distinguishd from crimes committed for personal gain or private vengeance or because of mental derangement. The political goals might be to punish or retaliate against an enemy or dissident elements or to destabilize an opposing government or organization.

Friends Committee on National Legislation, *Washington Newsletter,* May 1986.

Terrorists lacking state sponsorship, aid or safehaven tend to be extremely security conscious, keeping their numbers small to avoid penetration efforts.

State-sponsored or aided terrorist groups frequently are larger in numbers, have the advantage of protection by state agencies and are able to access state intelligence resources. Because of this host country-provided safehaven and the compartmented operations of terrorist organizations, it is extremely difficult to penetrate such groups. Moreover, they are subject to limited control by their sponsors and may be expected to carry out attacks for them.

State Support for Terrorism

The reasons for state support and use of such groups are many. Terrorism has become another means of conducting foreign affairs. Such terrorists are agents whose association the state can easily deny. Use of terrorism by the country entails few risks,and constitutes strong-arm, low-budget foreign policy. Growing government assistance in arms, explosives, communications, travel documents, safehaven and training of fanatics are the types of aid that state-supported terrorists receive.

Some individuals or groups may choose to engage in terrorist violence in the context of activities such as national insurgency, especially when they may be losing a conflict, to try to create a special effect, embarrass opposing leadership, or change the pace of events.

The most deadly terrorists continue to operate in and from the Middle East. In 1985 they were involved in roughly 50 percent of the total worldwide terrorist incidents. The two main sources are militant Shi'ites from various Middle Eastern countries, especially Lebanon, supported to varying degrees by Iran or Syria; and radical Palestinian elements, principally offshoots of the Palestine Liberation Organization (PLO), often with direct support from Libya, Syria or Iran. Others, such as independent agents of governments like Libya, also conduct terrorist operations.

Middle East terrorist groups have three main targets: Israel; Western governments and citizens, particularly the United States, France, Italy, and the United Kingdom; and moderate Arab governments and officials, particularly those of Jordan, Egypt, Kuwait and Saudi Arabia.

Many terrorist organizations have continued to operate in Europe during the past decade, including the Italian Red Brigade, French Direct Action, German Red Army Faction and the Provisional Irish Republican Army. The latter has been and remains the most active.

Terrorists Worldwide

Established leftist groups in Spain, Portugal and Greece continue their terrorist campaigns, while a new group has surfaced in Belgium, a country hitherto relatively free from terrorism. Recently, there have been disturbing indications that leftwing terrorists of several nationalities are beginning to cooperate and coordinate their attacks. Of the 812 incidents worldwide in 1985, over 200 took place in Western Europe.

In Latin America, social, economic and political turmoil have prolonged existing patterns of insurgency as well as international and domestic terrorism in several countries, particularly El Salvador, Colombia, Guatemala, Chile and Peru. Nicaragua and Cuba also have been implicated in terrorist activity in the region. During 1985 there were more terrorist incidents (86) directed at U.S. citizens in Latin America than anywhere else.

Certain governments have demonstrated a growing propensity to use, support and exploit terrorism as an instrument of national policy. This trend toward the alignment of interests between certain states and terrorist groups has markedly elevated threat levels worldwide, as state and financial resources have expanded terrorists' capabilities. . . .

During the past decade, terrorists have attacked U.S. officials or installations abroad approximately once every 17 days. In the past 17 years, terrorists have killed as many U.S. diplomats as were killed in the previous 180 years. . . .

Terrorism is political theater designed to undermine or alter governmental authority or behavior. The apparent inability of established governments to respond effectively to incidents affects the confidence of citizens and allies alike. America's foes take comfort in the apparent weaknesses of our society that terrorism exposes.

Our vulnerability lies, ironically, in the strength of our open society and highly sophisticated infrastructure. Transportation, energy, communications, finance, industry, medicine, defense, diplomacy and government itself rely on intricate interrelated networks. Given these inherent vulnerabilities, and the fact that Americans are increasingly the targets of terrorist attacks outside the United States, it is apparent that a potentially serious domestic threat exists. Recent threats such as Qaddafi's statement that Libyans will attack "American citizens in their own streets" only serve to underscore this worsening climate. . . .

Current Policy

The U.S. position on terrorism is unequivocal: firm opposition to terrorism in all its forms and wherever it takes place. Several National Security Decision Directives as well as statements by the President and senior officials confirm this policy:

- The U.S. Government is opposed to domestic and international terrorism and is prepared to act in concert with other nations or unilaterally when necessary to prevent or respond to terrorist acts.
- The U.S. Government considers the practice of terrorism by any person or group a potential threat to its national security and will resist the use of terrorism by all legal means available.
- States that practice terrorism or actively support it will not do so without consequence. If there is evidence that a state is mounting or intends to conduct an act of terrorism against this country, the United States will take measures to protect its citizens, property and interests.
- The U.S. Government will make no concessions to terrorists. It will not pay ransoms, release prisoners, change its policies or agree to other acts that might encourage additional terrorism. At the same time, the United States will use every available resource to gain the safe return of American citizens who are held hostage by terrorists.
- The United States will act in a strong manner against terrorists without surrendering basic freedoms or endangering democratic principles, and encourages other governments to take similar stands.

U.S. policy is based upon the conviction that to give in to terrorists' demands places even more Americans at risk. This no-concessions policy is the best way of ensuring the safety of the greatest number of people. . . .

Alleviating Causes of Terrorism

Terrorism is motivated by a range of real and perceived injustices that span virtually every facet of human activity. The resulting grievances provide the basis for recruitment and the terrorists' justification of violence. A cooperative international effort to mitigate the sources of grievances, such as pursuing the peace process in the Middle East, is an essential yet complicated and long-term objective. The issues are complex, highly emotional and seldom amenable to outside solutions. However, efforts that promote democratic societies with guaranteed personal freedoms continue to be the cornerstone of U.S. foreign policy.

"Individuals and groups have the right to fight, if necessary, for their freedom; and the act of rebellion itself, even against America's friends, is not, [necessarily] terrorism."

All Political Violence Is Not Terrorism

Charles William Maynes

Following the April 1986 US bombing of Libya, many US citizens were upset at the lack of support from Western Europe. In the following viewpoint, Charles William Maynes argues this reaction was not from cowardice or disinterest, but rather because the US definition of terrorism is too broad and insupportable. He believes that the US is taking sides in what are essentially civil wars in the Middle East and Central America and should expect to be attacked for their involvement. Mr. Maynes is the editor of *Foreign Policy* magazine.

As you read, consider the following questions:

1. What is wrong with the US' "sweeping definition of terrorism," according to the author?
2. Does the author support US actions in Lebanon? Why or why not?
3. How does the author believe the US can best fight terrorist states?

Charles William Maynes, "Testing the U.S. Definiton for Terrorism," *Los Angeles Times,* April 20, 1986. Reprinted by permission of the author.

An infuriating aspect of the recent military clash between the United States and Libya was the lack of international support for the U.S. response. Why do foreign governments refuse to support the U.S. position on terrorism?

Perhaps Americans should understand that one reason is the unusual way the United States defines the phenomenon. In February, 1986, for example, the Administration released the report of the Vice President's Task Force on Combatting Terrorism, officially defining terrorism as "the unlawful use or threat of violence against persons or property to further political or social objectives."

Such a sweeping definition enables the Administration to denounce as terrorist such self-proclaimed national liberation movements as the African National Congress, the Irish Republican Army or the Palestine Liberation Organization. In addition, the definition enables the United States to denounce as terrorist all attacks worldwide on American officials, civilian or military.

But its sweeping terms could also be used to brand as terrorists such figures as George Washington, Robert E. Lee, the French Resistance and even those who broke German law trying to assassinate Adolf Hitler during World War II. Obviously, such a definition is untenable.

Legal Remedies Must Be Tried

The traditional American position is that individuals and groups, after legal remedies have been exhausted or denied, have the right to resort to violence in resisting foreign oppression or overthrowing domestic tyranny. And in today's world there is much of both.

To start with the more sensitive cases, blacks in South Africa or, to a lesser extent, the Palestinians on the West Bank and Catholics in Northern Ireland, face intolerable oppression. So do the Shias in Lebanon who are trying to end the domination of their country by a determined Christian minority. So do countries in Eastern Europe that have tried to throw off the Soviet yoke.

The list can be continued. The Afghan and Cambodian resistance movements have the right to try to drive the foreign invader from their country. Those in Nicaragua or El Salvador who find the government an oppressive tyranny also have the right to revolt.

Yet if a group's resort to violence under certain conditions is not *a priori* terrorism, what then constitutes terrorism? The recent bloody American experience in Lebanon may offer an answer.

Reagan's Terrorism

In Lebanon, the Reagan Administration became a participant in a civil war by using the guns of the U.S. battleship New Jersey to support the Christian minority against the Muslim majority. The Muslim response was the devastating car-bomb attack on the

23

Marine barracks, another on the American Embassy and several kidnapings of U.S. civilians.

The United States denounced all these as acts of terrorism. But the car bombing of the Marine barracks was more in the nature of a military counterattack. Even the bombing of the embassy was not clearly an act of terrorism, since the U.S. diplomats in Lebanon were official agents of a government participating in a civil war against the Shias. The seizure of the innocent hostages certainly was an act of terrorism because the American citizens in question had absolutely no connection with U.S. policy. One reason the United States enjoys so little international support for its approach to terrorism is that it defines the problem in ways that force others to take sides in what are in effect civil wars: All acts of violence, including those against military targets, become, in American eyes, terrorist actions. There is, however, one mammoth exception: Attacks against civilians in Afghanistan, Angola, Cambodia or Nicaragua are tolerated on the grounds that the fight involves freedom from communist rule.

Put Terrorism in Perspective

We may or may not choose to deal with how we are viewed and why we are attacked. But we cannot avoid the knowledge that terrorists will win if, through inflated rhetoric, we multiply their role a thousandfold. To be serious about putting terrorism in its place, the President must begin by putting it in perspective.

Robert E. Hunter, *Los Angeles Times*, April 24, 1986.

In the Middle East, the United States, through its strategic consensus agreement with Israel, has become a participant on Israel's side in the war between the Israelis and the Palestinians. The U.S. position is that the Palestinians do not have the right to resort to violence under any circumstances, even if they are permanently denied their political rights on the West Bank.

A US Mistake

The West Europeans are determined to avoid what they regard as a U.S. mistake. No amount of American pressure for Europe to accept the U.S. definition of terrorism will work because the West Europeans have decided that they will not join the United States as a participant on Israel's side. The most the United States can expect is neutrality. The stakes for Western Europe are too high. Effects of the Israeli-Palestinian civil war have already spilled onto European soil. By becoming direct participants in that struggle, West Europeans would simply increase the number of terrorist acts on their territory.

24

Central America presents a different problem for Western Europe: America's double standard leads the Reagan Administration to denounce all attacks against civilians by the IRA or PLO while excusing such attacks by the *contras*. For Europeans this is especially troubling because many terrorist acts by the *contras* have been directed against Europeans working in the area. In February, for example, *contra* forces murdered a Swiss employee of a Catholic charity. Many of the *contra* attacks have singled out European medical technicians in the area.

Concrete Goals

In addition to the conceptual problems posed by the U.S. approach to terrorism, there remains the special case of countries like Iran or Libya, each motivated by forms of religious or political fanaticism. Most political movements employing violence seem to have a concrete goal: a free Afghanistan, a united Ireland, a Palestinian state. The leaders of Iran and Libya employ violence to promote a total religious or political transformation of society. Avoiding participation in their struggle is difficult because they are determined to carry it to other countries.

There are only two solutions in such cases: work to overthrow the government or attempt to isolate the state sufficiently to persuade it to alter its behavior.

In the case of Iran, a policy of isolation has begun to show some success. In June, 1985, Iran played a helpful role in resolving the TWA hijacking crisis in Lebanon; and the following month the Speaker of the Parliament, Hashemi Rafsanjani, called on the United States to take the initiative in resuming relations with Iran. Unfortunately, the Administration's reaction was President Reagan's July, 1985, denunciation of Iran as a terrorist state. . . .

Fighting for Freedom

And for the larger issue of terrorism, perhaps there are some common sense rules: First, individuals and groups have the right to fight, if necessary, for their freedom; and the act of rebellion itself, even against America's friends, is not, *a priori*, terrorism. Second, the existence of this right does not mean outsiders have to support it. Third, acts of violence in a struggle for freedom should be directed against agents of the oppressive government, not against innocent civilians. Fourth, the struggle should be confined to the territory in question. Finally, means should be appropriate to ends.

A sound definition of terrorism does not itself bring sound policy, but it is difficult to have the latter without the former.

"Terrorist acts are . . . very small matters which can be blown up in the imagination to monstrous proportions."

Terrorism Is Criminal Activity

David G. Hubbard

David G. Hubbard began his research into skyjacking while a psychiatric consultant to the Medical Center for Federal Prisoners at Springfield, Missouri. He has interviewed hundreds of skyjackers and other terrorists all over the world. Through the Aberrant Behavior Center, which he founded, he has served as a consultant to the Federal Aviation Administration and the airline industry. He also heads the Behavioral Research Center in Texas and is the director of Icarion, an international network researching physiological causes of behavior. In the following viewpoint, Mr. Hubbard claims terrorism is no more than ordinary crime with a political motive. By defining terrorism as a serious threat, the US and the world give terrorism far too much importance.

As you read, consider the following questions:

1. What reasons does the author give to support his belief that terrorism is not serious?
2. How does Dr. Hubbard's understanding of terrorism differ from other authors in this chapter?
3. How is the US encouraging new acts of terrorism, according to the author?

David G. Hubbard, excerpted from *Winning Back the Sky: A Tactical Analysis of Terrorism.* Dallas, TX: Saybrook Publishing Company, 1986. Reprinted by permission of the author.

Mother: An elephant is frightened by a mouse.
Child: Ho Ho—silly elephant.
Mother: Chicken-Little is scared the sky is falling in.
Child: Ho Ho—silly Chicken-Little.
Mother: The princess is inconvenienced by a pea under thirty-seven mattresses.
Child: Ho Ho—silly sensitive princess.
Media: "An American citizen has been killed by terrorists in a foreign country."
Public: "Oh no, this is terrible. What are we going to do?"

In its reaction to the problem of terrorism, the American public has lately been as timid as the elephant, as foolish as Chicken-Little, and as sensitive as the princess. Terrorist acts are, like the mouse, the acorn, and the pea, very small matters which can be blown up in the imagination to monstrous proportions.

This may sound callous, but it is nevertheless true. The number of deaths caused by terrorism is statistically insignificant; compare it to the death toll from famine in sub-Saharan Africa, or the annual carnage on our own highways. Our problem is not the loss of lives, it is a loss of perspective. The real threat of terrorism is the disruption of our national character and goals, and this is a threat *we pose to ourselves.*

Stampeded by Terrorists

We must not allow ourselves to be stampeded by terrorists, or there will be a high price to pay, in damage to our domestic fabric, our institutions, our programs, and our strategic objectives. We *can* take control of the problem of terrorism, at least in so far as it affects us directly, but only by coming to a clear and balanced understanding of the terrorist and his acts.

The main reason why we do not yet have such an understanding is that the "establishment" has been very reluctant to go to the source of the problem for information. Years ago, when the skyjacking epidemic of the late sixties and early seventies was in full bloom, I was asked to attend a high-level meeting on the subject at the White House. I entered a room dominated by a long table, and saw that only one vacant seat was left.

"Gentlemen," I said, "this empty chair should be occupied by a skyjacker. We will learn about this problem only to the extent that we listen to the skyjackers themselves."

A very, very important man at the table said, "Dr. Hubbard, we are not here to listen to skyjackers; we are here to learn about skyjacking, a very serious matter. You are an expert on skyjacking. Please sit down."

Some time later, when terrorism in Germany was presenting a serious threat to that government, I heard this same response

27

delivered with a different accent. I encouraged the German officials to study the members of the Baader-Meinhof Gang who were being held in prison. "No one can study them," I was told. "They are animals. They spit, they slam doors. They will not talk." Yet when I finally got access to one of them, he was more than willing to tell me his story. . . .

Repugnance and Fear

Unfortunately, official attitudes still have not changed much. Those in charge give many reasons why they will not or cannot listen to terrorists. But beneath these rationalizations, I believe, lies a more fundamental reason: repugnance and fear. The terrorist's attitude calls into question the lifelong habits and values of those whom he attacks. Every terrorist act essentially intends to question those who rule and their right to do so. Terrorists not only consider themselves to be outside the structure of the society they challenge, they have no desire to enter. Such an attitude is predictably threatening to those in power, who are accustomed to dealing with people who want very much to be accepted, successful within the system. This familiar quality in others they can understand and use to get what they want; it is their leverage.

But terrorists refuse to play by our rules. They will not submit to control. They are frightening because they are free of the constraints that most of us take for granted, constraints of order, conformity and morality. Or at least that is how it appears from the outside.

Terrorists Are Bandits

Terrorists, despite their political motivation, can be legally classified as bandits or criminals. Within the law, there is no distinction between a terrorist who seizes hostages for a political end and a kidnapper who holds them for ransom. This is why nations can and do issue arrest warrants for terrorists such as Abu Nidal and Mohammad Abbas.

Stephen V. Cole, *Conservative Digest*, April 1986.

In reality, the world of the terrorist is not at all as we imagine it. The behavior of the terrorist is not merely bizarre and willfully antisocial; it is a reflection of deep-seated personal and cultural pathologies. To see this deeper level, it is necessary to delve into the terrorists' own psychological world. . . .

Today we seem to be faced with a new kind of skyjacker, one who is part of a larger problem: world terrorism. The problem of terrorism has been becoming more clearly defined in the last decade, and it has also become in the last few years more directly threatening to Americans. As a result, we are now awakening to the realization that "something must be done." That "something" is not, however, to break out our massive naval force and pound to fragments any country which we suspect might harbor or support our adversary. . . .

What Is Terrorism?

In a very basic sense, all terrorism can be described as the addition of ideology to ordinary crimes of violence such as murder, theft, kidnapping, extortion and so on. Any person or group willing to commit a crime to back up its political (or religious) position can be terroristic. This includes governments as well as guerrillas. Terrorism can be exerted from above by governments which use policies of terror to subjugate the public, or from below by revolutionaries who use tactics of terror to attack the establishment. Not infrequently, the same people get to exercise both forms of terrorism, first using it to bring down an existing government or win power from a reluctant populace, then forming a new government which continues to use terror against its citizens in order to maintain itself. This is exactly what Hitler did, using the terroristic Brown Shirts to topple the Weimar regime, then creating the SS terror network to maintain the power of the National Socialist government.

Dictators and totalitarian governments, as terrorists from above, arrogate unto themselves a monopoly on the possession of arms and the use of force. When a state owns terrorism, all other violence is taboo, and unrest is ruthlessly suppressed. For this reason, governments which are themselves terroristic are much less vulnerable to terrorism than governments which are not. The Soviet Union is an example of such a government today, one which has organized its use of force over a long period of time and made itself almost immune to internal dissent in the form of violence.

The Soviet Union consolidated its power at a time when there were only a few major players in the game of world politics. Since World War II, however, it has become much more difficult to build that kind of all-powerful state. The proliferation of "emerging nations" that resulted from the postwar collapse of the great colonial empires has complicated the game enormously by creating an influx of new players, many of them amateurs and all fiercely competitive. Terrorism from below has become institutionalized as guerrilla warfare, and revolution has become a constant theme of the Third World. Governments everywhere, good and bad alike, are besieged by terrorism, from Northern Ireland to northern India. And now the Soviet Union, secure in its own borders, has the leisure to export terrorism, through instruction, financial aid, and even, occasionally, military troops. Simultaneously, the United States, because of its alliance with anti-communist governments and counter-revolutionary forces, has become a major target of terrorist activity.

With these changes, the nature of terrorism, and the way we think about it, has also changed. In recent years, the word "terrorism" has taken on a particular meaning, describing apparently random acts of violence, directed unpredictably at *symbolic* rather than *real* targets. The terrorists' aim, as Secretary of State George Shultz observed early in 1985, is "to impose their will by force, a special kind of force designed to create an atmosphere of fear. The terrorists want people to feel helpless and defenseless." And so they place a bomb in a crowded London department store or kidnap a university professor in Beirut or gun down Marines eating dinner in El Salvador. Since the victims are victims not because of anything they personally have done, but just because of their associations, or even just their location at the moment of the crime, everyone can identify with their fate. The fear-inspiring question is "Will it be me next time?"

Cutting Terrorists Down to Size

It doesn't profit us to forget, as we contemplate the villains who commit terrorist acts, that we are looking at only one side of the coin. . . .

By seeing these men as evil, as satanic, we give them far more power than is due them. . . .

We would serve our own interests by cutting these men back down to size. They are not villains but deluded, inept would-be heroes, who cannot be important unless we make them so.

David Hubbard, *Winning Back the Sky*, 1986.

Americans find it very difficult to understand the "logic" of this kind of terrorism because it comes from a way of thinking which is much older than the one we usually employ. Terrorism is a course of action which reflects an eighth-century rather than a twentieth-century mind; the attitudes of terrorists are converted to dramatic acts which express that archaic state of mind. This way of thinking might be called "symbolic transference"; the hatred that is felt for an enemy—say, Israel—is transferred to anything which symbolizes the hated quality of the enemy—for example, an American jetliner. Airplanes are nothing more than a means of transportation, to the contemporary mind. But to the powerful symbolic imagination, they may be emblems of the hated West, of slavery in the colonial past, of the destruction of treasured values by encroaching modernization. America, moreover, is the friend of Israel, and in eighth-century terms, "the friend of my enemy is my enemy."

Of course, more sophisticated arguments can be made from the terrorist's point of view. The individual or group may see themselves as having the right, when strong political beliefs and goals are involved, to unilaterally declare "war" on the enemy, and make all its citizens and property subject to acts of war. From this perspective, all the lives and belongings of the enemy "should" be fair game for the terrorist, just as London was for German bombers, or Dresden for the Allies. But underlying this rationale is a way of thinking about the world which differs substantially from the modern outlook of the Western world, a way of thinking which casts good and evil in stark contrast and gives "good" the absolute right to attack *whatever* is not clearly identified as "good."

An example of this sort of thinking can be found in the act of a Black Muslim in Washington, D.C., in the seventies. Suffering the loss of his wife and children, who had been killed by a different sect of the organization to which he belonged, he drew up a mighty—but unclear—plan for revenge, and gathered a number of his fellow Black Muslims into action. He and the others, armed with firearms of all sorts, and scimitars, the great curved Arab swords, occupied three public buildings: the City Hall, the B'nai B'rith building, and the Islamic Center. Whom did he mean to threaten—or punish—with such a strange collection of hostages? The killers of his loved ones must be punished, he said, but the "punishment" was actually visited not on the real killers, but on strangers who symbolized the evil he sought to destroy. The one person killed in the occupation was a black news reporter.

Pre-Civilized View of the World

No matter what theories of political activity terrorists may construct for themselves, they all proceed from this same deep base of associative thinking and polarized attitudes—in short, a pre-civilized approach to the world. In attempting to understand the terrorist and his acts, we must accept this psychological premise, and stop looking for rational interpretations and reasonable responses. We have to look behind the revolutionary rhetoric to the primitive urges and images from which terrorist activity springs.

The basic brew of international terrorism has been bubbling for a long time, but recently a new element has been added, and just as a nidus dropped into a super-saturated solution precipitates an impressive array of crystals, this new element has created new organizations of terror. The element is, of course, Islamic fundamentalism. Religious zeal has often been associated with terrorism (witness the Inquisition), especially where the separation of church and state is weak or nonexistent. Islam, then, where religion and politics are closely aligned, is a perfect breeding ground for terrorism. The accumulated tensions of the Middle

East, where the structures of the colonial past have been rapidly—and violently—disintegrating since 1948, when the British abandoned the protectorate of Palestine, create an atmosphere in which the escalation of terrorist activity is almost inevitable. . . .

Feeding Off Fear

Terrorism feeds off the fear it creates, and the media can amplify this fearfulness far beyond what a few men with a gun or a bomb could hope to create without such massive free publicity. Flight 847, perhaps the most extravagantly covered incident in the history of skyjacking (as of this writing), may represent a new phase in the evolution of aviation-related crime. By focusing our fears of terrorism on the hijacking of an aircraft, through the magnifying lens of the media, we may be in the process of giving new impetus to skyjacking, encouraging even bigger spectacles in the future.

"The United States must recognize the recent escalation of. . . violence from the level of a criminal act or political nuisance to a matter deserving serious international attention."*

Terrorism Is International Warfare

Robert H. Kupperman

Robert H. Kupperman is executive director of the Science and Technology Committee at the Center for Strategic and International Studies at Georgetown University in Washington DC. He was head of the 1980-81 transition team for the Federal Emergency Management Agency and has been Chief Scientist at the US Arms Control and Disarmament Agency as well as chairman of the agency's committee on government-wide studies of US counter-terrorism policies and objectives. In the following viewpoint, Mr. Kupperman argues that, far from over-reacting to the nature of terrorism, the US is under-reacting. He believes that terrorism has become a method of international warfare, and its ultimate aim is to bring down the democracies of the US and Western Europe.

As you read, consider the following questions:

1. What does the author believe are the advantages of terrorism?
2. Where do terrorist groups receive their support, according to the author?

Robert H. Kupperman, "Terrorism and Public Policy: Domestic Impacts, International Threats," in *American Violence & Public Policy*, ed. by Lynn A. Curtis. New Haven, CT: Yale University Press, 1985. Reprinted by permission of Yale University Press.

Terrorism is one aspect of political violence. Usually, terrorists belong to quasi-independent groups, which are at times manipulated by Libya and other rogue governments. These organizations create incidents intended to destabilize democratic governments and to perpetuate their ideological goals by exploiting the electronic and written media. There can be no sharp distinction between terrorism and related political violence. It is axiomatic that virtually all governments either commit or commission acts of violence in pursuit of political goals. Thus, for example, the Bulgarians and the Soviets have been accused of having arranged the assassination attempt against the pope and the Central Intelligence Agency is alleged to have sought the assassination of Fidel Castro. . . .

International terrorism is a new class of violence, beyond the norms of common criminality, that exploits today's advanced technologies, especially jet transport and instant global communications. Regrettably, it is becoming established as a worldwide steady state phenomenon.

Although the United States has not so far been a primary target of attack, any optimism that this benign state of affairs will continue is misplaced. Terrorism has, among other things, become part of the arsenal of international warfare, recognized as a useful tool of low-intensity conflict. As a surrogate means of warfare, terrorism also becomes a tool of strategic importance. We must recognize the promotion of such violence from the level of a criminal act or political nuisance to a matter deserving serious national attention.

Terrorist Acts a Daily Occurrence

Hardly a day passes without a terrorist incident occurring somewhere in the world. It pervades the fabric of contemporary civilization. But the significance of the terror act has been raised exponentially by several different but interrelated factors. First, the tools available for destruction are suddenly much more lethal and much more frightening than ever before. Second, the media attention focused on terrorism is immediate, global, and usually undisciplined. Third, motives for terrorist attack today span a spectrum that includes, at the extremes, personal grudges and superpower ambitions of global hegemony—and there is little certainty as to which underlying motive may really be at play in any particular case. . . .

The Threat to America

Although the U.S. government has not so far been a primary target of international terrorists, both threats and actions have been directed at it from time to time. Take a recent year, like 1982. Puerto Rican Nationalists carried out killings on their island and a spectacular bombing on Wall Street in New York. Trials of IRA members on charges of arms smuggling were underway. Harassment of foreign national students on American campuses by both Libyan and Iranian groups continued. And domestic terrorists continued bombings of commercial facilities, particularly in California. In addition, of course, Americans and American facilities abroad continued to be prime targets for international terrorists. Finally, the Tylenol poisoning case, while not itself inspired by any terrorist group, was a fearsome reminder of the type of media-magnified "terror theater" that could all too easily occur here. . . .

Terrorism as a Strategic Tool

The cause for concern is very real. America itself and American interests abroad are already direct targets of occasional actions. The future seems to promise more frequent and more serious acts. As the age of great power dominance is replaced by more open patterns of international relations, the traditional mechanisms of restraint are likely to become decreasingly effective. We should expect that the very diversity of actors on the world stage—each pursuing his own interests—will enhance the attractiveness of unconventional means of conflict. For the relatively weak, the high-level/low-cost factor is essential because they cannot afford to compete militarily or economically. For the more powerful, the high-leverage/low-risk element is decisive since the costs of large-scale conventional or even nuclear confrontations are unacceptable.

Terrorism Is War

It would be a mistake for us and our allies to view terrorism any differently from its perpetrators: Terrorism is a form of war. . . .

If we do nothing, the result will be more murders, more hostages, more tragedy. If the day comes when Western nations watch the cold-blooded murder of their citizens and fail to act for fear of more terrorism, the terrorists will have won. The future of the world, at that point, would be one of intimidation and violence; there could be no hope for stability and peace.

John K. Singlaub, *USA Today*, April 23, 1986.

International terrorism may become one of the dominant tools of unconventional warfare. Used as a strategic weapon, the vectored terrorist threat offers certain unique advantages in pursuit of foreign policy objectives. Although unimpressive in firepower, it is profound in leverage. Too, the initial uncertainty about the origin of attack often limits the full range of diplomatic and military response. And for the Soviet Union, its proxies, and certain radical national and subnational groups already on the terrorist scene, terrorism may offer an irresistibly low-cost/low-risk means of engaging America in low-intensity conflict.

The recent Libyan death threats against the U.S. president and the attacks against high-ranking NATO officials highlight the use of terrorism as a strategic instrument of policy influence as well as a tactical tool of social disruption. Whether or not a Libyan hit team actually existed is irrelevant; the threat itself forced the president to retreat into a "steel cocoon" and seemed to paralyze the American government. The dramatic and overplayed media coverage made the incident appear almost a self-inflicted act of terror with Colonel Kadaffi as the catalyst.

Incidents such as this and the kidnapping of General James Dozier raise the possibility of ever stronger leverage, an even broader scope for terrorist attacks. Increasingly, terrorism has become a strategic tactic, whether employed by neonihilistic or subnational groups or by nation-states.

These incidents also make clear that America is not immune to the terror event, either at home or abroad. If the usually random act of violence can paralyze a government, the strategically directed terrorist attack is potentially devastating. The United States appears unready to cope effectively with either tactically or strategically inspired terrorism, and that very unreadiness invites attack. In the immediate future, America can expect to join its European allies as a victim of major terrorist acts, playing the unwilling costar in a media event that undermines the government's credibility internationally and weakens it in the eyes of the domestic electorate. Unless the United States learns to deal at home and abroad with the phenomenology of terrorism in the longer term, it should expect to see its substantive strength sharply reduced as terrorism replaces conventional hostilities in the international allocation of power.

Terrorists as Surrogates

The new class of "violence manipulators" we can expect to see grow in importance over the next few years includes: subnational terrorist groups, harbored willingly or unwillingly by various states, which seek to disrupt Western societies; Third World countries willing to exploit the tools of terrorism directly for their own ends; and larger powers, which desire to manipulate international events without running the risks of formal military confrontation.

Terrorist groups are known to receive substantial financial and military support from cooperative governments. There are, of course, many ways a government may support terrorist activities, ranging from the apparently passive provision of safe haven or use of air space to actively promoting and supporting terrorists with money, arms, or training. The list of nations that are now

36

WW III

Reprinted with permission.

or have recently been involved in supporting terrorism includes Libya, Cuba, the Soviet Union, China, North Korea, Algeria, the People's Democratic Republic of Yemen (Aden), Tanzania, Congo, Zaire, Egypt, Syria, Iraq, and Lebanon.

Among the most active has been Libya, which supported and continues to support a wide range of nationalist groups of various ideologies. Much of this backing has been covert, but in the summer of 1972, Colonel Muammar Kaddafi, Libya's dictator, began openly to boast of his contributions to world terrorism. He added that he would be happy to supply weapons to American blacks, "Unfurling in the United States the banner of the struggle against American racism." . . .

Finding a Smoking Gun

While there is incontrovertible evidence of Soviet support in training and equipment, the administration has not produced an actual "smoking gun'—direct control of terrorist's policy or actions. Terrorism, on the whole, is too complex an issue to be easily explained away as an example of Soviet interventionism. Even if the Soviet Union withdrew all patronage, terrorist activity would certainly continue, perhaps unabated. Terror has other independent patrons, currently the most prominent being Libya. . . .

Moreover, subnational terrorist groups have matured into self-sustaining organisms; there is no organic need for a master conspiracy. Terrorist organizations are not mirror images of each other, even when there is a broad intersection of interest. Each group learns from the experience of others, its tactics evolving in response to governmental countermeasures and in the spotlight of media publicity. Hence, a loose confederacy of terrorist groups operates quite successfully without the limits that centralization would impose.

Contemporary terrorism offers its proponents few grand visions of a better world. Increasingly, it has become a strategic tactic, whether employed by neonihilistic subnational groups or by nation-states. As a result, the days in which terrorism was confined to isolated instances of social disruption are over. The destabilized international system provides the opportunity for profound disruption while the vulnerability of the West, in terms of its unprotected technical and democratic political infra-structure, offers a tempting avenue of attack not only for subnational terrorists groups but even for nations like Iran, Libya, or the Soviet Union that might choose to use them as "plausibly deniable" surrogate forces. . . .

The United States must recognize the recent escalation of such violence from the level of a criminal act or political nuisance to a matter deserving serious international attention. More and more governments including the United States have become increasingly impatient with terrorist threats and acts. But if the United States cannot, out of indecision, or will not, out of ignorance, act now to meet future challenges, the costs in the decades to come could well be paid in the currency of national humiliation and social disintegration. Time is running out, but the question is for whom—the terrorist or the government?

"By now, the grievance . . . is known, and murder becomes simply murder."

Terrorism Is Murder

Charles Krauthammer

In December 1984, fanatical members of Iran's Islamic Shiite sect hijacked an Arabian airliner to Tehran. Once in Tehran, the terrorists killed two passengers and tortured many more. Using this incident as a stepping-stone to discuss terrorism in general, Charles Krauthammer argues that terrorism has become violent and meaningless. People are no longer sympathetic to the cause behind such acts, he argues, and terrorism has become unadorned murder. A senior editor for *The New Republic*, Dr. Krauthammer holds an M.D. in psychiatrics from Harvard and was Commonwealth Scholar in politics at Oxford University in England.

As you read, consider the following questions:

1. In what way does the author say the Tehran hijacking has changed people's attitudes toward terrorism?
2. Why are Americans no longer sympathetic toward terrorists, according to the author?
3. Does the author believe terrorism will continue?

Charles Krauthammer, "It's Simply Murder," *The Washington Post National Weekly Edition*, December 31, 1984. © 1984, Washington Post Writers Group, reprinted with permission.

The hijacking . . . of a Kuwaiti airliner to Tehran, marks an end of sorts for terrorism. Not an end of terrorist acts. These will continue so long as they can be carried out with little jeopardy to the terrorists or with marked effect on the victim.

Shiite terror has done well on both counts. Tehran set free earlier hijackers, and the latest batch emerged remarkably unhurt from the "storming" of their plane. And . . . it took only two suicidal fanatics to persuade the United States and France to quit Lebanon. . . .

Terrorism this successful will continue. The most recent drama marks a different end, an end of the idea of terrorism in the Western mind, where it has enjoyed a long and pampered history.

After Tehran, it is perhaps hard to remember this earlier romance. But it existed, in two forms. One celebrated the act itself. Jean Paul Sartre, for example, writing in defense of National Liberation Front terror during the Algerian War, said that "to shoot down a European is to kill two birds with one stone, to destroy an oppressor and the man he oppresses at the same time: there remains a dead man and a free man." Any European—like any American today, . . . would do. Authenticity has its demands.

A Morally Stupid Idea

Few, however, were so tough-minded. To celebrate political murder as in itself an act of liberation was, to paraphrase George Orwell, an idea so morally stupid that only the greatest of intellectuals could believe it. Hence the other, more modest school of apologist: it did not exalt terror, it merely excused it. The method was to look beyond the dead body of the victim to the "root causes"—oppression, desperation, frustration—that drove the killer. That sympathy, bred of an excess of understanding, was most evident in widespread toleration of Vietcong, Irish Republican Army and Palestine Liberation Organization atrocities, among others.

After the Kuwaiti hijacking, that kind of thinking [is] difficult to sustain. Barbarism so raw and unadorned is immune to romanticizing. The Tehran incident provided an anatomy of terrorism as graphic as, say, *The Gulag Archipelago's* exposition of the soul of Soviet communism. The idea of communism in the Western mind has not survived Solzhenitsyn's demonstration. Nor can the idea of terrorism survive the torture/murders at Tehran's airport.

No Interest in the Cause

Of course, Sartrean idealization of the terrorist *act* was rare anyway. The more important result of the Tehran drama is the death of any lingering interest in the *cause*. Press coverage of the hijacking was remarkable in that respect. The press did explain the demand for release of terrorists who had previously blown up American, French and Kuwaiti installations. But there was no great inclination to follow the chain of causes much further.

Why? For one thing, the chain does not lead very far. The grievance of Shiite terrorists is the existence of heresy, a broad complaint. They are at war with so much (secularism, the West, modernity itself) and so fanatically that they represent nothing more than Islamic nihilism. And nihilism is not a very attractive, let alone illuminating, explanatory principle.

State-Sponsored Murder

Second, state sponsorship, the dominant feature of terrorism in the '80s, has removed much of the glamor. In the '30s communist revolutionaries lost their sheen when they gradually became instruments of Soviet *Realpolitik*. Libyan assassins, . . . and Shiite bombers are driven not by root causes but by reasons of state. State sponsorship turns romantic heroes . . . into spies, mercenaries and ordinary hit men . . . . State-sponsored murder resembles nothing so much as organized crime.

"..AND FOUR MORE AMERICANS, INCLUDING A MOTHER, HER DAUGHTER, AND EIGHT-MONTH-OLD GRANDDAUGHTER!..."

Gary Brookins, *Richmond Times-Dispatch*. Reprinted with permission.

But perhaps the most important reason we no longer seek empathic understanding of terrorists is that horror has its limits. A weariness has set in. Terrorists have gone to the well of Western sympathy once too often. Murder as a form of advertising works once, perhaps twice. The audience tires on repetition. By now, the grievance, if any, is known, and murder becomes simply murder.

It is hard to imagine that anyone would write today, as Diane Johnson (characterizing a theme of a Dom Delilo novel) wrote in 1977: "Terrorist action is not so much an act of lawlessness as a comment on the rules." After Khomeini, we have come to prefer our commentaries written in something other than blood. We have even grown to like the rules, like the ones against torture. Terrorist's esthetics are no longer interesting.

Terrorism will no doubt continue. But now it will have to do so on its own, without apology, without extenuation, without even curiosity from the West.

Distinguishing Primary from Secondary Sources

A critical thinker must always question sources of information. Historians, for example, usually distinguish between *primary sources* (a firsthand or eyewitness account from personal letters, documents, or speeches, etc.) and *secondary sources* (a "secondhand" account usually based upon a "firsthand" account and possibly appearing in newspapers, encyclopedias, or other similar types of publications).

A man's explanation of how he placed a bomb near a cash register in a department store is one example of a primary source. A television report on the increase of terrorism in the US which includes excerpts from this account would be an example of a secondary source.

It must be noted that interpretation and/or point of view also plays a role when dealing with primary and secondary sources. For example, the television reporter will use only those parts of the primary account which fit her story and may also interpret the incident. The primary source must be questioned as to interpretation or underlying motive as well. The bomb carrier may try to downplay the violence of his actions or claim that he was not really responsible.

This activity is designed to test your skill in evaluating sources of information. Pretend that your teacher tells you to write a research report on what motivates terrorists. You decide to include an equal number of primary and secondary sources. Listed below are a number of sources which may be useful in your research. Carefully evaluate each of them. Then, *place a P next to those descriptions you believe are primary sources*. Second, *rank the primary sources* assigning the number (1) to what appears to be the most objective and accurate primary source, the number (2) to the next most objective, and so on until the ranking is finished. *Repeat the entire procedure, this time placing an S next to those descriptions you feel would serve as secondary sources and then ranking them.*

If you are doing this activity as a member of a class or group, discuss and compare your evaluation with other members of the group. If you are reading this book alone you may want to ask others if they agree with your evaluation. Either way, you will find the interaction valuable.

_____ 1. An interview with a recently released hostage about how she was treated while captive. _____

_____ 2. A review of terrorist activities in the last year in *Time* magazine. _____

_____ 3. A newspaper article titled "Why Terrorism Against the West Is Wrong." _____

_____ 4. A speech by a terrorist leader explaining his methods and motive. _____

_____ 5. A translation of Islamic holy writings which some terrorists claim to be their inspiration. _____

_____ 6. A movie called *Rebel, Rebel* about a Palestinian boy fighting poverty and prejudice in Israel. _____

_____ 7. A speech by a US general in which he explains how easily terrorist actions could be stopped by relentless military force. _____

_____ 8. The testimony of a captured terrorist in an international court. _____

_____ 9. A textbook which includes many opinionated articles about different aspects of terrorism. _____

_____ 10. An interview with a man crippled by a bomb in a commuter train. _____

_____ 11. A history of Ireland which concentrates on clashes between English and Irish nationalists in the twentieth century. _____

_____ 12. A videotape of a hostage in which he explains his captors' demands. _____

_____ 13. Photographs of a police car bombed in Belfast. _____

_____ 14. A book called *The Terrorist Handbook* found in a terrorist's belongings. _____

_____ 15. A speech by a Northern Irish member of Parliament describing the damage done to his house by IRA terrorists. _____

Periodical Bibliography

The following list of periodical articles deals with the subject matter of this chapter.

March Bell	"The New Warfare," *Eternity*, September 1985.
Wayne Biddle	"It Must Be Simple and Reliable," *Discover*, June 1986.
Thomas L. Friedman	"State-Sponsored Terror Called a Threat to US," *The New York Times*, December 30, 1983.
Brian Michael Jenkins	"The Future Course of International Terrorism," *The Rand Paper Series*, September 1985.
Charles Krauthammer	"The New Terrorism," *The New Republic*, August 13 & 20, 1984.
Flora Lewis	"Definition of Terrorism," *The New York Times*, March 30, 1986.
Charles William Maynes	"U.S. Policy on Terrorism Is Confusion," *Los Angeles Times*, January 5, 1986.
William McGurn	"Terrorism Can Be Defined," *Wall Street Journal*, June 20, 1986.
John McLaughlin	"Superpower Impotence," *National Review*, July 26, 1985.
Robert B. Oakley	"Terrorism: Overview and Developments," *Department of State Bulletin*, November 1985.
George Shultz	"Secretary's Interview on 'Meet the Press,'" *Department of State Bulletin*, January 1986.
Conor Cruise O'Brien	"Thinking About Terrorism," *The Atlantic*, June 1986.
U.S. News & World Report	"Mideast Terror Strikes Americans," June 24, 1985.

What Are the Causes of Terrorism?

TERRORISM

"[Terrorist] attacks [are] not from love of violence, but from expressions of rage and frustration over an inability to achieve some form of freedom or independence."

Terrorists Act to Achieve Freedom

Robin Wright

Robin Wright is the author of *Sacred Rage: The Wrath of Militant Islam*. In the following viewpoint, Ms. Wright argues that the US has a history of reacting to each individual act of terrorism. Instead, it should attempt to pursue and correct terrorism's cause—a frustrating lack of political and personal freedom for people in many countries. Terrorists are not bloodthirsty murderers, she argues, but people motivated by dreams of freedom and independence, not unlike America's founders.

As you read, consider the following questions:

1. Why does the author believe that government security measures taken against terrorists will not work?
2. What does the author think the US must do to end Middle East terrorism?
3. The author believes that terrorism has definite, correctable causes. Do you agree?

Robin Wright, "Address the Causes, Not Just the Effects," *Los Angeles Times*, October 20, 1985. Reprinted by permission of the author.

In 1957, a young American senator said, "The most powerful single force in the world today is neither communism nor capitalism, neither the H-bomb nor the guided missile. It is man's eternal desire to be free and independent."

The senator might have been predicting the recent wave of terrorism, for his remark explains much about the motives behind the hijacking of the *Achille Lauro* [a Greek pleasure boat]. It also applies to the deaths of almost 300 Americans in suicide bombings over the last three years at a Marine compound and at embassies in Lebanon and Kuwait, and the kidnapings of nine Americans, six of whom are still held hostage.

In each case, the attacks were not from love of violence, but from expressions of rage and frustration over an inability to achieve some form of freedom or independence.

The Rev. Benjamin M. Weir, freed in September [1985] after being held hostage for 14 months by Shia extremists in Lebanon, said, "I shy away from the word 'terrorist,' a loaded term that tends to set up opposites. Actions of governments, including my own, can sometimes be classified as terrorism as terrible as that of individuals." Or, as an adage goes, "One man's terrorist is another man's freedom fighter."

America May Be Terrorist Target

In an age of nuclear weaponry, terrorism has become the idiom of expression among the weak and desperate in confronting superpowers they feel are not listening. That does not mean terrorism should be condoned; but it does mean the reasons behind it must be understood—or the violence will only escalate. Indeed, experts now predict that terrorism, once limited largely to foreign shores, may soon target American officials and installations at home.

The dramatic midair interception of the four hijackers gives cause to celebrate, but only temporarily. Nabbing a mugger does not eliminate the motives behind street crime. The problem goes deeper.

Rather than being obsessed by the mechanics and personalities—the hows and whos—of terrorism, the United States must focus on the whys.

So far, the United States has been unrealistic in dealing with the complexity of terrorism. Spending $3.3 billion for the biggest embassy-rebuilding program in U.S. history to improve security at 139 diplomatic posts will not end the threat. Nor will warning Americans against using international airports with lax security. And offering $500,000 to individual informers is unlikely to tempt the committed opponent.

Nor will retaliation work. As the Israelis discovered in south Lebanon, the eye-for-an-eye approach can backfire disastrously. During Israel's three-year occupation, more than 600 soldiers died.

Indeed, the use of force—either in retaliation or to preempt future attacks—only escalates the cycle of violence, providing new motives for expression of rage, raising the timbre and stakes.

Shlomo Gazit, a former chief of Israeli military intelligence, states, "There is no technical-military solution to the problem of terrorism. There is only a political solution."

During its 40 years as a superpower, the United States has usually dealt only with effects of specific incidents. It is time for Washington to stand back from the passion and fury that follows each incident and begin looking at the roots of violent opposition.

Terrorists Are Victims

Blowing up a lot of innocent people just to prove that we won't "give in to terrorists" will mean nothing to people who feel so brutalized that they will run a suicidal mission against a Marine barracks or an American embassy. . . .

A hard-nosed raid that sacrifices innocent lives only provokes more terrorism, more suicidal attacks by those who have become increasingly irrational in their enmity toward Israel, the United States, the British, an overweening Soviet Union or the long-dominant oligarchs in Central America.

We are never going to stop terrorism, in Northern Ireland, Central America, the Middle East or any other troubled area. We can increase the anguish, the dying, by glandular lapses into an escalation of the violence, or we can reduce it by sticking with tedious efforts to fashion peace and do justice to those who feel abused and trampled upon.

Carl T. Rowan, *Los Angeles Times*, October 11, 1985.

Policy-makers could start by not lumping incidents together as if a monolithic anti-American force were at work; that is as errantly simplistic as Iran calling the United States "the Great Satan" and condemning everything American. Somehow the capture of the *Achille Lauro* hijackers is now being perceived as partial compensation for the impotence felt during the 17-day trauma of TWA 847. In fact, the two are unrelated.

Two Strains of Terrorism

Two strains of terrorism, with separate goals and different tactics, emanate from the Middle East today.

The first involves the kind of Palestinians who hijacked the *Achille Lauro*. Their cause is a homeland. Their terrorism is designed to frighten or pressure Israel and its ally, the United States, into recognizing them and what they feel are their rights.

The second involves Islamic militants, particularly Shia Muslims, who are responsible for . . . the suicide bombings and

49

the abductions of Americans in Lebanon. Their terrorism is aimed at eliminating what they say is foreign domination and encroachment on every aspect of their lives, particularly by the United States, over the last 40 years.

Within both movements are many branches, each with specific, often different, flash points. Ironically, the two broad groups have been at odds, particularly in Lebanon, where fighting between Shias and Palestinians has killed hundreds.

The danger for the United States, however, is that these two disparate forces will some day act in unison, intentionally or indirectly, as a result of anti-American fervor, unleashing a force so potent that costly and humiliating attacks so far will seem small by comparison. . . .

Diminishing Terrorism

To end or at least diminish terrorism from the Middle East, the only lasting solution lies in tackling, with urgency, the two basic problems in that volatile region.

First, the United States needs, finally, to get the Arabs and Israelis to the peace table—without being waylaid by rhetoric or the often-violent advance posturing. Before the spate of recent incidents—the murder of three Israelis by Palestinians in Cyprus, the Israeli air strike on PLO headquarters that killed 60 and the piracy—the United States and Jordan's King Hussein appeared to be making progress. Attempts to end a 37-year dispute should not be aborted because of the heat of the moment.

Second, the United States and its Western allies need to begin defusing the tension with Islamic militants who say they have been increasingly overwhelmed and manipulated by the West since Napoleon Bonaparte conquered Egypt almost 200 years ago.

Neither act involves "conceding" to terrorism, but rather emphasizes constructive rather than destructive policies.

And neither will be done easily, quickly, or, probably, without further bloodshed. But the United States needs to take the initiative in rooting out causes of terrorism rather than simply reacting to attacks. The United States has the resources and the power; it lacks only the confidence and determination.

The same senator who spoke of freedom and independence, John F. Kennedy, told the United Nations after he was elected President, "If we can all persevere, if we can in every land and office look beyond our own shores and ambitions, then surely the age will dawn in which the strong are just, and the weak secure and the peace preserved."

"Far from being a bearer of freedom, the terrorist is the carrier of oppression and enslavement."

Terrorists' Causes Are Lies

Benzion Netanyahu

Benzion Netanyahu is professor emeritus of Judaic Studies at Cornell University. He was the founding editor of *World History of the Jewish People* and founding chairman of the Jonathan Institute, an independent terrorism research organization. In the following viewpoint, Mr. Netanyahu argues that terrorist causes are pretense, designed to delude and gain sympathy from a naive public. Terrorists do not fight for freedom, but fight to instill their own form of despotism.

As you read, consider the following questions:

1. What tactics does the author say terrorists use that freedom fighters would never use?
2. What examples does the author give to show that governments deposed by terrorists do not result in free societies? Do these seem like credible examples?
3. What does the author think is wrong in the public's attitude toward terrorism?

Excerpts from "Terrorists and Freedom Fighters," by Benzion Netanyahu from *Terrorism: How the West Can Win* edited by Benjamin Netanyahu. Copyright © 1986 by The Jonathan Institute. Reprinted by permission of Farrar, Straus, Giroux, Inc.

Any attempt to address the problem of terrorism entails a grave responsibility. For in discussing terrorism, we seek to determine the stand we should take in a hard and crucial struggle which touches not only on our current security but also on the worth of our future lives. Indeed, as I see it, what is involved is nothing less than the survival of free society itself.

Several years ago, few in the West realized all the implications of terrorism. Now there are many in the free societies who recognize its essence and what it entails. Today we see leaders of the free world, especially the leading statesmen of America, approaching the front lines of this battle and seeking ways to put a halt to the blight. This is certainly a heartening development whose importance cannot be overestimated.

At the same time, however, we see leaders in the West, and many in the press and the public at large, who are still hesitant about the stand they should take toward terrorism and those who fight it. Still others believe that the proper course to follow is one of political accommodation with the terrorists, though admittedly they are not at all sure that such an accommodation is feasible.

A United Front Is Necessary

Both these attitudes are extremely harmful, since both prevent the West from closing ranks and forming a common and united front, which alone can cope with the terrorist menace. We certainly would like the doubters and accommodationists to join the advocates of active resistance. But before we can expect to convince them to do so, we must comprehend the motives and arguments of those who refuse to take a clear stand against terrorism, let alone meet it head-on.

Some maintain that this position derives from the immediate advantages, political or economic, which the statesmen concerned hope to reap for their countries from a compromise with the terrorists. That such considerations play a part in this matter is indeed hard to deny; yet it is equally hard to conceive that they alone determine such attitudes. It is not easy to assume that Western statesmen, whose patriotism must be held above question, would agree to ignore long-term dangers in exchange for short-term gains. It is more likely that the indecision of some statesmen, and the readiness of others to bend toward the terrorists, stems partly from confusion about the true nature of terrorism, and partly from a belief that the terrorists have a case—perhaps a just case—and that they can be reasoned with and finally won over by adequate concessions. *Realpolitik* is surely there, but behind it there is a *moral* consideration which is based on a misconception of terrorism and what the terrorists are after.

This misconception must be cleared up if we are to make any headway against terrorism. In doing so, we must bear in mind that we are dealing here with a crafty, potent enemy who operates not only with physical but also with psychological weapons, with persuasive arguments and captivating slogans. Thus, to delude the peoples of the free world, the terrorist appears as the bearer of *their* ideals, as the champion of the oppressed, as the critic of social ills, and, more specifically, as a fighter for freedom. The last claim, especially, is the sure catch which springs the trap for the credulous. Since freedom fighters have also used violence in their struggles, and since freedom is so dear to free men, many in the democracies are almost automatically filled with sympathy for the terrorists and their causes. Some young people in the West are even moved to join their ranks. Others, more observant, more critical, ask: *Who* are these men? Are they really freedom fighters as they claim to be, or are they merely using a pretense, a ruse, a guise under which they hide their real face—the face of quite another type of fighter and another type of man?

We Must Deal Swiftly with Terrorists

One of the most fashionable criticisms of the new American policy of responding to terrorism with force is that it fails to address "the underlying cause" of terrorist violence. Underlying causes should certainly be treated whenever possible, but those who urge understanding as an alternative to a military response err in several respects.

First, we must not be diverted from dealing directly and swiftly with terrorists when they can be identified and found. Those who would divert attention from the assassin and bomb-thrower weaken international resolve to punish lawlessness and prevent a breakdown of world order. Just as we do not delay law enforcement in order first to understand the psychological deprivations that motivate criminals, so we must not delay our response to terrorism.

Kenneth J. Bialkin, *The New York Times,* May 1, 1986.

To answer these questions, we must first determine the nature of modern terrorism and how it relates to what is generally known as the struggle for human freedom. Terrorism was defined (in the 1979 Jonathan Institute conference on terrorism) as "the deliberate and systematic murder, maiming, and menacing of the innocent to inspire fear for political ends." This, we believe, is a correct definition, and it should have been sufficient for our purposes. But what definition, however perfect, cannot be submerged, evaded, or distorted by a campaign of shrewd demagogues proclaiming gross untruths from all the major forums of the world?

We should, therefore, sharpen that definition. More stress must be placed on the word "innocent," which, when properly underscored, cannot fail to expose the sham of the terrorist claims.

For in contrast to the terrorist, no freedom fighter has ever deliberately attacked innocents. He has never deliberately killed small children, or passersby in the street, or foreign visitors, or other civilians who happen to reside in the area of conflict or are merely associated ethnically or religiously with the people of that area. This was not just a matter of tactics but one that related to his basic aim. For this aim, proclaimed in his title, implied the following simple syllogism: *To fight for freedom means to fight against oppression; oppression means violation of man's rights; hence to fight for freedom means to oppose such violations.* Consequently, no freedom fighter could stand for these violations, let alone perpetrate them himself.

Yet that is precisely what the terrorist does—and that in the most brazen and brutal manner. Hence he is not what he claims to be. Since he tramples underfoot all the rights of man, he cannot be regarded, by any stretch of logic, as a fighter for freedom. But then what is he? What is he fighting for?

It may be argued that he fights for the liberation of his own people, for *their* inherent rights, without regard for the rest of the world. This notion is belied by the actual record of the terrorists' conduct. The PLO, for instance, claims to be the "sole representative of the Palestinian people." We shall not examine here the merits of this claim. But nobody can deny that there has been *opposition* to the PLO among the Arabs, and no one who stands for man's basic freedoms can question the right of that opposition to its opinion. Does the PLO respect this right? The answer is given by the many Arabs who were cruelly liquidated by PLO killers for having merely expressed disagreement with their views, or were just suspected of such disagreement. And what about the right of free thought and expression *within* the ranks of the PLO itself? There, too, differences of opinion are settled by the assassin's bomb and gun. Remember how the terrorists in Lebanon fought each other to death over "questions of policy," as they put it. And remember the case of the PLO dissident Issam Sartawi, who advocated coexistence with Israel and was assassinated by PLO gunmen.

Terrorist Society Not Liberating

Of course it will be said that all this is unavoidable, that it is part and parcel of the "mechanics of revolution," which is allegedly the necessary *means* of liberation. Let us then consider the promise of free life the terrorist holds out for his "liberated" people *after* the "revolution." We can judge that promise by the performance of regimes in countries where the terrorists have prevailed. Look at Angola, at Libya, at Vietnam; look at Cambodia, at Cuba, at Iran—is there freedom there or despotic rule which employs all forms of oppression? The subjugated populations of these countries are so terrified by their ruling "liberators" that they do not even utter a whisper of protest against any of the abuses of their rights.

Yet some advocates of the terrorists still argue that it is better for a group to be subjugated by its own members than by members of a foreign people. When was this proven to be the rule? Oppression is oppression from whichever side it comes, and intolerable oppression remains intolerable even when practiced by your own kind. In fact, it is often far worse. When Mazzini, after Italy's liberation, was asked for his view about the possible establishment of a Marxist regime in Italy, he answered: "I would rather see the Austrians return to Italy than see the Italians slaves to themselves."

But we must also consider a third factor which shows clearly what the terrorist is. I refer to his patrons, promoters, and overlords, all of which are states with repressive regimes in which freedom has no place. The terrorists' connections with countries of the Middle East such as Syria, Libya, Iraq, and Iran are well known. These regimes have earned the title of terrorist states because they habitually use terror to further their aims. Not so well known, and often obscure, are the ties of the terrorists with the Soviet Union. And these are by far more important, more decisive, and more crucial for the future of the free world.

Soviets Disclaim Responsibility

To be sure, the Soviets have repeatedly disclaimed their responsibility for the rise of terrorism in the world, but their deeds indisputably refute their denials. It is sufficient to note their treatment of the PLO, which has rightly been labeled the "core of world terror." They support them *politically* on an unprecedented scale. They support them *militarily* by offering them training in numerous bases within and outside the U.S.S.R. And they support them *legally* by preventing the effective implementation of an international convention for extraditing terrorists. There can be no doubt about the Soviets' motive. Terrorism is the first general attack upon a free society which the enemies of freedom plan to take over. When they succeed—that is, when the country attacked falls into the hands of the terrorist assailants—that country becomes a satellite of Soviet Russia and another launching ground for its political expansion.

The conclusion we must draw from all this is evident. Far from being a bearer of freedom, the terrorist is the carrier of oppression and enslavement. The three distinctive signs we have just mentioned—his method of warfare, which includes the murder of children; his oppressive rule over his own people; and his alliances with tyrannical regimes—indicate this unmistakably. If we point out these signs repeatedly, we should be able to destroy, as we must, the myth of the terrorist as a freedom fighter. But this is not enough. We should not only indicate what the terrorist is *not*; we must also show clearly what he *is*.

The terrorist represents a new breed of man which takes humanity back to prehistoric times, to the times when morality was not yet born. Divested of any moral principle, he has no moral sense, no moral controls, and is therefore capable of committing any crime, like a killing machine, without shame or remorse. But he is also a cunning, consummate liar, and therefore much more dangerous than the Nazis, who used to proclaim their aims openly. In fact, he is the perfect nihilist.

The harbingers of this type of man had already appeared a century ago, and then, too, they portrayed themselves as champions of "progress" and "true liberty," as the new wave of the approaching future. At that time, of course, it was difficult to see where all of this would lead. But a few great men did. One of these was Dostoevsky; another was Max Nordau. This is not the place, of course, to analyze the statements uttered by the heroes of Dostoevsky's novel *The Possessed*. But we can cite here Nordau's clear prognostications. Shocked by the sight of those terrible humans, and seeking to unmask them and reveal their aims, Nordau sounded the great alarm in his famous, and much misunderstood, *Degeneration*. "They are not the future," he cried, "but an immeasurably remote past. They are not progress, but the most appalling reaction. They are not liberty, but the most disgraceful slavery." Were their influence not destroyed, he added, the future would not bring the hoped-for brightness of day, but "the dusk of the nations, in which all suns and all stars gradually wane, and mankind with all its institutions and creations perishes in the midst of a dying world."

Terrorist Causes Are Nullified

However noble their cause, however sincere their intentions, however deserving of redress the wrongs done to them, terrorists nullify these claims by their refusal to operate within civilized norms. To defeat them, moreover, the West must have enough faith in its system of values and enough confidence in its forces to meet the challenge.

William McGurn, *The American Spectator*, December 1985.

Today we can see that this was no apocalyptic vision but a forecast of a stark reality. Nordau did not speak of the death of mankind by nuclear destruction. The atomic bomb was then not yet envisioned. But civilizations may be subject to moral diseases which may destroy them as surely as any bomb can. Our attitude toward terrorism and the way we treat it, the way we are getting *conditioned* to its horrors, and, above all, our reactions to the dangers of enslavement represented by the terrorists and their masters—all these are symptoms of a serious moral sickness that debilitates our capacities to act as free men. And yet we feel within ourselves the power of recovery and the ability to emerge triumphant. May God grant us the wisdom to cure ourselves before the dusk of the nations is upon us.

"Terrorism is a violent way of expressing long-felt, collective grievances."

Terrorists Struggle Against Oppressive Governments

Eqbal Ahmad

Eqbal Ahmad argues that the causes of terrorism are multiple, but that these causes are all related to government indifference and violence. In the following viewpoint, he claims that young people turn to terrorism to release the feelings of anger and hopelessness their living conditions generate. Eqbal Ahmad is a fellow at the Institute for Policy Studies, an independent research organization in Washington.

As you read, consider the following questions:

1. Does the author believe that terrorists strike randomly?
2. Why has terrorism been on the increase, according to the author?
3. Do you think the author is sympathetic to terrorists? Why or why not?

Eqbal Ahmad, "Just What in the World Makes Terrorism Tick?" *Los Angeles Times*, July 8, 1985. Reprinted by permission of the author.

"Why," people ask, "do so many youths grow up to be terrorists?"

The causes are multiple, and the cure is more complex than the champions of swift retribution imagine. If the threat of serious punishment does not prevent non-political terrorism—serial murders, gang wars and so forth—what can be done with the political terrorist, who is far more obdurate?

Several factors may be ascribed to non-official, political terrorism:

The need to be heard is crucial. Terrorism is a violent way of expressing long-felt, collective grievances. When political means fail over a long period, a minority of the aggrieved community acts out violently, often soliciting the sympathy of the majority. Thus, after Palestine became Israel, the Palestinians' struggle for self-determination was largely political. Twenty years later, they had gained little but refugee doles and a dozen U.N. resolutions. The world behaved as though Palestine had truly been a "land without a people." Then, between 1968 and 1972, the Palestine Liberation Organization pulled the world up by the ears. Today, no one denies that there is a question of Palestine.

It is significant that by the summer of 1981, when the PLO accepted and observed a U.S.-mediated cease-fire with Israel, it resembled other liberation movements. Its debacle in 1982 and renewed isolation should have caused thoughtful concern, not rejoicing.

Violent Retribution

The combination of anger and helplessness produces the impulse for retributive violence. "I have pounded a few walls myself when I am alone," President Reagan said during the hijacking crisis; an aide later described him as wishing "to kick somebody in the rear end." To his credit, the President muted this emotion, for reprisal and terrorism have a similar root.

The politicians and pundits who counsel retribution surrender to sentiments that can only yield further violence.

The connection between terror and counterterror is often direct: "They kept yelling about New Jersey," said Judy Brown of Delmar, N.J., after her release by the Beirut hijackers. "I was afraid to tell them where I was from. Why are they so mad at New Jersey?" It was not the state; it was the U.S. battleship New Jersey, which had hurled car-sized bombs into Muslim districts of Beirut after the suicide raid on the Marine compound.

Experience of violence by a stronger party has historically turned victims into terrorists. Battered children often become abusive parents. On a larger scale, state terror often breeds private terror.

Typically, the most notorious Zionist terrorist groups—the Stern and Irgun—were composed of youthful immigrants from Eastern Europe and Germany who had been victims of pogroms and the

Holocaust. Similarly, the young Shias who hijacked [a] TWA aircraft were witnesses to violence since childhood; most are believed to be refugees in Beirut from Israel's bombings and invasions, since 1976, of southern Lebanon.

Lacking External Targets

Violence is internationalized when identifiable external targets become available. When clear-cut external targets are lacking, the violence of underprivileged people tends to be internalized.

What Reagan said at his June 17 [1985] news conference holds true for the Lebanese too: "It is frustrating. But . . . you can't just start shooting without having someone in your gunsight." The Shias did not attack Israelis until Israel became the occupying power. And, although the civil war in Lebanon had been going on since 1975, the United States came under attack only after Israel's full-scale invasion of Lebanon in June, 1982, and the U.S. Marines' perceptively pro-Israeli, pro-Falangist deployment there.

Example spreads terrorism. The highly publicized Beirut hijacking was followed by a flurry of bombs directed at air travelers. Hurried, ill-planned and without a defined goal, these imitations can be deadly, as they were at Frankfurt Airport and on the Air India flight.

Eliminate Terrorism's Causes

Terrorists often claim that only through violence will their grievances be addressed. That is not so. Diplomatic and international channels exist for a peaceable working out of legitimate grievances.

One way to blunt terrorism in the long run is to address fundamental inequities, of which the world has many, at an early stage and in a peaceable manner. This could prevent the accumulation of frustration which ultimately leads some persons to commit terrorist acts.

Christian Science Monitor, July 10, 1985.

The more serious examples are set by governments. When practiced and supported by powerful states, terrorism is legitimized as an instrument of attaining political objectives. Today, those who condemn terrorism the most are among its primary sponsors. The Nicaraguan *contras,* armed and aided by the United States, are terrorists by any definition. So is the Israeli-sponsored South Lebanon Army, which held 22 Finnish U.N. observers hostage. So are the militant Israeli settlers in the West Bank and Gaza.

With violence being viewed as the means of demonstrating a strength and attaining political goals, terrorism has become a norm, not an aberration, in international politics.

The absence of revolutionary ideology enhances a group's propensity toward international terrorism. It is noteworthy that ideologically and territorially rooted revolutionary movements (such as the Chinese, Algerian, Vietnamese, Cuban, Angolan and Nicaraguan) rarely operated outside the contested territorial boundaries. Nor have these countries provided haven to hijackers. Revolutionary violence theoretically eschews the indiscriminate, attention-seeking use of terror; it tends to be sociologically and psychologically selective. It strikes at widely perceived symbols of oppression—landlords, rapacious officials, repressive armies. It aims at widening the revolutionaries' popular support by freeing their potential constituencies from the constraints of oppressive power.

Why Now?

Oppression and injustices have existed for millennia. Why, then, this scourge of international terrorism in our time?

Modern technology and its proliferation have provided the physical elements of contemporary terrorism—the airplane, the compact but formidable hand-held weapon, the immediacy of electronic broadcasting. When hijackers put these three elements together, they have the world's attention. If their grievances are just, they get heard. The American Indians never had such an opportunity; they went without notice.

Although governments still favor history's invisible wars, technology has rendered them obsolete. This phenomenon suggests the fundamental problem of world politics: While the environment has drastically changed, the political minds of policymakers remain rooted in the past.

"The bottom line of . . . terrorism is that such activity is a cheap and highly productive way to wage a form of warfare."

Economics—Not Oppression—Motivates Terrorists

Bill Anderson

In the discussion of terrorism, there is often debate over the religious and/or political motivations for terrorism. In the following viewpoint, Bill Anderson, an economist, writes that this type of discussion is irrelevant. Terrorists care little about ideology or about the oppression of their fellow men. They are simply attempting to gain political and economic power in the least expensive way available.

As you read, consider the following questions:

1. Why does the author believe it is impossible to appease terrorists' anger at injustice?
2. According to the author, why don't terrorists participate in the political process?
3. Who does the author believe are most likely to become terrorists? Why?

Bill Anderson, "Terrorism," *The Freeman*, September 1985.

Political terrorism has become a sickening yet commonplace fixture of our modern world. In the past 15 years nearly 5,000 persons have died with scores more injured from deliberate terrorist attacks aimed mostly at persons from either western or pro-western nations. We can expect to hear on almost any news broadcast or read in a daily newspaper that a western diplomat has been gunned down, an American military officer kidnaped or a foreign business executive "executed" by a political extremist group that "claims responsibility" for its bloody actions.

Short of abandoning all laws and precepts that guarantee civil liberties, there is little that can be done to totally rid our world, and especially the free world, of political terrorism. The cost of eliminating terrorism would be, in the eyes of most persons, greater than the cost of living with the terrorist specter. However, it is important to understand the reality behind the actions of terrorist groups, what they want and how they can be slowed, if not stopped, from doing irreparable harm to our social fabric.

An Economic View

This article seeks to examine terrorism from an economic point of view. . . . The fundamental principle of economic theory—namely self-interest—is missing from most literature on terrorism. By assuming that terrorists are self-interested (like the rest of us), we can examine their motives and plans of action in a rational manner that enables us to understand their goals (though not agree with them) and, more important, predict their reactions to certain government policies.

For the most part, terrorist groups work under the guidance of Marxist-Leninist theory, although there are others who are fighting against communist regimes. What all the groups have in common, however, is that they seek or have sought either to seize power themselves or drastically affect the workings of the government in power. The source of their motivation, as well as the response government should make to terrorist attacks is the topic of dispute, not the actual makeup or ideology of the particular groups.

Traditional literature on terrorism, especially the literature dealing with terrorism from Marxist-led groups, makes a number of important errors. Economist Richard M. Kirk writes that . . . "political terrorists are assumed to be ideological zealots, willing to kill and be killed in order to further 'the cause'." This is not to say that ideology or the willingness to die for a cause is not a part of terrorism. Certainly the suicide bombers who killed 252 American soldiers in Beirut, Lebanon, in 1983 (and died in the process) knew they would not survive their attack. The problem here is that such attacks are depicted as a form of altruistic behavior, an action in which the attackers expected nothing in return. . . .

As a result of traditional analysis of terrorism, we find that

63

Steve Kelley, *San Diego Union*, reprinted with permission.

predictable views of government and its role in stopping terrorism prevail in most literature today. Terrorists, it is believed, work simply out of ideology; in that same vein of reasoning, it is also assumed that governments work ideologically. That is, what on the surface is a violent confrontation between terrorist groups and governments is, in reality, an outgrowth of a deeper ideological struggle. Solutions to terrorist problems, then, are placed in ideological frameworks; depending upon one's ideological biases the solutions run from expanding the welfare state to increasing powers of the particular nation's security police. . . .

Expanding the Government

In other words, . . . it is assumed that many terrorists, especially those on the left, have deep concerns for the poor and, in their desire to make an unwilling government (and the public it represents) bend to the just needs of the poor and oppressed, turn to terrorism as a last resort. Thus, terrorists may have their actions condemned by elements of society who at the same time might have sympathy for their ideology. For example, the infamous Patty Hearst kidnaping in 1974 by the Symbionese Liberation Army brought both condemnation for their tactics and praise for the SLA's "goals" of "helping the poor." The public forgot that the

64

act of kidnaping a young woman nearly destroyed her life; the public also forgot that the SLA had gunned down (with poisoned bullets) a popular black school superintendent in the San Francisco area. The perception that became popular was that of a misguided group of men and women whose hearts were in the right place.

Faulty Solutions

To change the breeding grounds of terrorism, it is then supposed, governments must change their ideology (provided they are not already leftist in scope) in order to facilitate the kind of justice that it is assumed will mollify the righteous anger of terrorists. . . .

The literature assumes [that] redistribution of wealth from rich to poor through taxation and regulation *will actually succeed* in reducing the wealth gap between rich and poor. Thus, it is believed, redistribution will bring stability to a society, ending poverty and eliminating the reasons that terrorists operate in the first place.

As one can see, the reality of terrorists and government does not match with the traditional explanations, which also means that traditional literature, far from helping solve the terrorist problem, actually helps contribute to its increase. By presenting false views of both the motives of the terrorists and of the nature of government, traditional writers on the subject simply do not offer the public realistic information. . . .

What Motivates Terrorists?

After peeling away the ideological skins and fig leaves that terrorists use to justify their violence, we come to the core reason for their actions: the terrorists' own desire for power and influence. Economist Thomas Sowell, following the murder in 1978 of Italian Premier Aldo Moro by the Red Brigades, was one of the few social commentators to recognize the terrorists' real motives. He writes:

> For several weeks a group of obscure young men became important. They carried out a deed that made headlines around the world. They had a famous man in their power, to abuse or taunt as they pleased and to kill when they felt like it. They saw the life of the country around them disrupted as police, workers, and others changed their daily routines in response to the event. The pope, the American president, and the United Nations recognized them with appeals and declarations. In normal times, they might never have gotten past the secretaries to see any of these people, much less expect to influence them. With one daring crime, they leapfrogged bureaucracy and protocal and elbowed their way into the headlines and even into history.

Why the violence? Is it, as some "experts" have declared, simply an act of insanity by members of terrorist groups?

To the second question, we answer "no." And because we believe that terrorists are making rational decisions, we can only assume that they carry out acts of violence because they have deemed such violence both more effective *and less costly* than standard participation in accepted political processes. Kirk notes: " . . . when the cost of gaining conventional political influence is high enough, or some other explicit or implicit barrier to entry into the political sphere exists, the use of violence in the form of political terrorism can become a profitable method of rent seeking."

Less Risk in Violence

In other words, the terrorists are seeking wealth transfers and/or power (all of which can be defined as economic or political *rents*) through violent means because they are not willing to pay the cost of participating in the political system. True, the political system gives no guarantees of success. Radical politicians, though they may be influential in their own small districts, usually do not sway enough voters to gain national offices or, should they be elected, are often forced to moderate their policies in order to achieve the needed political compromises that permit them to govern effectively.

Many Avenues Open

As to terrorism being the only recourse of the terrorist, I say hogwash. There are many more avenues open that will more than accomplish the desired goals of all parties involved. All terrorism accomplishes in the end is to further widen the already wide chasm that now exists.

Henry S. Siemsen, *Los Angeles Times*, May 17, 1986.

Potential terrorists (or actual ones) are faced with the following dilemma: They can either pay their dues in the political system, thus perhaps reaping the rewards but also shouldering the greater risks of failure, or they can seek power by other means, that being violence. True, violent activity has the inherent risks of death or imprisonment, but in the terrorist's mind, the rewards gained from terrorist activity outweigh both those risks and the rewards that could have been gained had he or she simply participated in the political system like everyone else. The act of terrorism gives the individuals involved a chance to gain the kind of significance that most likely could not be gained by legitimate channels. Sowell writes:

The media and intellectuals tend to judge terrorists in terms of the effects of their acts on what the terrorists themselves define as their cause—the "avenging" of this or the "liberation" of that. Usually the terrorists' acts don't have a ghost of a chance of achieving their proclaimed goals, but they can give a lot of importance to a lot of otherwise insignificant people in the meantime. And these are not merely insignificant individuals: they are often insignificant individuals who grew up surrounded by people with wealth, power, or recognition which they would be unable to duplicate through normal channels for many long years.

In this passage, however, even Sowell underestimates the accomplishments of the terrorists. Yes, many of them are insignificant individuals who crave attention and power; but, no, they are not simply acting to gain attention the way a two-year-old child throws a tantrum to get Mommy's attention.

Terrorism can alter the way a government does business, and it can also alter the plans of those who originally wished to be involved in government but change their minds because the inherent risks of kidnaping and/or assassination become high. Democratic nations have seen some erosions of their civil liberties because of terrorist violence. And some European airports have sections that resemble armed camps instead of passenger terminals. . . .

State-Sponsored Terrorism

In the past few years we have seen increasing evidence of terrorism backed by national governments, the bombing of the U.S. Marine barracks in Lebanon in the fall of 1983 being a vivid example. Author Claire Sterling in her best-selling book *The Terror Network* documented the involvement of the Soviet Union, its Eastern-Bloc allies, Cuba, North Korea and other communist states in terrorist activities aimed at the West. Iran, it has been recently learned, is also playing a major role in helping terrorist groups such as the PLO and Islamic Jihad attack both Israel and other representatives of western nations, especially the United States.

The bottom line of state-sponsored terrorism is that such activity is a cheap and highly productive way to wage a form of warfare. The risks to the Soviet Union are minimal (witness the number of disbelievers in the western news media after strong evidence was presented that the U.S.S.R. played a role in the shooting of Pope John Paul II in 1981) and the opportunities for disruption of western societies excellent.

Again, western politicians and opinion makers must not fall prey to the idea that state-sponsored terrorists are simply acting out an ideological cause in controversial fashion. Rather, it is imperative for the West to realize that both the terrorists and their parent governments are using terrorism as a means to snatch political and economic gains that might not be obtained through normal diplomatic channels and are not worth the risk of all-out warfare.

And in response to the terrorist threat, western governments should steer clear of "solutions" which include liberalized wealth transfers toward the guilty hostile nations (e.g. liberalized government-to-government loan agreements, subsidies, etc.) or agreements that "give away the store" militarily. As in the case of domestic terrorism, the expansion of wealth transfers will only serve to bring about increased levels of violence.

In the 1960s many liberals were advocating vast increases in welfare and other transfer payments as well as increasing poverty programs in order to appease what they saw as growing unrest in poor—and especially black—communities. What the nation received in payment for its increased Federal largess was the most violent social upheaval in nearly a century. What was not accomplished was what liberals hoped would be accomplished: the elimination of poverty.

The same analogy can be applied to terrorism. Should our leaders continue to try to appease terrorists by using welfare state expansion, what they—and the rest of us—will reap is more violence.

"If the media were not there to report terrorist acts and to explain their political and social significance . . . terrorism as such would cease to exist."

Media Publicity Causes Terrorism

John O'Sullivan

John O'Sullivan is deputy editor of the *Times of London*. A long-time journalist, he was the editorial page editor of the New York *Post* and the editor of *Policy Review*. In the following viewpoint, Mr. O'Sullivan enunciates his belief that terrorists need and thrive on media attention. He explains further that the media exaggerates terrorist situations, thereby causing public apprehension and panic.

As you read, consider the following questions:

1. Does the author believe reporting terrorism is inevitable with a democratic free press? Why or why not?
2. Why is the media essential to terrorists, according to the author?
3. Does the author think that the media should try to discredit terrorists?

Excerpts from "Deny Them Publicity," by John O'Sullivan from *Terrorism: How the West Can Win* edited by Benjamin Netanyahu, Copyright © 1986 by The Jonathan Institute. Reprinted by permission of Farrar, Straus, Giroux, Inc.

A terrorist is a criminal who seeks publicity. This sets him far apart from what British officials in Northern Ireland have taken to calling the ODC, or Ordinary Decent Criminal, who understandably shuns the limelight. Indeed, it is an understatement to say that terrorists seek publicity. They *require* publicity. It is their lifeblood. If the media were not there to report terrorist acts and to explain their political and social significance (the motives inspiring them and so forth), terrorism as such would cease to exist. Each terrorist act would then be seen merely as an isolated criminal event. It would not be interpreted as an integral part of a pattern of political violence, the likely prelude to other bombings and shootings, something to be seriously discussed by politicians, bureaucrats, and television sociologists.

The media find terrorism a sensational news story and are therefore inclined at first to overreport it, to write admiringly of the terrorists' "daring," even while morally condemning them, and to exaggerate their significance. The media exploit terrorism as a good story, but they could do without it. If it were not there, however, other equally newsworthy topics would be at hand—wars, demonstrations, elections, congressional battles, the marriages of pop stars, and, of course, ordinary decent crime.

What benefits does the terrorist seek from media publicity? In what way does he hope to make the media his accomplices? There are three types of unwitting media assistance. They help the terrorist spread an atmosphere of fear and anxiety in society, they provide him with an opportunity to argue his case to the wider public, and they bestow an undeserved legitimacy on him.

Spreading Fear and Anxiety

Let us take the first, the spreading of fear and anxiety through society. This seems to be achieved principally by simple media coverage of the terrorist's act. Such reports naturally arouse public concern; it would be alarming if they did not. In a free society, however, nothing is to be done about this. A regime like that of the Soviet Union can suppress all news of its occasional hijackings, as it does news of airline crashes and major industrial disasters. If events do not become known, they cannot influence public opinion. (Even this argument cannot be pushed too far; if terrorist acts were sufficiently frequent, they would become known through gossip and hearsay even in the most effectively censored society.)

Is panic contrived by terrorists, then, simply the unavoidable price of living in a society with a free press? I do not think so. For it is not the mere succession of terrorist acts which when reported arouses public anxiety. Statistically, these are usually a very trivial threat to the lives and limbs of anyone in particular. Rather, the media heighten tension by reporting not just the terrorists' acts but also their threats of *future* violence, by describing

70

in often lurid colors the campaign of terror that will ensue if the government does not meet terrorist demands, giving the impression that endless violence and upheaval lie ahead.

Supermarket Terrorism

This spreads panic and anxiety in two ways. First, it directly increases the ordinary citizen's fear that he may fall victim to a bomb in a restaurant or a supermarket. But also, more subtly, it conveys the message that society is in moral chaos, that its laws, rules, standards, and securities no longer provide any protection against random violence. There is an instructive comparison from the world of crime. People are murdered all the time without arousing any public feeling more profound than a prurient curiosity. But when a killer like the Yorkshire Ripper not merely kills people but also mutilates them and then mocks society and the police for their inability to stop him, a genuine fear based on moral uncertainty grips the public. In short, the media can magnify terrorist violence so that its impact on public opinion is disproportionate to the actual physical harm it does. . . .

I turn now to the second way in which the media unwittingly

© Uluschak/Rothco

assist terrorism: they provide the terrorist with an opportunity to broadcast his views to the wider public. This is an opportunity which he would not generally enjoy if he were to use the conventional channels of democratic politics, because the support he would generate would not warrant that kind of media attention. But the use of terror gives him a platform. The reason is, once again, straightforward journalistic curiosity. Who are these people blowing up restaurants, shooting policemen, hijacking planes? Why are they doing it? What are their aims, intentions, philosophies? And what are their demands? The press assumes that the public is clamoring to know the answers to such questions, and seeks to provide them. The terrorists themselves so arrange their affairs as to make life relatively easy for the media. They arrange press conferences, publish "communiqués" and statements of ultimate aims, and give exclusive interviews. In Northern Ireland, the so-called Republic Movement is divided into a terrorist wing which murders people, the IRA, and a political wing, Sinn Fein, which is available to the media to explain why these murders were regrettable necessities. The PLO has a similar arrangement, complementing its terror apparatus with a full-fledged international press operation.

Forcing the Media to Report

We can judge the importance which the terrorists attach to the media by the fact that they often force the media to present their case by threatening to kill hostages if the media refuse. In 1975, for instance, the Montaneros terrorists in Buenos Aires released a Mercedes-Benz director after his company had published advertisements in Western newspapers denouncing the "economic imperialism" of multinational corporations in the Third World. . . .

It is, however, the concentration by the media on the terrorist's "case" that gives rise to the third, and perhaps most difficult, problem: the unwitting bestowal of respectability upon terrorist groups. Talking about the aims and philosophies of terrorists inevitably conveys the impression that they are a species of politician rather than a species of criminal. We begin to think of the terrorist in relation to economic or foreign policy rather than in relation to kneecapping, amputations, and point-blank murder. Yet it is what the terrorist *does* rather than what he *thinks* (or says he thinks) that makes him a legitimate object of media attention. After all, some people *like* killing and hurting and frightening others. That insight might be a far more reliable guide to the terrorist's "motivation" than some parroted guff about social or political justice and institutionalized violence. It might also be a better guide to his future actions.

Television presents this problem of legitimacy in a particularly acute form, for it conveys a sort of respectability upon the terrorist simply by interviewing him. Television is a leveling and homogenizing medium by its very nature, and the process of interviewing someone, whether he is a terrorist or a foreign diplomat or a government official, is essentially the same process. The producer and interviewer might well go to considerable lengths to show the terrorist in a bad light. No matter how aggressive the questioner is, however, he could hardly be more aggressive than, say, Robin Day interrogating Mrs. Thatcher or Dan Rather grilling Mr. Nixon. Even if the terrorist comes off badly, therefore, he will achieve his aim by being treated as someone whose contribution to public debate is worthy of attention. He becomes by degrees a politician.

Press Must Denounce Terrorism

Unless the press takes the position that terrorism—defined as the indiscriminate attack on innocents to achieve political ends—is absolutely indefensible, a moral corruption begins that is irreversible. If we compromise that principle, then our profession that we stand for certain values is hollow, because high among those values is the belief that civilians ought to be exempt from attack. If there are people on our side who engage in the murder of civilians—for example, the gangsters who practice terrorism in El Salvador—they have to be condemned with as much vigor as those who do it in the name of another ideology. . . .

Journalists must recognize that there exists a unique class of political events, media terrorism; these acts acquire importance by, and often are undertaken with the sole intention of, being broadcast over the media. Because of the symbiotic relationship between the media and terrorist acts, because these acts are created or at least greatly amplified by media coverage, journalists must exercise self-restraint—call it censorship if you like. The rule of thumb I propose is this: In covering terrorist events, reporters ought to concentrate on who, what, where, and when. They should leave the question of why to the historians and the psychiatrists.

Charles Krauthammer, *Harper's*, October 1985.

Is there some compensating advantage that justifies such interviews? I do not believe there is. The blunt truth is that a terrorist is an advocate of murder and that the advocacy of murder is, or should be, beyond the acceptable boundaries of public discussion. The justification commonly advanced is that "we need to know what these people think." But that is nonsense. To begin with, we invariably know what they think long before they appear on television to tell us. Is anyone unaware of the aims and beliefs of the PLO, or of the IRA, or of the Red Brigades? Secondly, what they say on television is not necessarily what they think (which, as I have argued above, is much more accurately conveyed by what they do). It is sugared propaganda. Finally, even if we needed to know what the terrorist thought and could rely on his honesty, a straightforward report and analysis by the journalist himself would be a more efficient and reliable method of conveying such information without the side effect of conferring legitimate respectability upon murderers. . . .

Press and Government Are Not Enemies

What attitudes in the media contribute to problems I have outlined? One attitude is the exaggeration of the reasonable view that press and government are necessarily antagonistic, the press bent upon exposure and defending the public's right to know, the government insisting upon its executive privacy. Whatever virtue this may have in the ordinary political rough-and-tumble, it is not an appropriate attitude when the authorities are coping with a campaign of murder. Leaks of government plans and ignoring official requests for a news blackout when lives are at stake represent a professional distortion of proper human priorities. Fortunately, this is not always so. In the Martin Schleyer kidnapping, for example, the media observed requests for strict silence on official actions.

Another problematic attitude is what Conor Cruise O'Brien calls "unilateral liberalism," which is as common in the media as it is in the new class. O'Brien describes this as the "kind of liberalism which is sensitive exclusively to threats to liberty seen as emanating from the democratic state itself, and is curiously phlegmatic about threats to liberty from the enemies of that state." It is this attitude that underlies the belief that, in some sense, the terrorists have a right to have their case presented, as if murder were a sort of opinion which the public should respect.

Finally, there is an attitude that requires little elaboration—the pursuit of commercial and professional competition, which allows no self-restraint in covering a dramatic story.

The most important contribution that the media could make to defeating terrorism would be changing such attitudes. Other aspects of media coverage would then change automatically.

6

"I believe the harm of restricting coverage far surpasses the evils of broadcasting even erroneous or damaging information."

The Media Must Report Terrorism

Katharine Graham

Katharine Graham is chairwoman of the board and chief executive officer of The Washington Post Company. In the following viewpoint, she admits that the media has been irresponsible in its reporting of terrorism in the past. However, she believes censoring a free press is not the answer. In a democratic society, an unhampered media is essential.

As you read, consider the following questions:

1. Ms. Graham outlines several reasons terrorism must continue to be reported. After reading her views and Mr. O'Sullivan's in the previous viewpoint, whose argument do you find more compelling? Why?
2. Ms. Graham believes the media and the government can cooperate on terrorism. Mr. O'Sullivan suggests that they are natural antagonists. With which view do you agree?
3. Why does Ms. Graham think terrorism will ultimately be the cause of its own demise? Do you agree?

Katharine Graham, "Terrorists Need the Press, But So Does a Free Society," *The Washington Post National Weekly Edition*, May 5, 1986. Reprinted with permission of The Washington Post Company.

Picture a warm and sunny day, not in Athens or Cairo, but in Washington. The Israeli prime minister is in town and is scheduled to meet the president.

At 11 a.m., the leader of an obscure Muslim sect and several accomplices armed with guns and machetes storm the headquarters of B'nai B'rith. Three other members of the group seize the city's Islamic Center and two more fanatics invade City Hall, killing a radio reporter in the process. Altogether, the terrorists take 134 hostages in three buildings at gunpoint, force them to the floor and threaten to kill them unless their demands are met.

The news media, as one might expect, descend on the scene en masse. Live television pictures carrying the group's warnings and demands soon go forth over the airwaves. One hundred and thirty-four lives hang in the balance, as reporters compete to get exclusive interviews with the terrorists.

This crisis actually happened, on March 9, 1977, when Hanafi Muslims staged a terrorist attack on the very day Prime Minister Yitzhak Rabin was meeting with President Jimmy Carter. Happily, it ended with the surrender of the terrorists and no further loss of life.

Terrorism Requires an Audience

The Hanafi incident illustrated a troubling fact about modern terrorism: It requires an audience. The terrorist has to communicate his own ruthlessness—his "stop-at-nothing" mentality—in order to achieve his goals. Media coverage is essential to his purpose. If terrorism is a form of warfare, as many observers now believe, it is a form in which media exposure is a powerful weapon.

As terrorism increases, we in the news media are being encouraged to restrict our coverage of terrorist actions. British Prime Minister Margaret Thatcher, for example, has proclaimed: "We must try to find ways to starve the terrorist and the hijacker of the oxygen of publicity on which they depend." Many people, including some reporters in the United States, share her view. Most of these observers call for voluntary restraint by the media in covering terrorist actions. But some go so far as to sanction government control—censorship, in fact—should the media fail to respond.

Full and Complete Coverage Necessary

I disagree. I am against any government-imposed restrictions on the free flow of information about terrorist acts. Instead, I am in favor of as full and complete coverage of terrorism by the media as is possible. Here are my reasons:

• Terrorist acts are impossible to ignore. They are simply too big a story to pass unobserved. If the media did not report them, rumor would abound. And rumors can do much to enflame and worsen a crisis.

• There is no compelling evidence that terrorist attacks would cease if the media stopped covering them. On the contrary, terrorism specialists I have consulted believe the terrorists would only increase the number, scope and intensity of their attacks if we tried to ignore them.

• Our citizens have a right to know what the government is doing to resolve crises and curb terrorist attacks. Some of the proposed solutions raise disturbing questions about when the United States should use military force.

"Oh, Come Now"

Now I hear that TV has become the terrorists' ultimate tool. This is a daffy and irresponsible charge. The competitive zeal with which the networks chased after the story of the hostages should be celebrated as an example of what's right about the democratic system, not what's wrong with it.

There were, to be sure, some unruly and odious excesses. But such indiscretions are a worthwhile price to pay for a precious freedom that does not exist for more than 80 percent of the world's citizens.

The argument emerging in newspapers and newsweeklies is that the granting of air time to the terrorists and to the events they stage-managed was akin to giving a credit card to assassins and bomb-throwers with which to shop the Free World for sympathy and support.

Oh, come now.

The intense coverage of terrorist acts in recent years has certainly not won armies of American converts to that frightening form of political expression. If terrorism is a deadly cancer, then the obvious way of combatting it is to focus on it, even if that glare of attention makes some people and some governments feel uncomfortable.

Morton Dean, *Minneapolis Star and Tribune*, July 14, 1985.

In covering terrorism, however, we must also recognize that we face very real and exceedingly complex challenges. There are limits to what the media can and should do. Three critical issues, in particular, must be addressed. All touch the central question of how the press can minimize its role as a participant in the crisis and maximize its role as a provider of information.

The first involves knowing how to gather and reveal information without making things worse, without endangering the lives of hostages or jeopardizing national security. One television news executive bluntly explained to me: "Errors that threaten loss of life are permanent; others are temporary. If we have to make mistakes, we want to make the temporary kind.''

In the early days of covering urban violence and the first terrorist attacks, the media would descend on the scene in hot pursuit of the news. Sometimes we didn't know what could put lives at risk. And we were often less than cooperative with the police attempting to resolve the crisis.

During the Hanafi Muslim siege, there were live television reports that the police were storming a building when, in fact, they were merely bringing in food. Some reporters called in on the public phone lines to interview the terrorists inside the building. One interview rekindled the rage of the terrorist leader, who had been on the point of surrender.

These potential disasters led to discussions between the police and the media, and to a more professional approach and mutual trust on both sides. For example, most authorities now know that at the beginning of a crisis, it is best to establish a central point where reliable information can be disseminated quickly. And the media, knowing that the authorities intend to help them obtain the information they need, are much more willing to cooperate.

The Media Is Not Exploitive

I want to emphasize that the media are willing to—and do—withhold information that is likely to endanger human life or jeopardize national security. During the American embassy crisis in Iran, for example, one of our Newsweek reporters became aware that six Americans known to have been in the embassy were not being held by the Iranians. He concluded that they must have escaped to the Swedish or Canadian embassies. This in fact had occurred. However, we (and some others who also knew) did not report the information because we knew it would put lives in jeopardy. Similarly, when a group of Lebanese Shiites hijacked TWA Flight 847 with 153 hostages aboard ..., the media learned—but did not report—that one hostage worked for the U.S. National Security Agency.

Tragically, however, we in the media have made mistakes. In April 1983, some 60 people were killed in a bomb attack on the U.S. embassy in Beirut. At the time, there was coded radio traffic between Syria, where the operation was being run, and Iran, which was supporting it. Alas, one television network and a newspaper columnist reported that the U.S. government had intercepted the traffic. Shortly thereafter the traffic ceased. This undermined efforts to capture the terrorist leaders and eliminated a source of information about future attacks. Five months later, apparently the same terrorists struck again at the Marine barracks in Beirut; 241 servicemen were killed.

This kind of result, albeit unintentional, points up the necessity for full cooperation wherever possible between the media and the authorities. When the media obtain especially sensitive information, we are willing to tell the authorities what we have learned and what we plan to report. And while reserving the right to make the final decision ourselves, we are anxious to listen to arguments about why information should not be aired.

A second challenge facing the media is how to prevent terrorists from using the media as a platform for their views.

I think we have to admit that terrorist groups receive more attention and make their positions better known because of their acts. Few people had even heard of groups such as the Hanafi Muslims or Basque separatists before they carried out terrorist attacks.

The World Must Know

What is the responsibility of the press in covering terrorism? If a representative of a terrorist group approaches the *Washington Post* and says, "I want to try to explain to you who we are and what we are," Bob Woodward can write a gripping story describing who the terrorists are and what they believe. By writing this story he does not prevent the police from taking action against them. But if the government then forces him to betray the confidence that made the story possible, while a few people may be arrested, he will never get that kind of story again. Some of us still believe that journalists are people committed to the idea that the world must *know*. We believe that our job is to explain who terrorists are— whether they are right-wing terrorists or left-wing terrorists— without accepting the view of any one side. The free press can be destroyed very easily if it is polarized in the way that some have suggested here. We should examine the press in countries where it tries to satisfy the prejudices of particular groups—in France, the Soviet Union, Syria—before we start making new rules for ourselves.

Daniel Schorr, *Harper's*, October 1985.

The media must make every attempt, however, to minimize the propaganda value of terrorist incidents and put the actions of terrorists into perspective. We have an obligation to inform our readers and viewers of their backgrounds, their demands and what they hope to accomplish. But we must not forget that terrorists are criminals. We must make sure we do not glorify them, or give unwarranted exposure to their point of view.

Maximizing Media Exposure

We often think of terrorists as unsophisticated. But many are media savvy. They can and do arrange their activities to maximize media exposure and ensure that the story is presented their way.

To influence media coverage, terrorists have arranged for press pools; granted exclusive interviews during which favored reporters have been given carefully selected information; held press conferences in which hostages and others have been made available to the press under conditions imposed by the captors; provided videotapes portraying events as the terrorists wished them to be portrayed; and scheduled the release of news and other events so that television deadlines could be met.

There is a real danger, in short, that terrorists hijack not only airplanes and hostages, but the media as well.

To guard against this, the television networks in our country rarely—almost never—allow terrorists to appear live. They also resist using videotape provided by terrorists. If there is no alternative, our commentators continually report that the material is "terrorist-supplied" so that viewers can evaluate its veracity and meaning. Likewise, when terrorists make hostages available for interviews, our commentators repeatedly indicate—or they should—that the captives are speaking under duress.

When one network reporter interviewed some of the hostages in last year's TWA hijacking by telephone, he said: "Walk away from the phone if you're under duress, or if you don't want to talk." One of them did walk away. Even when there is no evident coercion, the networks repeat that terrorists are standing by, although they are not visible on the screen. We also try to identify carefully and repeatedly the backgrounds and biases of the people we interview, including the hostages.

Forbidding terrorists their platform goes beyond using specific techniques. It is more an issue of exercising sound editorial judgment.

Terrorist Manipulation

Over the years, the media constantly have been confronted with attempts at manipulation. In the days of the Vietnam war, for example, we would get calls from protest groups saying, "We're going to pour chicken blood all over the entrance to Dow Chemical Co. Come cover this event." We didn't. But we did cover a Budist monk who wished to be filmed setting fire to himself.

How did we make the distinction? Here it was a question of trivial versus serious intent and result, of low versus high stakes. Clearly, the suicide was of cataclysmic importance to the monk.

The point is that we generally know when we are being manipulated, and we've learned better how and where to draw the line, though the decisions are often difficult.

A few years ago, for example, a Croatian terrorist group in a plane demanded that its statement be printed in several newspapers, including The Washington Post, before it would release 50 hostages. In the end, we printed the statement in agate, the smallest type size we have, in 37 copies of the paper at the end of our press run. Now I'm not so sure we would accede to this demand in any form.

That brings me to a third issue challenging the media: How can we avoid bringing undue pressure on the government to settle terrorist crises by whatever means, including acceding to the terrorists' demands?

State Department officials tell me that media coverage does indeed bring pressure on the government, but not *undue* pressure. However, I believe there are pitfalls of which the media should be exceedingly careful.

One is the amount of coverage devoted to a terrorist incident. During a crisis, we all want to know what is happening. But constant coverage can blow a terrorist incident far out of proportion to its real importance. Overexposure can preoccupy the public and the government to the exclusion of other issues.

During the TWA crisis, our networks constantly interrupted regularly scheduled programming with news flashes of dubious importance. And one network devoted its entire 22-minute evening newscast to the crisis. Many important topics were ignored. . . .

These problems of covering terrorism are serious. But in spite of them, I believe the benefits of full disclosure far outweigh any possible adverse consequences. I believe the harm of restricting coverage far surpasses the evils of broadcasting even erroneous or damaging information.

American democracy rests on the belief, which the centuries have proved true, that people can and do make intelligent decisions about great issues if they have the facts.

But to hear some politicians talk, you wouldn't think they believed it. They appear to be afraid that people will believe the terrorist's message and agree, not only to his demands, but to his beliefs. And so they seek to muzzle the media or enlist their support in the government's cause.

I think this is a fatal mistake. It is a slippery slope when the media start to act on behalf of any interest, no matter how worthy—when editors decide what to print on the basis of what they believe is good for people to know. It's dangerous if we are asked to become a kind of super-political agency.

I believe that terrorism is ultimately a self-defeating platform from which to present a case. Terrorists, in effect, hang themselves whenever they act. They convey hatred, violence, terror itself. There was no clearer image of what a terrorist really is than the unforgettable picture of that crazed man holding a gun to the head of the pilot aboard the TWA jet. That said it all to me—and, I believe, to the world.

Publicity may be the oxygen of terrorists. But I say this: News is the lifeblood of liberty. If the terrorists succeed in depriving us of freedom, their victory will be far greater than they ever hoped and far worse than we ever feared. Let it never come to pass.

Distinguishing Bias from Reason

The subject of terrorism often generates great emotional responses in people. When dealing with such a highly controversial subject, many will allow their feelings to dominate their powers of reason. Thus, one of the most important basic thinking skills is the ability to distinguish between statements based upon emotion and those based upon a rational consideration of the facts.

Most of the following statements are taken from the viewpoints in this chapter. Consider each statement carefully. *Mark R for any statement you believe is based on reason and a rational consideration of facts. Mark B for any statement you believe is based on bias, prejudice, or emotion. Mark I for any statement you think is impossible to judge.*

If you are doing this exercise as a member of a class or group, compare your answers with those of other class or group members. Be able to defend your answers. You may discover that others will come to different conclusions than you. Listening to the reasons others present for their answers may give you valuable insights in distinguishing between bias and reason.

If you are reading this book alone, ask others if they agree with your answers. You will find this interaction very valuable.

R = *a statement based upon reason*
B = *a statement based upon bias*
I = *a statement impossible to judge*

1. The motive behind terrorism must be understood or the violence will only escalate.

2. One danger for the US is that the Moslem extremists and the Palestinians will some day act in unison, unleashing a force so potent that costly and humiliating attacks so far will seem small by comparison.

3. A terrorist tramples underfoot all the rights of men.

4. The subjugated populations of Vietnam, Cuba, and Iran are so terrified by their rulers that they do not even utter a whisper of protest against abuses of their rights.

5. The cost of eliminating terrorism would be, in the eyes of most persons, greater than the cost of living with it.

6. Terrorist actions often incite terrorist responses.

7. Terrorists are motivated by a desire for power and influence.

8. The media find terrorism a sensational story and are inclined to write admiringly of the terrorists' "daring."

9. The results of all polls taken on the subject indicate that most people in the US support the death penalty for captured terrorists.

10. The media provide the terrorist with an opportunity to broadcast his views to the wider public.

11. The process of interviewing someone, whether he is a terrorist or a foreign diplomat, is essentially the same process.

12. To even listen to a murderer's demands gives him more credit than he deserves.

13. What terrorists say on television is sugared propaganda.

14. There is no compelling evidence that terrorist attacks would cease if the media stopped covering them.

15. Tasteless invasion of privacy can result from too frequent interviews with the families of terror victims.

16. The use of terror probably lessens the chances of the terrorists having their views considered.

17. The terrorist has no moral sense, no moral controls, and is capable of committing any crime without shame or remorse.

Periodical Bibliography

The following list of periodical articles deals with the subject matter of this chapter.

Abdullahi Ahmed An-na'im — "Muslims Are Challenging the Forces of Repression," *Los Angeles Times*, January 17, 1986.

David Bar-Illan — "Israel, the Hostages, and the Network," *Commentary*, September 1985.

Crime and Social Justice — Special Issue, "International Lawlessness and Search for Justice," Nos. 21-22.

Harper's — "Terrorism and the Media: A Discussion," October 1985.

Jeane J. Kirkpatrick — "Lost in the Terrorist Theater," *Harper's*, October 1985.

Micah Morrison — "Prime Time Terror," *The American Spectator*, September 1985.

Rod Nordland and Ray Wilkinson — "Inside Terror, Inc.," *Newsweek*, April 7, 1986.

John B. Oakes — "Reagan Isn't Buoying Freedom Abroad," *The New York Times*, April 6, 1986.

Robert L. Phillips — "The Roots of Terrorism," *The Christian Century*, April 9, 1986.

Raymond A. Schroth — "'These People Are Fighting for My Mind,'" *America*, February 1, 1986.

Kenneth Slack — "'Terrorvision' Censorship?" *The Christian Century*, August 14-21, 1985.

Lewis Snider — "U.S. Image as a Belligerent," *Wall Street Journal*, June 12, 1986.

Cal Thomas, Drew Middleton and Philip Geyelin — "Appeasement Will Not Quell Terrorists," *Los Angeles Times*, January 9, 1986.

James M. Wall — "Culture Clashes Need Cautious Interpretation," *The Christian Century*, April 16, 1986.

James M. Wall — "Terrorism Tempts TV to Waive Noble Right," *The Christian Century*, July 3-10, 1985.

Is Terrorism
Justified?

TERRORISM

"The amount of terror inflicted by 'terrorists' . . . is a thimbleful compared to official, legally-sanctioned terror."

Terrorism Is Sometimes Justified

Martin Oppenheimer

Martin Oppenheimer is associate professor of sociology at Rutgers University in New Jersey. A long-time political activist, he is the author of *The Urban Guerrilla* and the co-author of *A Manual of Direct Action*. His latest book is *White Collar Politics*. In the following viewpoint, Mr. Oppenheimer argues that terrorism is merely a label applied by governments to actions of legitimate protest. If governments were just and humane, there would be no terrorism.

As you read, consider the following questions:

1. Mr. Oppenheimer writes that terrorism is always a response to "institutional terrorism." What does he mean by that term? How does it differ from other definitions of terrorism in this book?
2. Can distinctions be drawn between violent acts, according to the author?
3. Which society does the author believe is the most violent in the world?

Martin Oppenheimer, "Defining Terrorism." Reprinted with permission from the May-June 1985 issue of *The Nonviolent Activist*, the magazine of the War Resisters League.

Terrorism is a label applied to certain criminal acts when the state doesn't like the criminal's politics. When the state, and those who support it, do like the politics, the label becomes more benign: freedom fighter or patriot. When politics are absent (or the state pretends that they are) the label becomes bandit, psychopath, or thug. Any act, violent or nonviolent, can be labelled criminal, and hence part of a terrorist conspiracy, when the state defines such behavior as dangerous.

Types of Terrorist Acts

Generally, we have come to think of terrorism as threats or acts of violence directed towards people in order to coerce them, or others (including governments), to change their policies. The terrorist seeks to prevent or stop some action. If necessary, this will be accomplished by the physical elimination of the actors, or by their forced withdrawal from a particular geographical area. Such terrorist acts include assassinations, kidnappings, sabotage, beatings, mutilations, cross-burnings, and other forms of harrassment. It also includes the broad category of vigilantism—when communities "take the law into their own hands" in the absence of official police, or when community values are in conflict with those of the law. Vigilante actions include night riders, mob lynchings, death squads, and pogroms. Robberies committed to further political goals are labelled terrorism; other robberies, no matter how much they terrorize, are just robberies.

Terrorism is often one of a panoply of tactics in a wider underground resistance and/or guerrilla national liberation movement. It is sometimes the first stage in the development of such broader movements. In such cases, the objective of terrorist acts may be more to raise political consciousness than to inflict injury or destruction. Some forms of terrorism may be ignored, condoned, encouraged, or even unofficially sponsored by the government or some part of it, to foster policies which it cannot officially acknowledge. Examples of this include the suppression of labor unions, keeping minority groups in "their place," and supporting exiles who carry out illegal actions in line with government policy.

Institutional Terrorism

Terrorism is always a response to institutional terror. It is an evasion to label some acts as terrorism, while ignoring the institutional terror which underlies this form of protest. This is true even though terrorist acts may be misdirected at scapegoats, who are sometimes provided by those responsible for the institutional terror.

The amount of terror inflicted by "terrorists," no matter how dreadful, is a thimbleful compared to official, legally-sanctioned terror. An example of state terror is the deliberate starvation of a population, as in Ireland during the potato famine. Other examples come all too readily to mind in this century; the brutalization of a population through poverty; child labor; slavery; the expulsion of a people from their lands; genocide based on religious, political, ethnic, and sexual identities; aerial bombardment; police brutality; official torture; the prison system in general and capital punishment in particular; and the systematic violence done by industry. To paraphrase Alfred McClung Lee from his recent book, *Terrorism in Northern Ireland*, more terrorists wear three-piece suits, ride in Rolls Royces, and sit in the seats of corporate power and government than lurk in dark alleys.

The Roots of Violence

The hijacking[s], like the car and truck bombings that have become an almost daily occurrence in Lebanon, . . . [are] best understood as an act of desperation by a people who have seen their homeland invaded and destroyed by forces infinitely more powerful than themselves. Faced with the overwhelming military power of Israel, which is sustained and encouraged by the world's most powerful nation, there is little the victims can do other than to strike back randomly through individual, frequently suicidal attacks.

In These Times, June 26-July 9, 1985.

Different kinds of disorder are defined in different ways by ruling groups. What rulers choose to do about any politically deviant behavior hinges on how they assess the danger, or the advantage, of such disorder. The survival of the established order requires the acceptance of the ruling class' definition of reality. The ruling class will enforce the definitions that are functional to it: black rioters or revolutionaries are defined as terrorists and shot, while more recently Ronald Reagan and New York City mayor Ed Koch had both refused to label other criminal acts as terrorism. These refusals have served as a quasi-official method of repressing certain subordinate and potentially dangerous populations: pro-choice women, the black "underclass," etc. The fact that these acts, like all vigilantism, have the support of a community of people makes them easier to ignore or downplay. . . .

Drawing Distinctions

At one level, as some pacifists argue, all terrorism is violent and therefore equally reprehensible. However, distinctions can, and should, be drawn. The concept of terrorism should exclude sabotage directed carefully and solely at property. The damaging of draft board files or missile components, while illegal, is non-violent in that the consequent suffering, if any, is undertaken solely by the perpetrator. This is clearly not the case for the abortion clinic bombers, whose sabotage disregards the danger of death or injury to persons, even uninvolved bystanders. . . .

In crossing the threshold of violence, caution is in order. We are talking about times when the police appear blind in their right eyes, so to speak. Laws exist to protect us, but are not enforced. Nazi gangs terrorized German streets while the police looked the other way. Klansmen burned the Freedom Rider buses, as police and FBI watched. The houses of voter registration volunteers in '63 and '64 were bombed and shot at; calling the sheriff was futile. Peasants and farmers are legally evicted from lands farmed by their ancestors. When the law works to stop the Nazis, the Klan, and the landlords, and ceases to define their victims as "terrorists" for fighting back, then we will have law and order, and armed defense will no longer be utilized. Until then, some people will defend themselves with weapons of violence. Decency requires that we not lump them together with those who terrorize them. . . .

Community Values

Other forms of terrorism cannot be stopped, short of the kind of fundamental changes that eliminate the dissatisfactions which are its seedbed. This implies a serious reallocation of resources and vast changes in public ideology. Terrorist groups can survive for very long periods even in countries which overwhelmingly reject their goals. This is true even under conditions in which population movement is thoroughly monitored and civil liberties are far more restricted than in the U.S. West Germany is one such example, where there is widespread support for strict counter-terror methods.

The U.S. is a relatively loosely-organized, poorly policed society with a long tradition of vigilantism. Today it is the most violent society in the industrialized world. Paradoxically, its citizens have, on paper, more protections from arbitrary police power than those of any other country in the world. It is clear, however, that these protections are hardly applied impartially. Whether it be street crime or "terrorism," the suppression of domestic disorder by the state requires the abrogation of rights. As the clamor for order increases, the differences between the U.S. and other nations will decrease. The state will define street crime, as well as political disorder of which it does not approve, as "terrorism," and order, imposed by both the police and by vigilante groups, will tend to supplant law.

The alternative is to develop methods of community order which are both independent of the state, and nonviolent; that is, incorporating an ethic of problem-solving and reconciliation. Neighborhood anti-crime patrols may be a first step for some communities—a form of nonviolent vigilantism. On a wider scale, the task is formidable to say the least. After all, violence is as American as apple pie.

89

"The practice of regarding an entire population as potential and legitimate targets is terrorism's defining principle."

Terrorism Is Never Justified

William McGurn

William McGurn is editorial features editor of the *Wall Street Journal's* European edition. In the following viewpoint, Mr. McGurn argues that in many war-related situations, violence can be justified. However, acts of terrorism cannot be included in these justifiable situations. Terrorists knowingly target innocent civilians and therefore transcend all rules of just warfare.

As you read, consider the following questions:

1. Why are most people confused by terrorism, according to the author?
2. Why does the author believe terrorism is "irredeemably evil"?
3. Does the author believe terrorists represent the people? Why or why not?

William McGurn's, "The Terrorist Outlaw," Reprinted with permission from *Catholicism in Crisis*, September 1985.

Terrorism has become the accepted model for the modern use of force, with terrorists themselves often enjoying more moral credibility than the democratic states they are trying to bring down. This growing acceptance of what is by definition an outlaw activity poses a graver threat to the liberal democratic polis than nuclear weapons. . . .

What makes terrorism a graver threat than nuclear weapons is its nature. Whereas nuclear weapons are means that can be shaped according to human will and strategies, terrorism rejects the foundation of all Western ethics: the conviction that even the noble cause has limits.

That terrorism has achieved success far out of proportion even to the extensive carnage left in its wake can be measured by the pronounced impotence in the face of this threat. In its most naked form, there is the lack of any coherent (much less co-ordinated) response to Col. Moammar Qadhafi's remarkable public assertions that he reserves the right to hunt down those Libyan exiles who do not share his vision. Lest this be thought another instance of Third World braggadocio, the colonel's record . . . shows him true to his word: Libyan assassins have killed in Germany, Italy, and Switzerland, not to mention the gunning down of a British policewoman by a sniper within Libya's London embassy, and their much-publicized failed assassination in Egypt.

George Washington a Terrorist?

However bad this lack of response to Qadhafi is, worse still is how this impotence has filtered down into the discourse of ordinary Americans. Two good examples are the everywhere-repeated platitude that "one man's terrorist is another man's freedom fighter" and the equally facile sugestion that "George Washington was a terrorist" because his troops fired at British soldiers from the woods. With statements like these, is it any wonder that Americans can call for us to "recognize the PLO" or are confused by the Reagan administration's support for the Nicaraguan contras? . . .

If Western governments are to triumph over bloodshed and chaos, they must meet the threat head-on. In this, they ought to take a cue from the terrorists themselves, who have no illusions about their incompatibility with the assumptions of the Western order. Having taken the-end-justifies-the-means to its logical conclusion, the terrorist has enshrined the monstrous twentieth-century notion of total warfare, the idea that anything goes. It is at once the root of their power and the source of their name, for terrorism is the practice of sowing terror into a population.

The practice of regarding an entire population as potential and legitimate targets is terrorism's defining principle and represents a clean break with all Western norms on the use of force. Whatever the past depravities of national or private armies, or resistance

"I can't understand why no one seems interested in our problems."

movements like the French Resistance or revolutionary forces like America's Continental Army, never in principle did they repudiate the right noncombatants had to safety from direct attack. This is not to say that noncombatants were never harmed or killed by some groups. It is to say, however, that in the past (with the notable exception of the French revolutionaries) the Western world was united on the principle that warriors must operate within certain ethical confines. To search for a parallel threat to civilization, one must go back to Huns, Goths, Vandals, Turks and their attacks on Europe. The prayer "Deliver us from the barbarian invader" is remarkably apt for our time, when the grocer has as much to fear as the general.

Confusion About Terrorism

At bottom, the present ambivalence about terrorism—the tendency to think of it in terms of whose ox is being gored—derives less from acceptance than from confusion, the fruit of our abandonment of just-war thinking at the moment it is needed most. Part of this is due to the false notion that just-war criteria represent a neat equation yielding a specific answer, when in reality they are simply the weighing together of various ethical principles, some of which may conflict. In contrast to circumstances, principles do not become outdated, and the just-war tradition centers on two: first, the propriety of going to war (*jus ad bellum*); second, the propriety of the belligerent's subsequent conduct (*jus in bello*). . . . The classic line boils down to this: permission, yet limitation.

Applied to terrorism, the first principle can be pretty much dropped, though it will become important when evaluating the claims of guerrillas, i.e., those who fight within accepted means. For the first part of our tradition tells us that it takes much more than a worthy cause to legitimate the call to arms; as even the best and most justified war inevitably imposes terrible human costs, the presumption is always against it. It therefore rests on the belligerent to prove that force is necessary, and this raises questions of authority, proper goals, prospects for victory, etc.—serious objections by no means met by terrorists.

But the guerrilla may legitimately answer all these questions in his favor, and by virtue of having a weaker force will have to rely on unorthodox strategies of fighting. Assassination is a favorite tool of guerrillas and is not ruled out by just-war criteria; the German resistance plots against Hitler's life appear eminently just. So long as the guerrilla wages his war within the constraints of proportion (not using excessive force) and discriminations (not directly harming noncombatants), he is a guerrilla and not a terrorist. Since he aims only at legitimate military/political targets, the population at large does not feel terrorized by his presence.

Terrorists Reject Limits

The terrorist is, by contrast, defined by his means, and the ethical assumption behind this difference is the key to understanding why terrorism is irredeemably evil. By rejecting limits observed by guerrillas or other revolutionaries, terrorists place themselves outside the area of legitimacy; they are outlaws.

Thus far no public official today has made this point with the clarity of Secretary of State George Shultz. . . . Mr. Shultz quoted the answer given by the late Senator Henry Jackson. "The idea that one person's terrorist is another person's freedom fighter cannot be sanctioned," he said. "Freedom fighters or revolutionaries don't blow up buses containing noncombatants; terrorist murderers do. Freedom fighters don't assassinate innocent businessmen, or hijack and hold hostage innocent men, women and children; terrorist murderers do. It is a disgrace that democracies would allow the treasured word 'freedom' to be associated with the acts of terrorists." . . .

In a modern conflict, for example, a central communications center staffed by civilians, a munitions factory employing women, or a key port in an enemy supply line are all integral parts of the war effort. Given the right circumstances each might make a reasonable target, even if an unavoidable side effect was the taking of many innocent lives. But to extend this to include the targeting of the businessman who sells the enemy phone lines, the farmer who supplies the food, or indeed the mother who supplies them soldiers is a mockery of reason. The line admittedly is often fuzzy—but a fuzzy line is a line nonetheless. . . .

No Good Terrorists

Terrorism is the cancer of the modern world. No state is immune to it. It is a dynamic organism which attacks the healthy flesh of the surrounding society. It has the essential hallmark of malignant cancer: unless treated, and treated drastically, its growth is inexorable, until it poisons and engulfs the society on which it feeds and drags it down to destruction. . . .

There is no such person as a "good" terrorist, anywhere, at any time, in any circumstances.

Paul Johnson, "The Cancer of Terrorism," *How the West Can Win*, 1986.

If we are to defeat terrorism we must understand exactly what it is. With supreme faith in an abstract cause invoked to justify any action, terrorists cross that fuzzy line. Guerrillas, on the other hand, who may or may not be justified, have more or less traditional targets, and so the population is not directly threatened. Indeed, part of the criteria for a just guerrilla struggle is that the guerillas in some way represent the community—because it is from the community that they derive the authority to use force in the first place.

Terrorist claims to represent "the people" are therefore completely discredited, for if the people themselves may be objects of attack then any claim to represent them is merely a rhetorical convenience. Nor may the terrorist acquit himself of this guilt by invoking a worthy cause, since as we have seen it is imperative not only that there be a good reason to resort to force but that the force be used within certain constraints. And the first of these constraints is the exercise of discrimination. . . .

Terrorists Focus on Democracy

This is not too surprising, because the idea of limits on behavior—even on the righteous—is the basis of all law, international, civil, moral. So too it is not surprising to find that terrorism in practice reveals a horrible consistency: its targets have all been areas of vital importance to the West, and for the most part these targets are democracies. Theoretically, at least, terrorists could attack totalitarian regimes (though this is harder to do); in practice it is otherwise. Bombs do not explode in Moscow or Warsaw cafes; they go off in Paris, New York, Belfast, Jerusalem and Rome. I make no claims to the extent of Soviet and Soviet-bloc support for terrorism. My purpose is merely to note the marriage; how convenient the union between the war without limits and the state without limits.

In his book *Just and Unjust Wars*, Michael Walzer struck much the same chord. "In its modern manifestations," wrote Walzer, "terrorism is the totalitarian form of war and politics. It shatters the war convention and the political code. It breaks across moral limits beyond which no further limitation seems possible, for within the categories of civilian and citizen, there isn't any smaller group for which immunity might be claimed . . . Terrorists anyway make no such claim; they kill anybody."

Over the past few years, Western observers have begun to comment on the affinity between right-wing and left-wing terrorists, which parallels the affinity between Fascists and Communists. During John Paul II's trip to Holland, for example, numerous groups popped up offering to assassinate him, and no one was sure whether these threats were coming from the left or the right. But Western policy makers must not allow themselves to be distracted by this, because it really doesn't matter. Whatever the goals dividing the various terrorists, they are far less important than the premises that unite them. Left-wing and right-wing terrorists, in other words, are not merely similar—they are the same.

The *New York Times* ran on its front page an Associated Press newsphoto of an elderly Israeli woman who had been killed when a Palestinian bomb hit her bus. Pointing to the heavy parcels of food underneath her legs and her generally cramped position, my father noted it would have made a dramatic anti-terrorist poster: An innocent woman murdered as she brought home food for her family. It could have been my grandmother, he noted, or anyone's grandmother. But in the mind of the person who planted the bomb, this old woman was an enemy equal to Ariel Sharon. This is what is meant by terror.

"It's no crime and there's no moral wrong in lifting a stone, planting a bomb, raising a rifle against those who oppress our people."

IRA Terrorism Is Justified

John M. Feehan

While the struggle in Northern Ireland has many roots and causes, two warring factions are evident: The Protestant-backed unionists, whose members want Ireland to remain a British colony, and the Catholic-supported nationalists, who seek an independent Ireland, free from British intervention. This virtual civil war has been the inspiration for many brutal acts of violence on both sides. On the nationalist side is the notorious guerilla organization, the Irish Republican Army or IRA. Strongly-supported by many nationalists, it is equally deplored by many others because of its violent, anti-British tactics. In the following viewpoint, John M. Feehan argues that this radical group has no choice but to use violence to attain its goals. A native of Ireland, Mr. Feehan is the author of many books on the Irish political situation as well as biographies of Irish rebels, including *Bobby Sands and the Tragedy of Northern Ireland*, from which this article is excerpted.

As you read, consider the following questions:

1. According to the author, what type of terrorism is justified?
2. Why, does the author claim, do IRA members commit heinous acts such as murder and bombing?
3. Why does the author oppose the unionists' cause?

John M. Feehan, *Bobby Sands and the Tragedy of Northern Ireland*. Sag Harbour, NY: The Permanent Press, 1985. Reprinted by permission.

Violence is a word that has been bandied about a lot by speechmakers but it is a reality that has to be faced. The best definition of violence I have been able to find is that of the great South American Archbishop, Dom Helder Camera. Archbishop Camera shows that violence has three different yet indivisible tiers: *The Violence of Injustice, The Violence of Reaction* and *Institutional Violence*. Serious injustice in any state is in itself a major act of violence. This in turn produces the second tier, the reaction of the oppressed populace to injustice, which in turn produces the third tier, the reaction of security forces to the second tier. It is of course a waste of time trying to eliminate the second and third tiers while the first still exists. Contrariwise eliminate the first tier and you automatically eliminate the other two. So when I speak of violence, I speak of it in the context of these three indivisible dimensions. . . .

IRA Violence Well-Publicised

If it seems that I have not highlighted the extreme violence of the Nationalist paramilitaries it is solely because it has been so well blazoned and placarded already. What has not been so well publicised is the fact that the majority of acts of violence in Northern Ireland *were the result of institutional violence,* i.e. they were caused, not by the paramilitaries, but by the security forces. It is easy to be negative and to condemn but so difficult to try to understand, to construct, to build on whatever good is around. If there is ever to be peace in Northern Ireland, the ruling classes of both countries will have to sit down and talk with the men of violence. That again is *realpolitik.* Could a beginning not be made now? Could those who in their righteousness condemn, not recall the words of W.B. Yeats:

Too long a sacrifice
Can make a stone of the heart? . . .

Getting to Know the IRA

I had to talk with, amongst others, many of the men who are currently being termed 'thugs, murderers and criminals.' I was conditioned to expect a kind of seedy cross between Bill Sykes and Al Capone. The reality turned out to be quite different. Those with whom I spoke were reasonable, intelligent and dedicated young men. They would much prefer to live a normal life but this was denied them and they had come to the end of the road, to the point where they believed that only the gun produced results. Again and again they quizzed me as to what I would personally do if I had been treated as they and their families were. Again and again I funked the answer. Responsible elements within the British army itself privately admitted to admiring their dedication and self-sacrifice while publicly condemning them. There was nothing very secretive about them except their whereabouts. None of them were in the £20,000 a year bracket of most of their public critics. In fact, I doubt if any of them had little more than pocket money. They spoke freely to me and answered my questions, even though with my background they had no reason to trust me too far. In trying to help me many ran great personal risks. At their own request I am respecting their anonymity but despite this they will understand how deeply grateful I am.

It is at this point that many readers might expect me to pose the pompous and self-righteous question: How could such reasonable men carry out the killings they have? I spent fifteen years of my life in the army and I know the mind of a soldier and the way he thinks when a war is on. To those seeking an answer to this question, I suggest that they read any good military biography or indeed any good biography of Michael Collins, Tom Barry or Dan Breen. A soldier with a gun in his hand does not exactly think like a Child of Mary or a Jehovah's Witness. I am not recommending the way of the soldier but I think that *realpolitik* demands that we at least try to understand it. . . .

The British Must Be Ousted

I find it startling to hear myself say that I am prepared to die first rather than succumb to their oppressive torture and I know that I am not on my own, that many of my comrades hold the same. And I thought of my dead comrades again. My friends who had stood beside me one day and were dead the next. Boys and girls just like myself, born and raised in the nationalist ghettos of Belfast to be murdered by foreign soldiers and lecky sectarian thugs. How many have been murdered at their hands throughout the occupied Six Counties. Too many! One boy or girl was one too many! How many more Irish people would die? How many more lives would be lost before the British had decided they had murdered enough and were forced to get out of Ireland forever? Inside and outside of gaol it was all the same—oppression bearing down upon you from every direction. Every street corner displaying an armed British soldier, every street having endured its share of suffering and grief at their hands.

Bobby Sands, *One Day in My Life*, 1983.

It might be well to pause and examine broadly some of the uncertainties and inaccuracies in circulation which, if not understood, might easily distort our picture. . . . Most of these distortions are the result of a superb British propaganda exercise aided, perhaps unwittingly, by a number of Irish politicians and by sections of the Irish media.

The public outside Northern Ireland, and particularly in the South, are well and truly informed about what is happening there. . . .

One of the main objectives of the British is to portray the IRA as thugs and murderers with a lust for blood and in this objective they have been extraordinarily successful particularly in Southern Ireland. It seems therefore a great pity that the following statement issued by the Provisional IRA was not given the publicity that would enable the Irish people to weigh up for themselves if in fact they were thugs and murderers. This important statement was issued as early as 1973:

> Will talk achieve more than the gun? Yes, definitely yes. And the IRA are more than willing to talk. We have said many times that we detest this war with its suffering and misery and we speak from first hand knowledge of that suffering and misery. We would much rather settle our differences in a civilised way. But let one point be very clear. It is the British, not we, who still refuse to negotiate.

In 1981 there was scarcely a media outlet that did not highlight Danny Morrison's famous speech about the 'armalite and the ballot box.' What was never highlighted, however, were other words he uttered:

> We are a peaceful people. I repeat we are a peaceful people. But it needs to be said fearlessly, because it is the truth: after what we have come through for fifty years, the repression, the discrimination. . . . it's no crime and there's no moral wrong in lifting a stone, planting a bomb, raising a rifle against those who oppress our people.

One may agree or disagree with these statements. But surely the public are entitled to know that such statements were made. They should not be kept in the dark.

Again we have never been told that five hundred Nationalist pubs have been blown up, thirty bombing attacks on Catholic churches and forty thousand Nationalists bombed and burned out of their homes. The public are entitled to know of these happenings. . . .

I have given these few examples, out of literally thousands I have come across, of how vitally important news concerning Northern Ireland does not get over to the public and it is hard to see how such a public could make any kind of a reasoned judgment on the tragic affairs across the border when they are kept in the dark about such important matters. But do those who purvey this news really want us to make a reasoned judgment? . . .

Not a Religious Struggle

The struggle in Northern Ireland is a Religious Struggle.

This statement is an over-simplification and I think that most people now realise that the conflict has very little to do with religion. Catholics are not fighting Protestants and vice versa, simply on the grounds of religion. The conflict in Northern Ireland is basically between two groups of people, the Privileged and the

Underprivileged, the Haves and the Have-nots. It is an economic conflict. The Privileged are the Orange Order, their minions and supporters, the Underprivileged are the rest of the population. The Orange Order are the overlords—everyone else is the underling. But behind all one suspects the sinister hand of Britain keeping the statelet divided. . . .

The Unionists Are the Upper Class

One of the great myths of British propaganda is that in Ireland there are *two nations*. There are not two nations. There is one nation only, with different traditions. They say, with tongue in cheek, that because the Northern Unionists want to remain with Britain therefore it is a separate nation. The British know quite well that there is only one nation with a privileged group in occupation of one part of it—and they support that group for their own interests. There are of course two traditions in the North and to this one can only say "So what?" There are three traditions in the Republic, the Gaelic, the Irish and the Anglo-Irish. In Switzerland, Belgium, France, the United States and other countries there are several different traditions. The existence of different traditions in a country does not mean that each tradition must have its own political independence. The Bavarian Catholics can co-exist side by side with Prussian Protestants. In all these countries the various traditions are able to live and work in harmony, but the desire of one tradition to be overlord and to have all the goodies is the reason why the two traditions in Northern Ireland cannot work together.

The British Will Never Break Us

There is no way the British are going to break us. In order to obtain any social justice we simply have to destroy the Northern state and unite the country by any means open to us.

Orangeism [British rule] will never be halted by negotiation. It will only be halted by force, and even if the struggle has to go on for the next twenty, thirty, fifty years, we are ready for it. Remember that the IRA of today were only children in 1969 when the troubles started. We are now an ongoing and continuing force—and this is something that never before happened in the history of Ireland.

IRA member quoted in *Bobby Sands and the Tragedy of Northern Ireland*, 1983.

The politically immature speeches of some Southern Irish politicians that we must make fundamental changes in our constitution is an example of the pathetic grasp these politicians have of the whole Northern question. If we turned our constitution upside down and inside out it would not make the slightest difference. The Unionists want to hold on to their privileged position, their total domination of all aspects of life, and they have already treated with utter contempt any suggestion of changes in our constitution.

There is now a possibility that the Nationalists may soon outnumber them but Harold McCusker, Unionist MP recently made it clear that even in such an event they would not accept a United Ireland. Majority rule for Unionists only operates when it suits themselves.

The Unionists struggle in Northern Ireland is about 'goodies' and not about 'gods.' . . .

The British army is in Ireland as a peace-keeping force.

Outside Northern Ireland the British like to portray the role of the army as that of a kind of fairy godmother protecting the innocent, seeing them safely to their homes at night, if not exactly tucking them into bed. One young British officer in a military bar said to me: 'We are in Northern Ireland to try to preserve some form of civilised living.' I think he was hurt when I told him with some derision that very few people in Northern Ireland would accept that view, and indeed most would laugh at its naivety. . . .

Brutal Harassment

There is hardly anyone living in a Nationalist area that has not experienced . . . brutal harassment. But one can travel freely through the Unionist areas without seeing a British soldier. Regrettably, the British army have a long string of killings to their credit, and the few who ever appear in court are usually found not guilty. I have no later statistics, but up to 1980 the admitted figure of killings of *innocent* people by the security forces is 116. This figure *does not* include killings of Nationalists or other paramilitaries—just ordinary, innocent men, women and children. . . .

Forced into Violence

I think I could not be accused of exaggerating if I suggest that there is much more than a doubt hanging over the activities of the British army in Northern Ireland. And if the forces of law and order do not administer justice and are themselves guilty of criminal acts then one can begin to understand how young men . . . are forced to resort to violence. . . .

The British Army Occupation Begins

Initially the Nationalist population rejoiced and hoped that the army would protect them but unfortunately this hope proved unfounded. It turned out that the British army were merely a substitute for the B Specials.

When Bobby [Sands] was a child the British army were his TV heroes:

> The British army always fought for the 'right side' and the police were always the 'good guys.'

He was to wake up later to the hard reality:

As the unfamiliar sound of gunfire was still echoing, there soon appeared alien figures, voices and faces, in the form of armed British soldiers on our streets. But no longer did I think of them as my childhood 'good guys', for their presence alone caused food for thought. Before I could work out the solution it was answered for me in the form of early morning raids. From now on my heart pounded at the heavy clatter of the soldiers in the early morning stillness and I carefully peered from behind the drawn curtains to watch the neighbours' doors be kicked in, the fathers and sons being dragged out by the hair and being flung into the backs of sinister-looking armoured cars. This was followed by blatant murder: the shooting dead of our people on the streets in cold blood.

Now the Nationalist population, virtually unarmed, found itself faced not only by the police, but the British army as well. In this desperate situation they sought help from their friends in the South only to find that nothing was forthcoming. In the South the politicians might be said to have covered their heads in the sand, and the leader of the government refused all help to the Nationalists. This refusal almost broke their spirit. They felt totally and completely let-down and betrayed. With everything and everyone against them they saw nothing ahead but the road to extermination.

The Formation of the IRA

It was when they had reached this very gloomy point of despair that a new hope appeared, a new force came into being, a force which in effect said: 'Do not give up. We will protect you!' That force came to be known as the Provisional IRA, or for short, the Provos. The violence had now escalated from civil rights marches to virtual civil war. Here again one must honestly pose the terrible *realpolitik* question: Are the Northern Nationalists to be blamed for supporting the gun? What other option had they?

The Official IRA had been fighting spasmodically in the North since the foundation of the state without any real success. In the late 'fifties and early 'sixties largely, but not only, because they had been infiltrated by members of the British Communist Party who sought to use the Republican movement to set up a Marxist front for political and social agitation, they had neither the will nor the means to defend or help the beleagured Nationalists. The Northern Brigade, disgusted with this failure broke away and founded a non-Marxist political movement, Provisional Sinn Féin and a military wing, the Provisional IRA. It was to this new movement that the Nationalist population turned. Later Official Sinn Féin became the Workers Party and it is said that the Official IRA disbanded leaving the field to the Provos.

Over the next few months and years hundreds of young men and women joined this new force because they saw in it the only

102

means to defend their homes and families from the attacks of the Unionist gangs, the police and the British army. . . .

Most of the Nationalist population, particularly in the ghettos, saw in the IRA their saviours and protectors. These young men believed they were the inheritors of the oldest guerrilla force in the world who had waged a war against the British for more than sixty years. They did not see themselves as terrorists because their object, . . . was not to strike terror into civilians, but to shield and defend half-a-million Irish people from destruction and perhaps death and in the process to get rid of the occupying British whom they saw as the predominant cause of all this suffering.

Bombings Suit IRA Purposes

Quite frankly it suited IRA strategy to carry out selective bombings in Belfast, Derry, and other towns in Occupied Ulster. They see these actions as a legitimate part of war, the targets chosen being military and police barracks, outposts, customs offices, administrative and government buildings, electricity transformers and pylons, certain cinemas, hotels, clubs, dance halls, pubs, all of which provide relaxation and personal comforts for the British forces; also business targets e.g., factories, firms, stores (sometimes under the guise of CO-OPs) owned in whole or part by British financiers or companies, or who in any way are a contributory factor to the well-being of Her Majesty's invading forces, and in certain instances residences of people known to harbor or be in league with espionage personnel. . . . In many ways this campaign is reminiscent of that carried out by the underground Resistance in France during World War II.

In all cases IRA bomb squads give adequate warning though these warnings are sometimes withheld or delayed deliberately by the British army as a counter-tactic, with view to making optimum publicity out of the injured and the dead in their propaganda war on the IRA. In no instance has the "warning rule" been violated by the guerrilla forces in sharp contrast with the "no warning" methods used by the Unionist gangs and British army.

Freedom Struggle by the Provisional IRA, in *The Terrorism Reader*, 1979.

This is how the Provisional IRA began and I think it behooves us all to take a hard cold look at these circumstances and not be influenced by any propaganda from any quarter. We must also ask ourselves some *realpolitik* questions: Who are really responsible for the birth of the Provisional IRA? Do we, here in the South, share in that responsibility by our indifference and inactivity towards a people whom we constitutionally claim to be our own? Before we begin to throw stones perhaps we might examine the structure of the glasshouse! . . .

One of the hard facts, which so few people in the South seem to believe is that the Nationalist population accepted the new IRA—they housed them, fed them, hid them and whether we like it or not *this support continues down to the present day*. When I asked one young married woman living in a Nationalist area if she really supported the IRA despite the condemnations by church and state, she answered without hesitation: 'Of course I do and so do all my neighbours. Who else have we to protect us? You people in the South haven't a clue what it is like to live up here. If we hadn't the Provos we'd be as good as dead. Will you or your loud-mouthed politicians come up to help us?' I had no answer to her question. . . .

Goodwill of the People

In all guerrilla warfare the strongest weapon the guerrillas have is the goodwill of the people. It was this weapon that won the Anglo-Irish War in 1918-1921 and it was the absence of the same weapon that lost the Civil War for the Republicans in 1922-1923. In Northern Ireland the IRA were able to make full use of this weapon insofar as the vast majority of Nationalist homes were open to them, particularly in the ghettos and the rural areas, and I can find no evidence to suggest that such is not the case at the present moment. . . .

I came across a curious incident which intrigued me and gave me an unusual insight into the value of opinion polls. Some outfit or other was conducting a public opinion poll in Belfast as to the attitude of the people to the IRA. In one small house in a Nationalist area the housewife was asked if she approved of the IRA and in strong, vehement language she expressed her disapproval of them and everything they stood for and almost threw the questioner out for daring to ask such a question. The enquirer duly noted this for his statistics. What she did not say of course was that at that very moment two IRA men on the run were asleep in a room upstairs. Her native cunning had told her that there was a danger any answer she made might ultimately find its way into the computer at police headquarters, so she stretched the truth somewhat and the media were able to give us another researched statistic!

"The IRA fights not to bring freedom and life but terror and death."

IRA Terrorism Is Not Justified

Ian Paisley, Nora Bradford, and John Taylor

In January 1982, three spokespeople for the Unionists party of Northern Ireland spoke before the National Press Club in Washington, DC. Their speeches make up the following viewpoint. The first speaker is Mrs. Ian Paisley, who read a speech written by her husband, who had been denied entry into the United States because of his controversial reputation. Reverend Paisley is perhaps the most outspoken and well-known critic of the IRA. Although he has a large and tenacious group of followers, he also has numerous fervent critics, including many senators in the United States, which contributed to his visa denial. Mrs. Nora Bradford is the second speaker and one whose life was touched directly by the IRA when it assassinated her husband. The final speaker, John Taylor, is a Unionist party member of Parliament. In the following viewpoint, all three emphasize the terror, instability, and fear the IRA generates in Northern Ireland.

As you read, consider the following questions:

1. Mr. Paisley compares proportionally the IRA impact on Ireland to what it would be on the United States. Do you think his comparison is valid?
2. Why is the IRA a threat to the United States, according to Mr. Paisley?
3. What does Mr. Taylor beg US citizens not to do?

Mrs. Ian Paisley, Nora Bradford, and John Taylor, speeches made before the National Press Club in Washington, DC on January 18, 1982.

Mrs. Ian Paisley: First of all, I wish to thank you most sincerely for the privilege of addressing your august assembly even though I can only do so through my good wife. I must apologize, of course, for my enforced absence today especially as it denies you to see at first hand my devil's horns, hooves, and tail. But it appears that there are those in your State Department who feel it part of their public duty to protect you from such. Hence my absence. While I do not wish to dwell on the point, I must say that the serious implication of the State Department's action is that in this, the great country of freedoms, that most fundamental of freedoms, freedom of expression, has been denied to an elected representative of the majority community in Ulster. Whereas it appears to me that the IRA and its apologists can come and go from the USA without let or hindrance just as some of those Congressmen who played a part in having my visa revoked have often exercised in my country the very right they have seen fit to deny me. In pondering why the IRA and their supporters should be so determined to try and stymie this campaign on behalf of the Ulster unionists people, one can but conclude that militant Irish republicanism which for so long has peddled its propaganda free from challenge, fears the challenge which this delegation presents to them. And well they might, for we come to North America today to explode the IRA-spawned myth that Ulster is British by compulsion rather than choice and that the IRA are gallant freedom fighters rather than blood-thirsty terrorists.

IRA: Messengers of Terror

As members of this delegation can personally prove and testify, the IRA fights not to bring freedom and life but terror and death. Nora Bradford would not be here today in place of her late husband if he had not been savagely murdered by the IRA, nor would John Taylor bear the marks of IRA bullets. The wanton terrorism which has touched this delegation only typifies the horrendous terror to which the people of Ulster have been subject by those who refuse to accept the right of the community they terrorize to freely determine their own future. What the IRA cannot attain by the ballot it seeks by the bullet.

In order to convey to the people of America the position and plight of the people of Ulster, there is no better way than to translate what is happening in Ulster onto the American level. Northern Ireland has a population of one and one-half million people. During the last twelve years in our small land there have been 2,169 murders, 26,750 shootings, and 10,600 bombings. These are not mere statistics comparable to deaths caused on the roads, for this violence in Ulster has not been the result of fortuitous accidents. Rather it has been the consequence of a coordinated and deliberate campaign masterminded from headquarters in an adjacent country, namely, the Republic of Ireland, which aspires to take over the terrority of Ulster. How would citizens of the United States feel if, in the hope of bringing about a takeover of their country and placing of it under the rule of the government of another adjacent country, terrorists brought about a similar state of affairs in the United States? To put the possibility into perspective we take account of the fact that the population of the United States of America is one hundred and forty five times that of Northern Ireland. This would mean that in the past twelve years there would have been 315,000 deaths, 3,900,000 shootings and 1,500,000 bombings. If this happened in the United States, how would US citizens regard the country on whose behalf the campaign of murder and violence was being waged and from within whose territory it was being masterminded? And if some of the perpetrators of these violent acts were caught and put in prison, would you as citizens welcome demands from other countries that such prisoners should be given freedom to run their prisons according to their own wishes? And if it was clear that the perpetrators of violence were receiving arms and support from eastern Europe and had links with worldwide Marxist organizations, would you as citizens have more kindly feelings towards them? Would US citizens admire and patronize those who committed murders in such a campaign but ignore the widows and orphans of those who were murdered?

To even better appreciate the feelings in Ulster, consider how

AUTH, COPYRIGHT 1986 THE PHILADELPHIA INQUIRER. Reprinted with permission of Universal Press Syndicate. All rights reserved.

Americans would feel if such terrorism was concentrated in one state, say Texas, and the campaign was directed to the reunification of Texas with Mexico against the will of its citizens. What would be the attitude of most US citizens then to these troubles in Texas and this demand for its reunification to Mexico? Would they welcome senior officials of the British government declaring that the people of Britain were hoping and praying for the reunification of Mexico? Would there be much public support for those in the USA who supported the terrorist objective of transferring Texas to Mexico? One would like to think that the vast majority of American people would want the Texans to be allowed to retain the American allegiance and citizenship that they preferred and it is certain that most people in Britain would agree.

A Communist-Linked Organization

Let us also not forget the international security dimension of this whole issue. Northern Ireland is a part of the United Kingdom and the United Kingdom is the ally and partner of the USA in NATO. Does it really help the USA and its allies if a native American pressure group, to the undoubted satisfaction of Marxist terrorist groups throughout the world, advocates the cutting off of territory from the United Kingdom and the ceding of this territory against the wishes of its inhabitants to a country outside the alliance altogether, where the USSR maintains a surprisingly large embassy staff in the relatively small city of Dublin? Likewise, does it serve the American interest for such native American pressure groups to supply funds to Irish terrorists for the purchase of communist weapons? Yet, alas, and to the great personal cost not only to this delegation but the entire people of Ulster, this is precisely what has been happening. If by our visit we can do something to put an end to this funding of communist-linked terror, then not only will our time have been well spent on behalf of the people of Ulster, but also we will have served the real interest of all Americans who care for the standards and civilization which we in the west have created and are proud to uphold.

Nora Bradford: I come here today to tell you a little of the violence created by subversives in our province of Ulster. My husband should have stood here today. But as you know, he was murdered in cold blood by the IRA as he met with his constituents.

There are two reasons why I believe they killed him. Firstly, he was digging deep into their money-making rackets in Belfast from which they fund terrorist activities. These include allegations of embezzlement by computer of over one hundred thousands pounds from the Royal Victoria Hospital. Secondly, this very trip, which was largely Robert's brainchild, if successful, will nip off the very substantial source of funds from here and the

United States of America. We seek to persuade Irish-American politicians that their pressure to unite Ulster with Ireland against the repeatedly-expressed will of the majority misguidedly aids those who killed my husband. Robert's work was effective; therefore, he had to be removed.

We must realize that this struggle is not isolated to Ulster. When one looks at the world situation in terms of communist takeovers and terrorism, it becomes apparent that the terrorism that has taken my husband is part of a worldwide strategy. . . .

Those Other Terrorists

When is a terrorist not a terrorist? In the confused view of some, he's not a terrorist when he belongs to the outlawed Irish Republican Army. Many an Irish-American feels about the IRA the way the Continentals felt about George Washington (though it is not reported that Washington enjoyed blowing the arms and legs off Tory children). They even tithe to it through the Irish Northern Aid Committee. . . .

The IRA is a murderous, anti-democratic, pro-Soviet apparatus that has artfully capitalized on sentimentality and some legitimate resentments. . . .

The IRA deserves no consideration from any thoughtful American.

The Washington Times, May 14, 1986.

I am making this trip because I wish to see the purpose Robert intended fulfilled. Evil men thought they could harm Robert. They merely succeeded in sending this man of God to be with his lord, a state he has spent his entire life working towards. They who intended great evil only succeeded in doing great good. I end with a quotation that Robert was particularly fond of using: "All that is required for the triumph of evil is that good men do nothing."

John Taylor: Ulster is part of the United Kingdom since 1800 and intends to remain within the United Kingdom because that is the overwhelming desire of its people as stated clearly in every election in Ulster since the southern part of our island broke away from us and thus created the partition of Ireland. Partition exists not because of any action by Ulster or any change in the political attitudes of the Ulster people, but because the south really decided to oppose the Union of Great Britain and Ireland. The international border in our island between the United Kingdom and this new Republic of Ireland is no artificial line drawn at random across the island. It is a boundary freely recognized by the south of Ireland by the time it decided to partition Ireland, and represents the division between two peoples who happen to live on the same area of land. These people differ in religion, loyalties, aspirations, and nationality. In Ulster we are British as we have been for centuries. In peace and in war, we stand firmly with the United States and the West in the defense of freedom. Ulster opposes the narrow nationalism of southern Ireland, the imposition of one's religious teaching upon those of other religions as happens in the south, and the declared policy of neutralism by southern Ireland in the conflict of freedom and communism throughout the West.

US Ignores the Irish Majority

Today Ulster suffers from Irish Republican terrorism from IRA, political instability, and a weak economy with almost 20% of our people unemployed. . . . Because there is a large Irish-American lobby in the States, many will not have heard the other point of view, the Ulster point of view, which is the majority feeling throughout my province. It is natural that there should be considerable interest in the USA in Ulster not only because of the southern Irish lobby on the east coast but because of the very close links between Ulster and the USA over the past one hundred years. . . .

American Industry in Ireland

Ulster has become one of the main centers of investment in the European community by American industries. Some forty American firms in Ulster now employ over 30,000 people, and in addition, I am glad to say we receive over 40,000 American tourists per year to Northern Ireland. America therefore not only has an interest in Ulster, but it is actively contributing to Ulster's economy. We in Ulster welcome this American support. But . . . America can help Ulster further. The USA can ensure that IRA terrorism, opposed as it is by most people in Ulster and also by the Dublin government, does not receive financial support and encouragement from minority sections of the Irish-American community. The IRA has been responsible for more than 2000 murders in Ulster during the past ten years. It is detested by church and people in Ulster, and yet, unbelievably, IRA terrorism, through its kindred organization NORAID [Irish Northern Aid Committee] in the states, will receive over half a million dollars in 1981. This American support for IRA terrorism brings the United States into disrepute. We beg of the American people that they will not support this evil organization which has been responsible for the loss of so many innocent lives. The IRA is supported by communists from eastern Europe. It is its many members who wish to impose a socialist united Ireland on the Ulster people. It is closely linked to the PLO terrorists in the Middle East, where, it is recently confirmed by Foreign Minister Douglas Herd, many IRA terrorists are now trained. Above all, the IRA has no significant support from the Ulster people. It is not, and I repeat, NOT, a freedom movement and does not deserve the support of any country which respects the democratic wishes of the Ulster people and the right of Ulster to determine its own future.

Ireland Is a Victim of the IRA

[The IRA] have killed over a thousand people, most of them their own countrymen, since 1968. But the unitary Irish state is as far away as ever, and they themselves constitute the chief obstacle to its realization. Meanwhile, what has happened to the Irish Republic? . . . The very fabric of its state is under threat, and—since the IRA finances itself through the drug trade—Ireland now has one of the biggest drug problems in Western Europe. No harm of any consequence has been inflicted on Britain; it is Ireland and her people who are the victims of the men with guns.

Paul Johnson, "The Cancer of Terrorism," *How the West Can Win*, 1986.

The way I hear it . . . for Ulster, is for all interested parties to recognize that it is and will remain part of the United Kingdom. I welcome the recent moves by the Dublin government, belated as they obviously are, to introduce constitutional reform so that the south of Ireland may finally remove the arrogant and offensive articles 2 and 3 of its constitution which claim jurisdiction over our problems against the wishes of our people. Having accepted the reality of Ulster's position within the United Kingdom, then we in Ulster must work together to bring about the restoration of a devolved government, a similar system to that which exists in your states here in America. . . .

Ulster Suffers From a Remote Government

Devolved government in Ulster would not only satisfy the wish of Ulster people to remain British but it would also ensure participation and partnership of most parties and most religions in government, if not in cabinet. It would therefore create political stability, improve community feelings, isolate and reduce the impact of terrorism, and ensure a more efficient, on the spot government and administration of Northern Ireland. At present, we in Ulster suffer from a remote government from London by politicians who are neither elected by us nor answerable to us for their decisions. This is not democracy and it certainly has not been good government of Northern Ireland, for it has ensured that since 1972, Ulster is more divided, polarized, and economically deprived than it has been at any time under the government in Northern Ireland from 1912 to 1973. The way ahead is indeed to devolve government for us within the Union, the Union of Great Britain and Northern Ireland. Such a political solution would restore external confidence in Ulster and it would be my wish that America, wishing to help Ulster, would then find an even more attractive base for manufacturing industries in Europe, and also that we would become more popular as a holiday base for those in America who want to come back and see "the old sod" from whom so many families emigrated during the past few centuries.

Americans Should Hear the Other Side

I want to conclude in a final point and that is in relation to [the reasons for] our trip here. . . . One, is to appeal to those sections of the southern Irish community who are contributing funds via NORAID to the IRA. The second is to meet the press and media as we are now doing, and we appreciate your invitation. And the third, of course, is to meet those in Congress and in the administration. And I want to say that we have been disappointed that some of those Irish-American politicians who speak so freely about affairs in Northern Ireland and yet appear to know so little about the internal situation within Northern Ireland have up to now refused to meet us. . . . How can American politicians state the views on Ulster if they refuse to listen to both sides? Views which undermine the right of Ulster people to remain British. Views which give support and succor to the IRA terrorists, and views which run contrary to accepted western standards of civil rights and democracy. For far too long . . . Irish Republic propaganda has indoctrinated the American administration of Congress. The British-Ulster case is a just cause. I would throw down this challenge to the American politicians: . . . to meet with us, talk with us, speak and argue with us, but do not shut your minds to the Ulster-Unionists' viewpoint which is the majority viewpoint of the Northern Irish people.

"Justified struggle means the right of a people to seize and use all available means against the usurpers of their land."

The Palestinian Goal Justifies Terrorism

Abu Nidal

The Israeli/Arab conflict is primarily over the land of Israel. By United Nation's mandate, Jews were given the land formerly called Palestine to create a homeland, renamed Israel. This solution for the Jews created an impossible and impractical situation for the Palestinian people, many of whom had lived in Palestine for centuries. Many Palestinians have scattered to surrounding Arab nations, but millions still live in Israel and are constantly subject to Israeli mandates including forced evictions, and they cannot be legal citizens of the area their ancestors called their own. This volatile situation results in many bloody, tragic battles between Israelis and Arab nationalists within the Middle East, and also has its impact on Western Europe and beyond. In the following viewpoint, excerpted from an interview in the German publication *Der Spiegel*, avowed terrorist Abu Nidal explains why violent, armed struggle is necessary to achieve the goal of Palestinian liberation.

As you read, consider the following questions:

1. What does Mr. Nidal oppose?
2. Does Mr. Nidal claim he has ever murdered an innocent person?

Spiegel: Whom do you consider your enemy?

Abu Nidal: My enemy is the Zionist occupation of my homeland, Palestine. My enemy is imperialism in all its forms. My enemies are the divisions and factions in my Arab nation. Furthermore, my enemies are the chaotic situation in our Arab society as well as the oppression and misguidance of our younger generation.

I will tell you my dream: a united Arab nation that lives in freedom, justice, and equality.

Spiegel: Are explosive attacks and political murders legitimate means to realize this dream?

Abu Nidal: Entirely legitimate. That the Zionists have forcefully torn a part of my Arab homeland for themselves is in my eyes not even *the* crime. To me, *the* crime would be if we were to allow these Zionists to leave our homeland alive. That is my philosophy. I, Abu Nidal, consider myself the answer to Arab misfortunes.

Hatred of US Imperialism

Spiegel: Why do you hate the Americans so much?

Abu Nidal: If there is anything absolute in this world, it is our emnity against American imperialism. Without American help, the Zionist state would not still exist. The Americans get mixed up in the Gulf war and cause quarrels between Arabs. Should the Arab fight some day be victorious, we will not allow a single American to enter our territory.

I can assure you of one thing: if we get the chance to do the slightest damage to America, we will not hesitate to do so. Between the Americans and us, there can only be a war of life and death. In the next months and years the Americans will think of us.

Spiegel: What do you want to accomplish with your dark threats?

Abu Nidal: We only want for them [the Americans] to disappear from our land. They can elect President whomever they choose: a ballet dancer, a cowboy, an actor. But when the American planes drop bombs over our homes, that is terrorism and crime, and we will answer it with the same.

Spiegel: Have you put President Reagan on your death list?

Abu Nidal: Naturally. If we catch him, we can finally assign him for posterity his honored place in history. Reagan has spent hundred millions of dollars to secure the White House. We are pleased that he is so nervous; so he should remain.

Spiegel: Many Arabs welcome the American presence.

Abu Nidal: Unfortunately. I summon every king, every emir or sheikh in our region, to honestly admit whether he risks sleeping with his wife without first asking the Americans for permission. Who can honestly imagine that such a tiny state as [Arab] Qatar really owns its army, flag, and national hymn, if the Americans had not helped create this structure? . . .

Spiegel: You have made it absolutely clear that you are an irreconcilable enemy of imperialism and Zionism. But why do you attack Jewish schoolchildren, synagogues, and restaurants?

Abu Nidal: The question is not whether civilians or Jewish civil establishments are being hit, but rather that many such establishments which look innocent, in reality serve the Zionist secret service, Mossad [Israeli Secret Service]. . . .

Disagreements with the PLO

Spiegel: You were sentenced to death in absentia by Yassir Arafat [long-time leader of the Palestinian Liberation Organization]. How did this disagreement happen?

Abu Nidal: We have been in conflict since September 1970. We have never really understood each other. In the beginning we tried to lay our quarrel over Fatah [a faction of the Palestinian Liberation Organization] aside, but this democratic phase ended in March 1974. Arafat and his clique instigated a campaign against us, which led to bloodshedding. We quit Fatah.

For that more than 150 of our men had to give up their lives; Arafat's people murdered them in cold blood. Since this terror didn't get the desired results, Arafat arranged a show trial in our absence. My colleagues in the fight and I were sentenced, some of us to death, some of us to custody.

Arafat's people have tried many times to kill me. In the context of that, it is important to mention that not a single Arab nation protects me. We stand alone against the fury of Arafat.

Terrorism Can Be Used by the Poor

The reality is that terrorism has become part of a modern state's arsenal, just as much as nuclear armaments; but unlike such weapons, terrorist tactics are within the grasp of the poorest nations.

Since terrorism is only an instrument designed to achieve an end, Mideast terrorism can be controlled only be removing the *reasons* that groups and states use the weapon in the first place. The root cause of the problem remains the Palestinian question.

Spencer DiScala, *The Christian Science Monitor*, April 9, 1985.

Spiegel: How do you judge Arafat today?

Abu Nidal: The puppet Arafat dances to the commands of the Zionists and the Americans. Indeed, he believes he holds the strings. In reality, he himself struggles on the strings. Arafat is a marionette directed by the Fatah movement and certain Arabian regimes.

Spiegel: There were times when you worked together with the Iraqis. Why did your organization finally split with Iraq?

Abu Nidal: Our alliance with Iraq fell apart because of the machinations of the Vatican. We consider the Vatican the most secretive agent and biggest news center in our region. For tactical reasons, I refuse to go into detail on this issue. Listen and believe, though, that the Vatican is a Christian religious stronghold. . . .

Spiegel: Do you consider yourself a Syrian even though you are a Palestinian?

Abu Nidal: We are Syrian citizens. To us, Syria is the mother nation, Syria is our history, society, community, geography. Until recently half of Lebanon was a region of Syria. So you see, we are true Syrian citizens. I myself have Syrian parents; one parent comes from what is today Syria, the other from Palestine. . . .

Peaceful Negotiating Impossible

Spiegel: You have completely given up on peaceful negotiations leading to a settlement of the Palestinian question?

Abu Nidal: There is no such thing in the entire world as peaceful settlements. If you read Arab history, you will see that not once has the peaceful way to a settlement solved our problems.

Spiegel: Do you really believe then, that an armed fight will lead you to your goal?

Abu Nidal: I admit, the existence of Zionists in Palestine will last a certain amount of time—we don't indulge ourselves in daydreaming about that. For now, the entire Zionist society is mobilized, but nevertheless, our children will succeed in fighting the occupiers with stones and knives.

The peace accord from Camp David was concluded at the time of Sadat [President of Egypt] and has gone under with him. It is only a question of time, before Sadat's follower, Hosni Mubarak, will also pay dearly for his betrayal of Arab history. . . .

Spiegel: What is your real name?

Abu Nidal: Sabri Chalil el-Banna

Spiegel: There are often lists of your terrorist acts in the press. You have killed among others the Palestinians Said Hamami, Iss el-Din el-Kalak and Naim Chudr.

Abu Nidal: You have there a modest list, very modest. Let me make this entirely clear: every Arab or Palestinian who has contact or any sort of connection with Mossad will end as those three did—liquidation. We have carried out almost a hundred such actions, ones that we haven't widely publicized. The reason was always the same: contact with Mossad.

Spiegel: Have you erred and killed someone who was innocent?

Abu Nidal: Surely not. We first called to account every accused person. If he didn't listen to us we killed him. Said Hamami was, by the way, my nephew.

Murdering Traitors

Spiegel: What have you accomplished with the murders? Have you come any closer to your goal?

Abu Nidal: To me that is not the question. When someone betrays

116

his land, his people, his nation, he gets the same in return. All resistance fighters have handled things that way. What did the French resistance do with its traitors? We have never shot innocent people or journalists.

Spiegel: That's not true. You shot the well-known Egyptian journalist Sibai in Cyprus in 1978.

Abu Nidal: You give me the occasion to tell about this act for the first time. It concerned not only Sibai, but rather primarily his intimate friend, President Sadat.

Spiegel: How's that?

Abu Nidal: We had designed a plan to lure the Egyptian secret service, whose leader is Major Nabil, to Cyprus. Major Nabil was the chief of the so-called Republican Security, a secret service organization that was exclusively under the personal command of Sadat. Its main duty was to protect the life of the president at any cost.

Immune to Suffering

The Palestinians have a clear and simple cause. In their words: "We want to go home," to a country where they could run their own affairs: a Palestinian state, even a ministate. Since it is official Israeli—and U.S.—policy not to permit such a state, the cause will remain as a continuing challenge and inspiration. . . .

The attacks carried out . . . suggest the emergence of a new type of Palestinian gunman. He is younger, a member of the generation born and reared in the sordid misery of the Palestine refugee camps, less educated, less sophisticated and so not very efficient at his task, but much more bitter and so much more brutal. . . .

This new wave of gunman is motivated by a great load of suffering. One of the Rome airport messages [left by terrorists who bombed the airport] is worth quoting in full because many parts of the world are going to resound to these cries of rage and anguish: "As you have violated our land, our honor, our people, we will hit you everywhere, even your children, so that you should feel the sorrow of our children. The tears that we have shed will be washed away by your blood."

G.H. Jansen, *Los Angeles Times*, January 5, 1986.

So we shot Sibai in Cyprus and Sadat reacted exactly as we had expected. He sent special troops with military supplies to Cyprus, led by Major Nabil. They were to carry out a punitive expedition against us in Cyprus.

That left Sadat unprotected at home. The further plan for this action called for taking advantage of this, and killing Sadat and his confidantes. For certain reasons the second step of our plan could not be carried out. In any case, there was shooting at the airport in Cyprus during which Major Nabil and half of his elite troop died. At the state burial of Nabil and his people, Sadat, contrary to the announcements, didn't dare show himself.

Every Betrayal Punished by Death

Spiegel: Do you continue to do such things today?

Abu Nidal: Yes, for example with Ahmed Dscharallah, the chief editor of the Kuwaiti newspaper *El-Sijassa*. We have nothing against his commentaries and analyses. But his publishing house in Kuwait is no presshouse, but rather a whorehouse. We have asked him often by letter and by mouth, to pull his audaciously outstretched hand back away from Mossad. This corrupt man has decided to accept an invitation in occupied Palestine. Every Arab should know: every betrayal will be punished with death. The regime in Kuwait should not forget that Kuwait is an Arabic land and its oil is Arabic oil, not Zionist-American oil. We have shot at Dscharallah, he came away unharmed this time. We hope he has understood the message. . . .

Spiegel: Is every Jew and Israeli really your enemy?

Abu Nidal: Every Zionist is my enemy. I make a distinction between Zionists and Jews. Not every Jew is my enemy.

Spiegel: Don't you realize that there are forces in Israel that want peace with Arabs?

Abu Nidal: The so-called Peace-Now movement is nothing more than eyewash; we don't believe in it. Uri Avnery is a Zionist immigrant; he should go back to where he came from, near Hannover, Germany. If he really means it, he should emphatically distance himself from Zionist ideology. Then we would believe what he says.

Spiegel: Do you work together with underground organizations in Europe?

Abu Nidal: Certainly. With the French Action directly, the Belgian fighting communist cells, the Irish IRA, the Basque Eta, the German Red Army Faction, and so on. Why not, what's wrong with that? The imperialists have united and fight against all of us. So we have also united under the motto: "Oppressed, unite!"

Justified Struggle

Spiegel: What is the difference, in your eyes, between justified struggle and terrorism?

Abu Nidal: Justified struggle means the right of a people to seize and use all available means against the usurpers of their land. Terrorism is the liquidation of innocent people without cause by a group or organization or state-sponsored force, such as what happened in the Palestinian camps of Sabra and Shatila.

"The issue that should concern us is not whether in their heart of hearts, gunmen seek goals beyond the violence they perpetrate. The issue that should concern us is the violence itself."

Terrorist Goals Do Not Justify Terrorism

Jeane J. Kirkpatrick

Jeane J. Kirkpatrick is an American scholar and diplomat who served as ambassador to the United Nations from 1981-1985. Ms. Kirkpatrick remained a controversial figure during her tenure as ambassador, primarily for her position that the US should support authoritarian governments but not totalitarian governments. In the following viewpoint, Ms. Kirkpatrick calls upon the American public to reject terrorists' pleas for understanding of their political goals. She believes violence in any form is repulsive and unacceptable.

As you read, consider the following questions:

1. How does Ms. Kirkpatrick say that American culture differs from others in its attitude toward violence? Why is this significant?
2. Does the author believe US allies will help in squelching terrorism? Why or why not?
3. Compare Ms. Kirkpatrick's attitudes with those of avowed terrorist Abu Nidal of the previous viewpoint. Do you believe Ms. Kirkpatrick is right?

Jeane J. Kirkpatrick, "Terrorist Acts, Not Motivation, Is the Issue," *Human Events*, February 1, 1986. © 1986, Los Angeles Times Syndicate. Reprinted with permission.

Attack by murderous attack, terrorists are teaching us about the world: about the vulnerability of open societies to assault, about the complexity and violence of Middle Eastern politics, about the difficulties of protecting ourselves, about the limits of our alliances and the reluctances of our allies, about the limits of law in international relations, and about the limits of civilization as well.

"Of course," one thought before the attacks in Rome and Vienna, "the threat at airports begins after you check in." Not so. Travelers at airline counters are essentially unprotected. So are travelers at train stations, shoppers in department stores, pedestrians at red lights, students in classrooms, and churchgoers.

Most people are vulnerable most of the time to attack by violent men, especially those ready to die to accomplish their bloody missions. In civilized society there is a rarely articulated understanding—reinforced by law—that we will not kill each other as we go about our daily lives.

Terrorism shocks us because it is organized and because it is political. And in our political tradition and political culture, politics is not a violent activity.

"Oh señora, be careful," a Central American housekeeper said to me a decade ago as I left for a local political meeting, "politics are so dangerous."

"Not our politics," I explained to her. We are a democracy.

Violence and Government

Violence is, of course, the very antithesis of government by consent. But terrorists are not interested in the requirements of democracy. Some commentators tell us that Abu Nidal's group is not interested in politics at all. For them, it is said, violence is the end as well as the means, the goal as well as the method, a good in itself. "To kill Israelis" was goal enough for the men who murdered travelers in Rome and Vienna, or so a surviving attacker told his interrogators. Now some commentators are contrasting the nihilism of Abu Nidal's group with the "diplomatic" goals of Yasir Arafat and his followers.

The distinction is not relevant. Remember the *Achille Lauro* "mistake"? They told us later they never meant to hijack that ship. The plan called for landing at a crowded Israeli port, opening fire, and shooting until the attackers themselves had been killed— killing as many Israelis as possible in the process.

The man who planned that operation was an Arafat lieutenant who was released by Egypt, Italy and Yugoslavia, and is presumably today enjoying freedom in Iraq.

Arafat has denounced the Rome and Vienna attacks and accused Libya and Syria of sponsoring them to embarrass him and prevent a negotiated settlement with Israel. Libya, meanwhile, has taken to denying any responsibility for the attack. "Libya had nothing to do with it," said Qaddafi's foreign minister, who joined

Michael Keefe *The Denver Post*, reprinted with permission.

Arafat in deploring the attacks.

We know, of course, that Syria and Libya have tried to destroy Arafat's forces and that they support Arafat's rivals in a bitter struggle for power in the Palestinian movement. We know, too, that this struggle for power overlaps, but does not coincide precisely with the division between moderate and radical Arab states.

All PLO Factions Equal

But so far, the differences among Palestinian factions have little practical significance for peace, democracy, or Western interests in the Middle East. All these PLO factions deny Israel's right to exist, all utilize violence, all are closely tied to the Soviet Union and all actively support Soviet policies in Afghanistan, Angola, Nicaragua and around the world.

The issue that should concern us is not whether in their heart of hearts, gunmen seek goals beyond the violence they perpetrate. The issue that should concern us is the violence itself. Terrorist acts are the issue, not the motives or sincerity of those who commit them.

Some people and some governments excuse terrorists because they think them "sincere." Others excuse Palestinian terrorism because they approve the goal of a Palestinian state, or because they lack sympathy for Israel, or because they want to do business with the terrorists' sponsoring countries.

Most of our allies do not so much excuse terrorism as they try to deal with it privately under the table. The tradition of *sauve qui peut* (each man for himself) is more powerful among nations than the tradition of collective response. Most of our allies see their alliance with us as strictly limited to mutual defense against military attack, where we Americans see it as providing for mutual defense against all manner of ills.

Our Allies

Our allies declined to join in sanctions against Poland's repression of Solidarity. They declined to boycott the Beirut airport and declined to hold the murderer of Leon Klinghoffer for trial. Now they decline to join in sanctions against Libya. The British Foreign Office has already reiterated that it finds sanctions ineffective (except, presumably, when taken at Britain's behest—as in the Falklands war), the Germans have recommended caution, the French have alluded vaguely to other unnamed remedies available under international law.

It is one more lesson in reality.

I believe the President was right to impose a total embargo on U.S. economic relations with Libya and right to insist that Americans working in Libya come home. He was right to emphasize the barbaric character of the airport attacks and to inform the American people of the existence of "irrefutable evidence" of Libya's involvement in the December 27 [1985] attack. He was right to call on our allies for common action to isolate Libya. It all clarifies the situation.

These are appropriate steps in dealing with an outlaw regime. Sooner or later, however, it will be necessary to take on the terrorists themselves.

Can Terrorist Acts Be Justified?

This activity will give you an opportunity to discuss with classmates the conditions you and your classmates consider necessary in order to justify the use of violence. While most of us would agree that killing is wrong, terrorists argue that there are circumstances that necessitate its use.

Dana Summers, *The Orlando Sentinel*. Reprinted with permission.

The authors in this chapter debate the reasons for and against terrorist acts. The cartoon above, while a comic exaggeration, nevertheless represents the opinion of some that terrorists are fanatical, bloodthirsty, and that their acts are completely unjustified. Some of the authors in this chapter would agree, believing that no circumstances, including government oppression and violence can ever justify terrorism's use. Other authors, most notably the representatives of terrorist sects, would argue that the odds against them necessitate terrorism.

Part I

Consider carefully each of the examples below. *Mark J for each situation you think justifies the use of terrorism. Mark U for each situation in which a terrorist response would be unjustified.*

Incidents

_____ bombing a Nazi headquarters in Paris during the German occupation of France

_____ throwing stones and homemade pipe bombs at members of South Africa's apartheid police during a civil rights strike

_____ the systematic planning and assassination of Fidel Castro by the United States' CIA to prevent the communist influence spreading into Latin America

_____ the hijacking of an American cruise ship and the subsequent murder of several of its passengers by members of a Middle Eastern terrorist sect to protest US support of Israel

_____ the burning of a civilian village by American soldiers in Vietnam because the village was said to be harboring members of the Viet Cong

_____ the capture and torture of a member of a Middle East terrorist group by Israeli officials to gather information on an impending terrorist attack

_____ the murder of a pregnant Israeli woman by Shi'ite fanatics because she is carrying a future "Israeli soldier"

_____ the bombing of a Palestinian refugee camp by Israel in retaliation for the bombing of an Israeli children's hospital by the PLO

_____ the capture and torture of an American embassy official by fanatical Shi'ite terrorists to provoke the United States into releasing several of its members from prison

_____ the bombing of a British unit based in Northern Ireland by the IRA

_____ the assassination of a repressive dictator by guerrilla forces

_____ the assassination of an American president by someone who believes the president is a warmonger

_____ the bombing of a US military unit in Beirut by a terrorist organization to protest US involvement in the Middle East

_____ the bombing of a crowded British nightclub on a Saturday night by IRA terrorists

_____ the capture and murder by IRA members of a British informant who infiltrated the IRA

Part II

Step 2: Either working in small groups or as individuals, give a short, written rationale explaining why you feel certain acts are justified and some are not. Then, compare your answers to others in the class. Discuss the different reasons others give for their answers.

Step 3: After the general classroom discussion, attempt to determine some kind of criteria as to when terrorism may be justified. Look back at the viewpoints in this chapter. Which authors would disagree with your criteria? Which authors would agree?

Periodical Bibliography

The following list of periodical articles deals with the subject matter of this chapter.

Clinton Bailey — "The Tribal Side of Mideast Terrorism," *The New York Times*, July 7, 1985.

William O. Beeman — "Reagan Could Leave Legacy of Vengeance," *Los Angeles Times*, March 26, 1986.

Zev Chafetz — "PLO Sympathy Comes Home to Roost," *Los Angeles Times*, October 9, 1986.

Lawrence Davidson — "Terrorism in Context: The Case of the West Bank," *Journal of Palestine Studies*, Spring 1986.

Robert I. Friedman — "Nice Jewish Boys With Bombs," *The Village Voice*, May 6, 1986.

Thomas L. Friedman — "Armed and Dangerous," *The New York Times*, January 5, 1986.

Thomas L. Friedman — "The Power of the Fanatics," *The New York Times Magazine*, October 7, 1984.

Walid Khalidi — "A Palestinian Perspective on the Arab-Israeli Conflict," *Journal of Palestine Studies*, Summer 1985.

Daoud Kuttab — "When Violence Begets Violence," *Los Angeles Times*, October 11, 1985.

Jonathan Kuttab — "Justice Is an Illusion in the West Bank," *Los Angeles Times*, April 6, 1986.

Alfred M. Lilienthal — "Middle East Terror," *Vital Speeches of the Day*, February 15, 1986.

Judith Miller — "A Rare Glimpse of Colonel Qaddafi," *The New York Times*, January 11, 1986.

The Nation — "Desperately Seeking Solutions," July 6/13, 1985.

Benjamin Netanyahu — "Face Up to the P.L.O.'s True Nature," *The New York Times*, October 16, 1985.

The New Republic — "Interception, Fumble," November 4, 1985.

Rod Nordland — "Flake or Fox?" *Newsweek*, January 20, 1986.

Adran Abu Odeh — "'What We Need Most Is Peace,'" *The Plain Truth*, January 1986.

Do the Superpowers Sponsor Terrorism?

"The United States will stop private terrorism only when it stops sponsoring state terrorism in the Third World."

US Support of Terrorists Is Immoral

The Progressive

One of the most debated aspects of terrorism is whether or not the US, by supporting dictatorial leaders throughout the world, is sponsoring terrorism. In the following viewpoint, taken from *The Progressive* magazine, the author argues that the people living under these corrupt, US-sponsored dictatorships begin to despise and resent the US. Denied any legitimate form of protest, they turn to terrorism in a final attempt to achieve justice for themselves and their countries. Founded in 1909, *The Progressive* is a prominent liberal journal of opinion.

As you read, consider the following questions:

1. What, according to the author, motivates terrorists?
2. Does the author believe terrorism is a serious threat? Why or why not?
3. What should the US do, according to the author?

As the cycle of international violence spirals upward, the distinction between "terrorist" and "counterterrorist" becomes blurred:

Israeli troops occupy Lebanon to squelch Palestinian terrorism; the Shiite population responds with violence of its own. U.S. warships shell Beirut; the destruction is answered by an exploding truck at the Marine compound.

The Indian government moves against Sikh separatists; they assassinate Indira Gandhi and, in reaction, more Sikhs are murdered. Then an Indian airliner is blown apart.

Salvadoran forces, armed and trained by the Pentagon, level rebel-held villages; the fire is returned at cafes in San Salvador. Ronald Reagan responds by providing the Salvadoran army with "additional military assets."

The CIA, still in Beirut, establishes counterterrorist units made up of Lebanese citizens; one squad detonates a car bomb, killing eighty and wounding 200. (The intended target escapes harm.) Meanwhile, Israel imprisons 766 Lebanese and Palestinians in violation of international law. Shiite militants retaliate by hijacking an airplane full of Americans. Washington prepares to strike back.

Definition Encompasses Much More

If terrorism "is a war in which innocent civilians are targets," as President Reagan maintains, then the governments of the United States, El Salvador, Israel, and India, among others, are terrorists in every sense of the term. They deserve all the contempt and censure meted out to individuals and political groups that rely on weapons to achieve their ends. Reagan properly reviles "state-sponsored terrorism," but that menace encompasses much more than he acknowledges—Death Squads, "sweeps" of guerrilla strongholds, army massacres.

Almost every government, East and West, has committed or encouraged such atrocities. The perpetrators include Reagan and Gorbachev, Khomeini and Peres, Duarte and Mugabe. The nuclear powers, which threaten civilian lives every day and hold the planet hostage, are the ultimate terrorists.

To recognize the pervasiveness and brutality of official terror is not to minimize or excuse the behavior of nongovernmental terrorists. There is no rationale—ever—for threatening or taking human lives. But even as we recoil in horror from the violence perpetrated against innocent civilians, we are well-advised to try to understand the pain and frustration from which such violence arises. Oppression engenders resistance, often armed resistance. Dissident terrorists are motivated by the exploitation, alienation, and powerlessness they have been compelled to endure.

In the case of the Shiites, "they have traditionally been the downtrodden second-class citizens of Lebanon," reports *The Wall Street Journal*, "saddled with the worst land, crammed into the poorest slums, and stuck on the lowest rung of the political ladder." Is it any wonder that they seek redress? . . .

President Reagan [has] pulled out all the rhetorical stops. Terrorists, he said, are waging war "against all of civilized society." Members of his Cabinet and most of the mass media pundits parroted the line.

No Threat to Civilization

Such demagoguery is inaccurate—the Shiite hijackers, at least, had clearly defined political objectives—and it clouds the question of violence. David Barret, a leader of Canada's New Democratic Party, has noted, "It is misleading to talk of terrorism as a 'threat to civilization,' except in the sense that all violence, including war and state violence, is incompatible with a truly social and civilized condition."

M.G. Lord for Newsday. © 1986, Los Angeles Times Syndicate. Reprinted with permission.

The issue is not one of good versus evil, as Reagan would have it, but of violence versus nonviolence. On this score, the President has no moral standing to judge others, for he has bloodied his hands in Nicaragua, Lebanon, Grenada, and El Salvador. His proposed solution—to stop terrorism by escalating state violence—will only water the roots of terrorism.

U.S. military personnel and CIA officers are now training "anti-terrorist" commandos in about a dozen countries. (The ill-fated Lebanon squad was one such outfit.) Through this program, the police agencies of some of the most repressive regimes on Earth—

Turkey and Honduras among them—are being bolstered.

In Spring, 1985, the State Department acknowledged in Congressional testimony that it is "relaxing a bit the long-standing ban on aid to foreign law enforcement organizations." Put another way, the United States is reverting to the sordid practices of the 1950s and 1960s, when it routinely schooled Third World police in the techniques of torture and repression.

In El Salvador, for example, the U.S.-trained antiterrorist team was recently used to break up a strike by public hospital workers. The troops tied up many of the strikers and left them lying on the floor.

In Costa Rica, where 750 commandos are being trained by Green Berets, the new antiterrorism program serves as a smokescreen to conceal the militarization of that democracy. Costa Rica has not had an army since 1948. "We don't want a group of jack-booted young men here, goose-stepping, saluting, and clicking their heels," says former President Jose Figueres. "I see in this another U.S. mistake in Latin America in the making."

Administration officials also plan to expand U.S. intelligence-gathering efforts around the globe, sharing information about terrorism with allies. Inevitably, some of those governments will use CIA intelligence to stifle dissent, contending that "civil disorder" is the prelude to terrorism.

Restricting Freedom

At home, too, the Reagan Administration's initiatives threaten to restrict freedom. A comprehensive antiterrorism strategy is being developed by a Federal task force under the direction of Vice President George Bush. Even before the panel began its study, Bush hinted at what to expect: He professed admiration for the way Italy handled terrorism in the last decade.

The Italian method that drew such favorable attention at the highest level of the U.S. Government entailed an emergency law under which suspected terrorists could be jailed for up to twelve years without trial; authority for the police to conduct unrestricted wiretapping and warrantless searches; the arrest of journalists who tried to publish interviews with members of the Red Brigades; mistreatment and torture of prisoners, and controls on foreigners working in Italy.

With such martial measures, the U.S. Government could probably stamp out domestic private terrorism. In the process, it would come to resemble a police state, bereft of the pretense of democracy.

US Must Stop Terrorism

The primary challenge facing the United States comes from terrorism abroad, not at home. To cope effectively with violence directed at U.S. installations and traveling citizens, our Government will have to adopt a policy of nonintervention. It was this country's foreign meddling, after all, that triggered the current wave of lawlessness. The United States will stop private terrorism only when it stops sponsoring state terrorism in the Third World. Reagan's approach, intensifying the U.S. presence around the globe, will just intensify the problem.

No Conspiracy

There is no "international conspiracy" against the United States, but there is a growing international consensus that Washington should mind its own business. Whether or not the Ayatollah Khomeini officially sponsors terrorists outside of Iran, his example certainly inspires Middle East revolutionaries. Khomeini has shown that guns can topple a U.S.-backed ruler, in this case the terrorist Shah.

Terrorism Is Not Radical

Terrorism is commonly understood to be the indiscriminate killing or injury of human beings. It is condemned as being heartless, harming the innocent as well as the guilty. Nevertheless, terrorism is not always an individual act. It can be sanctioned by a government, officially or unofficially, as part of its policy. The murders and rapes in Nicaragua, perpetrated by the contras, furnish a case in point. . . .

The lesson is that we must reject the idea that terrorism is a product of radical thought. We must point out to our friends and neighbors what the real face of terrorism looks like. And we must organize to eliminate such depravity.

David Michaels, *Daily World*, November 30, 1984.

In Iran and then in Lebanon, the U.S. Government fueled terrorism by doggedly defending its perceived "interests" against the wishes of most of the people. The same mistake is being made in South Africa, the Philippines, El Salvador, and elsewhere. Americans will remain vulnerable to violent backlash until our leaders recognize that nonintervention is in this nation's highest interest. It is more important than markets, military bases, "listening posts," malleable governments, or even oil.

The suicide squad has been inside the White House all along.

"Americans have to realize that violent deeds conducted by surrogates are preferable not only to losing but also to direct U.S. involvement."

US Support of Terrorists Is Necessary

Geoffrey Kemp

Geoffrey Kemp, a senior fellow at Georgetown University Center for Strategic and International Studies, was special assistant to President Reagan for national security affairs from 1981 to 1985. In the following viewpoint, Mr. Kemp argues that in the struggle against terrorism, the United States should consider itself at war. As such, it is absolutely essential for the US to be less fastidious about the rebels it supports. The top priority of the US should be in protecting its own national security even if, in doing this, it must employ its own "terrorists."

As you read, consider the following questions:

1. What are the advantages to supporting the enemies of regimes that are anti-US, according to the author?
2. Does the author believe terrorism is a legitimate form of warfare? Why or why not?
3. Do you believe Mr. Kemp is right when he argues that the US may need to support terrorists? Why or why not?

Geoffrey Kemp, "When One Man's Terrorist Is Another Man's Freedom Fighter," *Los Angeles Times*, July 21, 1985. Reprinted by permission of the author.

During his 1985 visit to Southeast Asia, Secretary of State George P. Shultz met with large numbers of Cambodian refugees in Thailand, victims of the continuing civil war and the Vietnamese occupation of their country. In scenes reminiscent of Western leaders' pilgrimages to Afghan refugee camps in Pakistan, Shultz was warmly received by Cambodians who, like their Afghan counterparts, urged the United States to provide the means to liberate their country from a foreign invader.

Shultz's response was warm but noncommittal—in spite of a rather extraordinary series of measures taken by the House of Representatives while he was away. In voting to approve the foreign-aid bill, the House passed resolutions providing financial aid to Cambodian resistance groups who could be certified "non-communist"; to the Afghan resistance movement, and to the forces of the National Union for the Total Independence of Angola (UNITA, from its Portuguese initials) led by Jonas Savimbi which are fighting Cubans in Angola. The House remains hostile to funding arms for the Nicaraguan *contras*, but on most foreign-aid questions the mood on Capitol Hill is now decidedly hawkish.

This may explain Shultz's negative response to the House proposal to help the Cambodians. Shultz does not want to provide military aid to these resistance groups in part because he fears Congress can be fickle on these types of issues, denying tomorrow what it approves today and thereby undermining a carefully crafted policy. Unfortunately, the record of the past 10 years corroborates Shultz's pessimism.

Belligerent Mood in Congress

But are things changing? To make sense of the belligerent mood in Congress and to understand U.S. problems in funding resistance groups, two questions must be answered. First, is the shift in congressional opinion permanent or transitory? Second, what criteria should the United States and other democracies adopt when taking steps to support anti-communist resistance movements that differ widely in size, composition, ideology and international support and that may themselves use "terrorist" actions to pursue their objectives?

One explanation for the new hawkishness is that the Congress has overcome the traumas of Vietnam and Watergate that had such a divisive impact on the foreign-policy consensus. It now seems prepared to return to a more traditional bipartisan approach to national security issues. If this is the case, we might see the day when funding the *contras* will be *de rigueur*, even for liberal Democrats. . . .

While most observers would welcome a more permanent return to consensus in foreign-policy making, bipartisanship itself does not guarantee good policy—especially if U.S. goals and objectives are muddled. No arena is more susceptible to confusion, particularly moral confusion, than the question of supporting insurgents. Hitting back at *our* enemies by supporting *their* enemies has the advantage of not involving the United States directly in combat; but the disadvantage that we cannot control our clients. How can the United States assure that military assistance provided to non-communist Cambodians will not trickle down to another member of the resistance, namely the odious Pol Pot and his Khmer Rouge?

Anti-Communist Groups

This raises the tricky problem—that anti-communist resistance groups are by no means monolithic. While they have some common features, each has its own identity and badge of respectability in the international community. Despite the fact that some Afghan resistance groups adhere to the tenets of Islamic fundamentalism, they have become, as a whole, heroes in the United States and Western Europe, eulogized by the same people who express fear and loathing for Ayatollah Ruhollah Khomeini and his Shia zealots. On the other hand, Savimbi's fighters are highly controversial and disliked in many quarters because of the material support they have received from South Africa and their effective disruption of Angolan economy, which in turn causes disarray among the multinational oil companies. Most isolated and despised are the *contras*, who have virtually no support in Europe and are regarded by many Americans as an artificial creation of the CIA.

Using Bad Methods for Good Ends

We must beware of defining terrorism ideologically. Whether one is a terrorist has little to do with what side one is fighting on, only with the methods used. In fact, it's perfectly possible to be a terrorist and a freedom fighter at the same time—for the simple reason that it is possible to use bad methods for good purposes.

Joseph Sobran, *The Wanderer*, October 10, 1985.

Similarly, the regimes and military forces under attack from these resistance groups cover a wide spectrum, ranging from the well-trained, well-equipped Soviet Union and Vietnam to the less prepared and relatively poorly equipped Cubans in Angola and the Sandinistas. To come up with any simple description of the conditions of combat and conflict in these regions is exceedingly difficult. On the matter of values, ethics and the use of force, it requires wild leaps of the imagination to believe that the Afghan resistance, or any other group receiving U.S. support, will adhere to Queensberry Rules when using violence to defeat or intimidate their enemies. Hence the strong possibility that they will, on occasion, use terrorist methods to achieve their objectives. How should we react to this, given U.S. outbursts about the evils of such acts?

Americans Too Selective

The unpleasant fact is that Americans are highly selective about who is called a terrorist and what is defined as a terrorist act. One man's terrorist is another man's freedom fighter. In popular usage, "terrorist" has come to be associated with radical, anti-Western groups who use violence—including random violence—against civilians to change the political landscape. Yet terrorism is a form of warfare that can involve the regular armed forces of sovereign states. The Soviets probably kill more innocent Afghan civilians in one afternoon than all the civilians killed by the Lebanese Shias in one year. And Americans should not forget that a cornerstone of Western strategy today is a doctrine that calls for the massive, systematic annihilation of millions and millions of innocent civilians—a potential act of terror unparalleled in history.

No Clean Way to Fight Enemies

To become bogged down in a semantic debate about who is a terrorist is to miss the point. What the United States has to do is focus on the real problem, namely that certain political groups are, for different and complex reasons, at war with the Western world. If America is in a state of war, rules of behavior and engagement must be modified, just as they were during World War II. Rhetorical statements about the generic evils of terrorism run the risk of adding to the confusion because they focus on the deeds themselves rather than the perpetrators. We need to fight our enemies and if necessary use some of their methods—with the exception of the deliberate murder of innocent civilians. This may mean the United States will support groups that use unsavory methods. But Americans have to realize that violent deeds conducted by surrogates are preferable not only to losing but also to direct U.S. involvement, the massive use of American firepower and the increased risks of confrontation with the Soviet Union. In theory there is an alternative to surrender, direct escalation or support for such groups: namely negotiation. Yet the diplomatic record is dismal, despite intensive efforts, especially in southern Africa and Central America.

If the United States is going to be serious about dealing with the threat to its national interests, the country has to realize that there is no clean way to fight its enemies. And if the Congress is serious about providing aid to anti-communist resistance groups, its members should understand all the implications of what they are doing and be prepared to see the unpleasant business through to the end.

136

"The CIA and the comandantes *believed that sabotage, rape, execution and other atrocious tactics would terrorize the population into supporting the* contra *cause."*

US-Sponsored Contras Are Terrorists

Edgar Chamorro

The contras, the revolutionary faction who oppose the Sandinistan government of Nicaragua, have sparked a world-wide controversy over the issue of terrorism. The US government views the contras as freedom fighters, whose goal is to defeat communism and bring democracy to Nicaragua. Many other countries, including some in Latin America and Europe, argue that the contras are nothing more than terrorists, brutally maiming and murdering harmless civilians in their attempt to greedily wrest power from the legitimate Sandinistan government. In the following viewpoint, Edgar Chamorro, who served as a director of the Nicaraguan Democratic Force from 1982-1984, has emerged as an outspoken opponent of the contras. He describes how the violent, terrorist methods used by the contras ultimately disillusioned him from their cause.

As you read, consider the following questions:

1. What disillusioned Mr. Chamorro about US involvement in the contra movement?
2. Mr. Chamorro disliked the Sandinistas but changed his mind. Why?

Edgar Chamorro, "The Contras Were Born in Original Sin," *In These Times*, September 4-10, 1985. Reprinted by permission.

In recent weeks the U.S. Press has reported signs of a dramatic escalation of the *contra* war to overthrow the Nicaraguan government. This is a prospect to be feared, not celebrated.

Nothing positive will be gained from continuing to destroy the Nicaraguan people and their economy, because the *contra* in no way represent a democratic influence on Nicaraguan politics. A growth in *contra* strength to 20,000, 25,000, or even 30,000 men in the coming months would only add to the suffering of a war that since 1982 has left more than 12,000 Nicaraguans dead, 50,000 wounded and 300,000 homeless. Will the Reagan administration realize this after 30,000 have died? After 50,000? Why not stop the war now?

The *contra* army does not represent the democratic forces opposing the FSLN (Sandinista National Liberation Front). The FDN (Nicaraguan Democratic Force) was created, trained, financed and encouraged by the Reagan administration, repeating the same interventionist tactics that gave us Somoza and the National Guard from 1931 to 1979. This U.S. proxy force is the seed from which only new Somozas and a new National Guard can grow. By mid-1984, 46 out of 48 of the *contra comandantes* were former National Guardsmen.

Relying on Cuba as a Model

In 1979 the FSLN united and led the opposition that defeated Somoza. Six years later the social achievements of the new revolutionary society are many. But some people in the FSLN are abusing the original nationalistic concept, replacing it with Marxism-Leninism. Many Sandinistas have relied heavily on the Cuban model, which has led to excessive regimentation, planning and militarization. For example, the state farms, the literacy and health campaigns, and the CDS (Sandinista Defense Committees, neighborhood organizations) are carbon copies of the Cuban experience. Dependence on Cuba and the USSR is too strong, and there are indications that as U.S. hostility continues, Marxism's influence among the Sandinista leadership is growing. This has fueled Reagan's Cold War crusade.

Just Another CIA Employee

In 1982 I became a *contra* leader, one of seven directors chosen by the CIA to lead the Nicaraguan Democratic Force (FDN), the largest group fighting the Sandinista government. At that time the CIA told me that in only one year we would accomplish our goal of democratizing Nicaragua. I accepted the job believing I was a Nicaraguan patriot fighting for democracy in my homeland with the support of the U.S. It later became clear to me, however, that to the CIA, I was just another employee.

As a spokesman for the FDN Directorate in Tegucigalpa, Honduras, my interviews and press contacts were closely monitored by CIA operatives. The CIA had advised me to be careful of the "sharks" of the American press who "only want to make news and sell newspapers. . . ." The CIA regularly sent the station chief in Tegucigalpa a wire to reprimand and correct what I was saying to the media, as they did, for example, on April 5, 1983 and Nov. 7, 1983. On another occasion I was instructed to say that the FDN's objective was to put pressure on the Sandinistas to engage in political dialogue.

The Contras Are Murderers

The anti-Sandinista war has already cost U.S. taxpayers $150 million and is responsible for $250 million worth of damage in Nicaragua. More than a thousand civilians, including 150 children under the age of 12, are listed among the dead, and 130,000 people have been displaced from their homes.

After Anastasio Somoza was overthrown in 1979, more than 4,000 of his National Guardsmen fled to Honduras. Many of them became roving bandits, living as they always had, by terrorizing the local citizenry. The most famous and feared was Pedro Pablo Ortiz Centeno. He and his band of followers were arrested repeatedly in southern Honduras for theft and murder.

When the CIA began encouraging the organization of the *contras* in 1981, they joined ex-National Guardsmen such as Ortiz, also known as Commander Suicide, with Somoza's vice-president, Alfonso Callejas, Deshon, and others. . . .

Ronald Reagan refers to these close associates of the former dictator as our "brothers" in struggle, and "freedom-fighters."

Connie Blitt, Dennis Bernstein, *In These Times*, March 13-19, 1985.

In 1983 the CIA hired "Latin assets"—mercenaries from other countries, such as Argentina—to plant mines at Nicaragua's Port Corinto. In September the CIA station chief in Tegucigalpa brought me a communique written in perfect Spanish to be read to the international press. The statement said that the FDN was responsible for the Port Corinto mining.

Hiring Professional Criminals

After working regularly with the press, I became uncomfortable with the lack of credibility we had developed from such lies. I felt that the FDN needed dignity and integrity with the press, and I decided to challenge this deception and tell more of the true story. I opposed the recommendations made in the CIA "Psych-Ops" manual, which advised the *contra* to hire professional criminals and to create martyrs from our own supporters. I described to the press FDN's cooperation with the CIA. The more I asserted my independence and honesty, however, the more I was disliked by the men I was working with.

When I complained about the use of professional criminals advocated in the CIA manual, a replacement agent told me, "The mistake my predecessor made was that he put everything down in writing. Those things are done, but they don't get written down." It was this code of secrecy and lack of debate on planning that made me feel like a pawn of the CIA. I realized that the FDN had been reduced to merely a CIA front organization.

Contact with FDN fighters on the Nicaragua-Honduras border, perhaps more than anything else, made me decide against military efforts to overthrow the Sandinistas. I was told that in the *contra* war all prisoners were executed. A *comandante* said that he had a special rule of thumb to decide who would live and who would die. If the prisoner was caught with some ammunition remaining with him, he was spared.

But if he had none left that meant he had fired the last shot—that he had fought to the end. He had to be killed because this indicated that he was a brave and committed Sandinista.

Routine Killing

I learned that it was routine to seek out and kill people working for the Nicaraguan government. I heard repeated stories of executions of informers, collaborators, government agency workers, cooperative workers, bank workers—anyone suspected of being a Sandinista. The CIA and the *comandantes* believed that sabotage, rape, torture, execution and other atrocious tactics would terrorize the population into supporting the *contra* cause. Jimmy Carter's human rights, they said, were "out" and Ronald Reagan's big stick was "in."

I realize now that the FDN was born in "original sin," the original sin of U.S. intervention. I thought I was dealing with the democratic United States of America. I was wrong. I did not realize that anything the CIA does can be denied. Everything was carried out in such a secretive and totalitarian manner, and the CIA operatives' view of history was so simplistic, that I knew I was dealing with the same "ugly Americans"who carried out the dirty work of the counterinsurgency war against A.C. Sandino in the '20s and '30s. These men could only make Nicaragua less democratic. I would not accept being a puppet of their plans, and they fired me.

Polarizing Nicaragua

The U.S. *contra* war has only polarized the Nicaraguan conflict into two hostile camps. Legitimate political moderates have been forced to choose between equally undemocratic sides. If they try to exert a democratic influence within Nicaragua they are per-

YOU CAN HELP MAKE ROSITA AN ORPHAN, OR YOU CAN TURN THE PAGE.

WE'RE THE CONTRAS, AND WE NEED YOUR HELP. FINANCIAL HELP. YOU SEE, SINCE CONGRESS CUT OFF DIRECT MILITARY FUNDING WE'VE BEEN SEEKING MONEY FROM PRIVATE SOURCES. MONEY FOR GUNS. AND GRENADES. AND MINES.
WE'VE ALREADY KILLED MANY PEOPLE. PEOPLE IN VILLAGE MILITIAS, WHO SUPPORT A GOV'T WE DON'T LIKE. PEOPLE LIKE ROSITA'S FATHER. WOULDN'T IT BE A SHAME TO STOP NOW?

LET ME HELP! I WANT THE WEAPONS MY DONATION PAYS FOR TO CREATE A:
☐ BOY ORPHAN
☐ GIRL ORPHAN ☐ USE MY DONATION WHERE ITS NEEDED LEAST

Reprinted with permission from the Minneapolis Star and Tribune.

ceived as creating links to the *contra* and are repressed. If they join the *contra* they become tools of the CIA and U.S. intervention.

The Reagan administration's war to "Americanize" Nicaragua has denied Arturo Cruz, parts of the Catholic Church, the business group COSEP, the Conservative Party and other moderates any real national reconciliation. Democracy may never come to Nicaragua if this policy continues. It is time to end the insanity of this war. Too much of the country's blood has already been shed.

"A large share of the 'atrocities' of which we are accused are either fabricated by the Sandinistas or are in fact atrocities committed by the Sandinistas."

US-Sponsored Contras Are Freedom Fighters

Adolfo Calero, Arturo José Cruz, and Alfonso Robelo Callejas

Adolfo Calero, Arturo José Cruz, and Alfonso Robelo Callejas comprise the directorate of the United Nicaraguan Opposition. All three fought in the Nicaraguan revolution. Mr. Robelo and Mr. Cruz have held high positions in the Sandinista government. In the following viewpoint, the authors describe the contras as the "genuine voice" of the Nicaraguan people. They believe the contras fight for pluralism, freedom, and human rights.

As you read, consider the following questions:

1. Why do the authors believe the US should be disillusioned with the Sandinistas?
2. Are any atrocities committed by the contras, according to the authors?

Public opinion in the United States has a passion for "balance"—for believing that both sides in any conflict are at fault and blaming both in equal measure. In the case of the Central American conflict, this is leading many people astray.

There has been increased recognition in the United States of the fraud perpetrated by the Sandinistas. People hear increasingly urgent expressions of concern for the elected leaders of Nicaragua's neighbors, and there is growing awareness of the danger that the Sandinistas pose to peace and democracy.

This recognition is all to the good. The problem is that many North Americans worry that it is one-sided. They don't like the fact that it may lead Washington to support the Nicaraguan opposition—and so they look for a "balancing" argument. They suggest that, while the Sandinistas are bad, there are also grave problems with the anti-Sandinista fighters known as the "contras"—an incorrect label first pinned on them by the Sandinistas.

No Movement Above Reproach

This is an easy way out: No political movement is above reproach, and one can always point to disagreements and unsavory elements in the opposition. In truth, however, the facts do not justify the charges.

We in the United States Nicaraguan Opposition, an umbrella group known as U.N.O., are the first to admit that there are differences among our leaders. We respect our differences and are proud we do: This is what distinguishes us from the Sandinistas. U.N.O. has brought together a wide range of democratic groups—from all across the spectrum of those who joined in the revolution against Anastasio Somoza Debayle—struggling to prevent the consolidation of Sandinista rule, and we are proud to be united behind this objective. The organization was designed to preserve differences of opinion on economic and social questions and to preserve the groups that represent each point of view.

Contras Respect Human Rights

There is, however, one issue on which we brook no disagreement—human rights. Our commitment to respect human rights applies even while we are fighting against those who systematically violate the rights of other, innocent Nicaraguans. We agree across the board about the need for systematic procedures to insure that this commitment is implemented by our troops and that violations are punished. Such procedures have been in place for some time. They are continually tested and will continually be improved.

Only the very innocent imagine that we could fight a guerrilla war with no misconduct by our troops. But a large share of the "atrocities" of which we are accused are either fabricated by the Sandinistas or are in fact atrocities committed by the Sandinistas.

Beyond this agreement, the U.N.O. leadership is also united in its goals—peaceful solutions and national reconciliation. All the groups in the organization have repeatedly offered to stop fighting and start negotiating. That offer is still open.

The Contras Are Sincere

When the Sandinistas betrayed the revolution, many who had fought the old Somoza dictatorship literally took to the hills, and like the French Resistance that fought the Nazis, began fighting the Soviet bloc Communists and the Nicaraguan collaborators. These few have now been joined by thousands.

With their blood and courage, the freedom fighters of Nicaragua have pinned down the Sandinista Army and bought the people of Central America precious time. We Americans owe them a debt of gratitude. In helping to thwart the Sandinistas and their Soviet mentors, the resistance has contributed directly to the security of the United States.

Ronald Reagan, speech delivered to the American people, March 16, 1986.

The leadership of the Nicaraguan opposition has the right to disagree about many things, but we agree on the important points. We recognize that the only legitimate source of power is a free electoral process. We agree completely on the need to overturn the Sandinistas' totalitarian control of Nicaragua. We prefer to do so by negotiation, but we recognize the need now to fight for this objective. We are determined to respect human rights even at the height of the struggle, and we hope to establish a genuinely democratic system under which every Nicaraguan has the right to participate in the political process.

Self-Determination Key

The Sandinistas have failed historically because they became an instrument of foreign interests. We are not, and will never be, the instrument of a foreign power.

The Nicaraguan opposition is the genuine voice of the people of Nicaragua. It does not threaten a return to Somocism. Its strength comes from tens of thousands of Nicaraguan peasants and other young people from every social class who are willing to risk their lives to fight for it—to fight for pluralism and freedom and the protection of human rights.

"A considerable body of evidence has been accumulated to prove that the Soviets are active in the support of terrorism and guerrilla warfare."

The Soviet Union Sponsors Terrorism

Samuel T. Francis

Samuel T. Francis received a Ph.D. in modern history from the University of North Carolina. From 1977 to 1981, Francis was a policy analyst for The Heritage Foundation, a conservative think tank in Washington DC. He is currently a Legislative Assistant for National Security for Senator John East and has worked closely with the Subcommittee on Security and Terrorism. In the following viewpoint, excerpted from his book *The Soviet Strategy of Terror*, Mr. Francis documents Soviet involvement in various revolutionary movements throughout the world. He concludes that the Soviets support international terror in order to help achieve their ultimate goal, the takeover of the United States.

As you read, consider the following questions:

1. Mr. Francis claims the Soviet Union uses surrogates to foment revolution throughout the world. Who are some of these surrogates?
2. Does the author believe Soviet support of terrorists is motivated by political ideology? Why or why not?
3. What does the author believe the US should do to counter the Soviet threat?

Samuel T. Francis, *The Soviet Strategy of Terror*. Washington, DC: The Heritage Foundation, 1985. Reprinted by permission.

It is clear that the Soviet-terrorist connection must be examined . . . closely. The Soviet invasion of Afghanistan, the documented support of Cuba for the Nicaraguan Sandinistas and other Central American insurgencies, the connections between Iranian and Palestinian terrorists and the Soviets and the strong evidence linking Moscow with the attempted assassination of Pope John Paul II have generated far more skepticism about detente and the intentions of the Soviet Union than was fashionable in the 1970s. Moreover, the persistence of international terrorism—in southern Africa, Latin America, the Middle East, and Western Europe— has given rise to the belief that traditional approaches and solutions to the problem have not worked. The Western world now seems ready to reexamine much conventional wisdom, including the idea that terrorism is a spontaneous response to perceived grievances, that it is mere "mindless violence" that will eventually disappear, and that the Soviet Union has graduated completely to the status of a great power with a vested interest in preserving international stability.

This [article] rejects all of these ideas, and their rejection is part of the assumptions on which it is written. First, terrorism is indeed sometimes spontaneous and sometimes is a mere response to perceived grievances. Where this is all it is, however, it is usually suppressed easily and dies out quickly. Anyone familiar with the precision and complicated planning of such international terrorist incidents of the last decade as the Munich massacre, the Entebbe hijacking, and the kidnapping and murder of Hans-Martin Schleyer in West Germany and Aldo Moro in Italy will see at once that serious terrorism, far from being spontaneous, is well-planned, highly organized, and disciplined. These and other terrorist operations involved arduous training of the perpetrators, carefully designed support actions, and internationally coordinated movements of individuals and weapons. Some terrorism is indeed carelessly planned and executed by amateurs or mentally unstable elements, but the kind of terrorism that has become a threat to the public order of Western societies—the kind of terrorism that the Soviets and their allies support—is not.

Terrorists Are Rational Organizers

A related misinterpretation is that terrorism is "mindless" and the product of pathological irrationality. Again, some of it is, but much of it is carried out by men and women who have very distinct goals in view and who pursue these goals with brutally rational methods. Probably none of the most notable figures associated with international terrorism in the last decade—Arafat, Habash, Qadhafi, "Carlos," Meinhof, Khomeini, Agca and the like—could be considered entirely sane; some are clearly candidates for a straitjacket in any society. Yet, none is so far divorced from reality as to be unable to plan, organize, and command

146

the deadly and dangerous operations that have made their names feared (or in some places idolized) all over the world. The goals and methods which these individuals employ may be insane, but the pursuit of the goals and the execution of the methods usually have required a tenacious grip on reality. . . .

THE PUPPETEER –

Bob Dix, *The Union Leader*, reprinted with permission.

If we grant that Soviet purposes are aggressive, then it should come as no surprise that the government of the Soviet Union is involved in the support of terrorism, guerrilla warfare, and insurgency movements. To be sure, there is an ideological gap between the Soviet Marxist-Leninist and the nationalist, New Left, or reactionary ideologies of many insurgent and terrorist groups; but . . . there is sufficient overlap between the ideologies and ambitions of the terrorists and the Soviets for the former to be of use to Soviet aims. . . .

Soviet Support for Terrorism

A considerable body of evidence has been accumulated to prove that the Soviets are active in the support of terrorism and guerrilla warfare in many parts of the world. . . . Although the Soviets, through the KGB, the GRU, or the International Department of the Central Committee of the Communist Party of the Soviet Union (CPSU/ID), have directly supported terrorism in different ways, a far more common means of Soviet support has been indirect, through satellites or surrogates. These two terms are often used interchangeably; in fact they have distinct meanings. A satellite is a government, country, or organization that, while ostensibly independent, is in truth firmly controlled by the Soviet government. Examples of satellites would be Cuba, East Germany (the German Democratic Republic or GDR), Czechoslovakia, or the World Peace Council. A surrogate, however, is a government, country, or organization that, while perhaps independent of Soviet control, acts as a substitute for the Soviets in certain ways. Examples of Soviet surrogates would be the Palestine Liberation Organization (PLO), Libya, or North Korea, or a number of terrorist groups that are not orthodox Marxist-Leninist in ideology but which receive aid from and cooperate with the Soviet Union, its satellites, or their clandestine services. A surrogate can be a satellite, but it is not necessarily one.

The advantage of using surrogates is that it puts some distance between the Kremlin and the disreputable policies and actions that the surrogates must perform. Operations that conflict with the publicly stated goals or values of the Soviet Union, the Communist Party, or Soviet foreign commitments or which, if the Soviet role were known, would embarrass the Soviet leadership are assigned to surrogates that appear not to be closely tied to the USSR. Furthermore, operations that would require too much commitment of Soviet resources are also undertaken by surrogates. Thus, Cubans, East Germans, and others are involved in the training and support of guerrilla movements in southern Africa. The Soviets also make use of surrogates that enjoy a better reputation in some circles than the Soviet Union does. Among American leftists, for example, Castro, Cuba, and Vietnam are often regarded more favorably than Moscow, and in the Third World the Soviets are often distrusted for their notorious racial prejudice as well as for their ambitions as a great power. Thus, both American leftists and Third World states will sometimes be more cooperative with Cubans, North Vietnamese, or other surrogates than with the Soviets themselves. It is principally through the use of satellites and surrogates that the Soviets have provided support for terrorism around the world, and a regional survey of their activities and role can document this fact.

Cuba and Latin America

Although the Soviet Union has directly supported terrorist activities in some Latin American countries, since the early 1970s it has relied largely on Cuba for this purpose. . . .

As long as Cuba retained a vestige of independence, the Soviets were reluctant to allow Castro to support insurgency or terrorist movements in Latin America. However, once Cuba became a reliable satellite of the Soviets in the early 1970s, the Soviets were willing to use it as a surrogate for their political warfare operations. . . .

Soviet Link Irrefutable

Evidence of a link between the Soviet Union and terrorist activities around the world is "irrefutable," according to Dr. Joseph Churba, director of the Center for International Security. "They've been aiding terrorism both directly and indirectly. Directly in the political and diplomatic field and indirectly through the PLO," he said in an exclusive interview with *The New American*. "The Russians have been training PLO guerrillas in their own country in the number of some 7,000. The PLO in turn sets up bases and trains other nationals."

Kirk Kidwell, *The New American*, February 3, 1986.

The Cuban role in the support of insurgency movements and terrorism is well known in the case of Nicaragua, where, in 1979, the Sandinistas (FSLN) overthrew the U.S.-allied Somoza government. The FSLN was founded by Carlos Fonseca Amador, himself an alumnus of the Friendship University in Moscow, and according to what the Cubans told the present Nicaraguan Minister of the Interior, Tomas Borge Martinez, it was the first Latin American group to receive military training in Cuba. The FSLN made an alliance with the illegal Communist Party of Nicaragua, but its alliance broke down because of the tactical disputes between the terrorists, who advocated a pure "armed struggle," and the Party, which endorsed a "united front" and a political alliance with non-Communists. The Sandinistas also participated in the first Tricontinental conference of OSPAAAL in 1966. This early support for the FSLN was undertaken prior to the satellization of Cuba by the Soviets, but Cuban support increased dramatically in the mid-1970s. The FSLN, after remaining inactive in the early 1970s, began a series of terrorist attacks in late 1974 that lasted through 1975. In the state of emergency declared by Somoza following these attacks, two major leaders of the FSLN were killed and Borge himself was captured. His testimony revealed the breadth of Cuban support for the Sandinistas. . . .

North Africa and the Middle East

In [North Africa and the Middle East] the most useful surrogates for the Soviet Union's political war have been Libya under the regime of Colonel Muammar Qadhafi and the Palestine Liberation Organization (PLO). Neither is a satellite of the Soviet Union, and neither Qadhafi nor Yassir Arafat is a Marxist. Libya and the PLO, however, as well as other states and organizations in North Africa and the Middle East, have been highly useful to Soviet purposes and share Soviet hostility to "Zionism," "advanced capitalism," and "imperialism."

It is through the provision of training facilities, sanctuaries, and weapons that Libya has been most useful to terrorist operations around the world. Qadhafi purchased $2.5 billion worth of arms from the USSR between 1974 and 1979. This was the largest amount of Soviet weaponry provided to any African state, though other recipients of large amounts of arms from the Soviet Union have been Algeria, Ethiopia, and Angola (and, until 1977, Somalia). In a speech of March 2, 1981, Qadhafi stated that "almost all of our weapons are supplied by the Soviet Union. The Soviet Union gave us the most dangerous and the most modern weapons; we bought them from the Soviet Union." In early 1983 a Libyan publication claimed the presence of over 70,000 Soviet bloc personnel in Libya. . . .

Soviet-PLO Link

Yassir Arafat and the PLO have also been used by the Soviets as surrogates, and the Soviets have provided arms and training to the PLO in support of Palestinian terrorism. Between 1974 and 1980 over 1,000 PLO members were trained in terrorist techniques and guerrilla warfare in the USSR. Arafat himself attended the World Festival of Youth held in Prague in 1956 and between 1968 and 1981 made fourteen trips to the Soviet Union, ten of them since the 1973 Arab-Israeli War. In 1972, following one of Arafat's visits, the Soviets for the first time began supplying weapons directly to the PLO (previously it had obtained Soviet weaponry through intermediary Arab states), and since 1977 the Soviets have supplied the PLO with heavy weaponry. In 1974 the PLO was allowed for the first time to open an office in Moscow—an act that some writers have seen as indicating a Soviet commitment to the PLO similar to the commitment made to the NLF of Vietnam in 1964, when that group opened a Moscow office. Arafat had also had close relations with Fidel Castro and attended the conference of "non-aligned" nations held in Havana on September 3-7, 1979. At the conference he and the PLO delegation collaborated with Castro in seeking to turn the meeting into an openly pro-Soviet, anti-American movement. Although this effort was not entirely successful, the conference adopted the anti-Israeli resolutions proposed by the PLO. In July 1980, Arafat attended and was received with special honors at the first anniversary celebration of the Sandinistas' victory in Managua, where Castro was also present as a guest of honor. In 1972, not long after the Lod Airport massacre, *Pravda* quoted a declaration of the PLO that:

all attempts by the imperialists and reactionary circles to disrupt the friendship between the national liberation forces in the Arab world and the Soviet Union and other socialist states are incompatible with the interests of the Arab peoples. . . .

Soviet Support Is Not Ideological

The Soviets do not limit their support to groups that are pro-Soviet in their ideologies and aims; and indeed Soviet support is often extended to groups that are non- or anti-Communist with goals and ideologies at odds with those of the USSR. The purpose of Soviet and Soviet-surrogate support of terrorism is not therefore ideological, and the Soviets would seem to anticipate gains other than the consolidation of ideological solidarity by promoting terrorism. That the Soviet aid to terrorists is not merely occasional and that it is connected to the strategic objectives of Soviet political warfare is shown also by the nature of Soviet and Soviet-surrogate support facilities in the form of training, weapons, and propaganda—what one authority has called "the infrastructure of terror." . . .

US Must Support Targeted Regimes

The unequivocal support of the United States for targeted regimes, especially those that have traditionally supported the United States, on a diplomatic and political level, as well as economically and militarily, should provide the foundation for the U.S. response to the Soviet strategy of terror. The principal enemy of all terrorism is certainty—the certainty that a government or population will not be abandoned to atrocities and intimidation; the certainty that an economy will not be reduced to chaos by the driving out of investments, the expropriation of property, and the sabotage of business facilities; the certainty that an anti-Soviet government can count on the unquestioned support of the United States. There are indications that the U.S. government is gradually awakening to the nature of the Soviet threat and to the dangers of the Soviet strategy of terror, but the policies, orientation, and mentality of the United States government in the recent past have not been encouraging to those who have been aware of the threat. It will not be a simple or easy matter to reverse these policies and orientations, but it will be necessary to do so. The struggle, as the terrorists say, continues.

"A new Red Scare in the form of a 'Soviet-backed international terror network' has been vigorously pushed in the United States."

Soviet-Backed Terrorism Is US Propaganda

Edward S. Herman

Edward S. Herman is professor of finance at the Wharton School, University of Pennsylvania. In addition to co-authoring *The Political Economy of Human Rights* with Noam Chomsky, he has written *Corporate Control, Corporate Power*. In the following viewpoint, excerpted from Mr. Herman's latest book *The Real Terrorist Network*, he argues that the Soviet "terror network" is a US concoction to rally support for a new Red Scare.

As you read, consider the following questions:

1. Mr. Herman does not believe the Soviets use "surrogates." Why?
2. Why does the author believe a Soviet "takeover" of the US is highly unlikely?
3. The author believes it is hypocritical for the US to criticize Soviet involvement in terrorism. Why?

Edward S. Herman, excerpted from *The Real Terror Network*. Boston, MA: South End Press, 1982. Reprinted by permission of the author.

A new Red Scare in the form of a "Soviet-backed international terror network" has been vigorously pushed in the United States during the past decade. . . .

Soviet "Surrogates" Are Propaganda

The Soviet-network propagandists all rest their case heavily on the Soviet's use of "surrogates" or "proxies." Libya, Cuba and the PLO are Soviet "surrogates," so that whatever they do is done on behalf of their master. [Those people who support this theory] use these terms with great assurance, but never stop to define them or to discuss the details of why and how the Soviet controls these alleged proxies, if they control them at all. Are Libya and the PLO as closely linked to the Soviet Union as Brazil and Chile to the United States? . . . One obvious difference—Kaddafi was not installed in power with significant or decisive assists from the Soviet Union.

If the Soviet Union does not control these surrogates, but supports them because of some common interest, their terrorism may be carried out independently of, possibly even contrary to, Soviet desires. Thus the question of degree of control or influence is important and worthy of discussion. None of the three major surrogates allegedly controlled by the Soviet Union are controlled to the degree it controls, say, Czechoslovakia—where, as in the case of Brazil and Chile, the external power played an important role in the counterrevolution—and Soviet influence declines from Cuba to Libya and the PLO. Cuba, driven into Soviet arms by the U.S. boycott and continuous U.S. hostility and intervention, is economically dependent, but still retains at least some autonomy while trying to maintain warm relations with its benefactor. Western propaganda always presumes that Castro's actions abroad are a response to Soviet "discipline" (an assumption rarely made in reference to the actions of western satellites). But even in Angola, for example, the former head of the CIA's operations there, John Stockwell, stated that "After the war we learned that Cuba had not been ordered into action by the Soviet Union. To the contrary, the Cuban leaders felt compelled to intervene for their own ideological reasons." Stockwell points out that

> Moreover, the Cuban policy in Angola was consistent with Cuba's ideology and its international stance. Our Angola program, like the previous Bay of Pigs and *Operation Mongoose* war against Castro, was a direct contradiction of our public policies, making it essential that we keep the American public from knowing the truth. The Cubans weren't ashamed of their program and they didn't need to hide it from their own people, or from the world press.

As regards Latin America, the Castro-as-Soviet-surrogate theory has been contradicted for years by the fact that Soviet Latin American policy has accommodated quite cynically to an ugly

Ollie Harrington, *The Daily World*.

status quo, in sharp contrast with Castro's hostility to that status quo.

Libya is far more independent of the Soviet Union, and its classification as a "proxy" or "surrogate," implying that its behavior is a function of Soviet orders, is unsupported and implausible propaganda. Libya has bought a lot of weaponry, for cash, and has received some military training and diplomatic support from the Soviet Union. (It turns out that Libya has also gotten a lot of support, logistical, training and operational, from former CIA agents now in the business of servicing terrorists who are well heeled.) Kaddafi has, however, denounced the Soviet invasion of Afghanistan, even during his visit to Moscow (a point not discussed in the Free Press—possibly because it disrupts the "surrogate" view), and he has not only rejected Soviet requests for naval bases, he has also claimed territorial water rights inconvenient to Soviet as well as to U.S. maritime interests. His militant Islamic ideology is anathema to the Soviet leadership. He seeks Soviet support with reluctance, under the pressure of open U.S. threats. If the Soviets are willing to support him it is because he splinters a hostile Arab bloc of states and because his own isolation pushes him into a tentative reciprocal relation with them. Only an enormously biased press could convert this marriage of convenience into a control-surrogate relationship, with his terrorism accepted as a product of Soviet orders. The same point may be made as regards the PLO—a splintered group, whose supporters include Saudi Arabia as well as the Soviets, and whose more extreme groups espouse aims in the Middle East different from those of the Soviet Union (which favors a settlement that would include and ratify the existence of Israel). The Soviets support the PLO partly on ideological grounds as self-proclaimed leader of the oppressed, partly to build support among Arab nationalists and preserve a slim and weakened position in the Middle East.

In the view of Claire Sterling (*The Terrorist Network*), the international terrorists controlled from Moscow are trying to "destabilize western democracies." As many of these retail terrorists are extremely nationalistic and would appear to be pursuing local ends, the idea that they all have the global objective of "destabilizing western democracy" is classic terrorist pseudoscience, resting, as in . . . other Red Terror constructs of the past, on carefully selected "facts" and the final imaginative leap. . . . The imaginative leap is to a mysterious Soviet power of discipline and control that produces the common destabilization purpose. But even ignoring the false assumption of Soviet control, is this objective of destabilization compatible with Soviet methods and interests anyway? . . .

Destabilizing US Against Soviet Interests

Destabilization of democratic societies in the west appears to be quite contrary to Soviet interests. Destabilization would most likely bring into power rightist regimes more violent and more hostile than their predecessors. The Soviet leadership has been pressing for detente for many years because the military burden of the arms race is extremely heavy to the poorer country. Furthermore, it has been technologically backward in many fields and has been seeking trade and technological exchange for urgent economic reasons. Efforts to destabilize would damage Soviet efforts along these lines.

In the Third World, Soviet interests and intentions are more ambiguous. Part of the Soviet moral resources in the world arises from its claim, as the leading socialist state, to leadership and support of the oppressed. It can justify aid to the NLF in Vietnam, SWAPO in Namibia, and the indigenous Neto-led rebels of Angola, to take just three examples, on the grounds that the movements supported were popular, were resisting an oppressive old order, or were fighting against aggression from without. If the Soviets failed to support such movements they would lose face and status as leader of the anti-imperialist bloc.

Disregarding Morality

There are quite a few facts proving Washington's absolute disregard of morality, international order and the UN charter. Otherwise they would not have called the invasion of defenseless Grenada its "liberation," or the dirty war in Vietnam a "noble" act. . . .

Meanwhile, the USSR calls for eliminating regional conflicts through peaceful talks. It sharply denounces all forms of interference and state-sponsored terrorism. In this connection, the new draft edition of the Communist Party of the Soviet Union program says that the U.S. policy of imposing unequal relations on other states, supporting regressive anti-popular regimes and discriminating against the countries not to Washington's liking disorganizes international economic and political relations and hinders their normal development.

Yuri Gvozdev, *Daily World*, February 1, 1986.

Of course, the bias of the western media is so huge that Soviet and Cuban aid to an indigenous movement against an ancient colonialism in Angola, or against South African efforts to destabilize the successor regime, is a priori aggressive and evidence of Soviet "expansionism." . . . These premises of the natural right of the west to intervene anywhere on its own terms, and the inappropriateness of any Soviet moves beyond its borders (even in defense of people resisting external aggression), makes it easy to demonstrate enemy "terrorism."

Rationalizing the Terror

Even with this reliance on manipulated definitions and the premise of different natural rights to intervene as between us and them, the Soviet network analysts never provide numbers. This is because if they were obligated to get specific, the numbers would be relatively small and would reveal that Guatemala by itself is more of a terrorist problem than the entire (mythical) Soviet network. But the little stories of liberal-left middle class youth, with good intent, becoming cold-blooded killers, feeds well into western biases and helps rationalize the needs of the multinational corporation. By tying together resistance movements in the Third World and seemingly arbitrary and wanton hijackings, kidnappings and murders in Italy, and making them all part of a Soviet plot to undermine western democracies, a lot of needs are met— we turn attention away from western support of official terror in the National Security State, and we put pressure on the Soviet Union and Cuba to halt their support—not for the Baader-Meinhof gang or Red Brigades—but for the peasants of El Salvador, Guatemala and Namibia. . . .

Major Error of Fact

Claire Sterling and Walter Laqueur claim, as evidence of the Communist root of terrorism, that terrorists concentrate on the democracies and rarely disturb the Communist sphere. This is a major error of fact, made credible to the uninitiated only by grace of the major biases of the western mass media. South Africa's assaults on Angola and Mozambique during the past five years are cross-border terrorist attacks beyond anything suffered by any western democracy. But as South Africa is part of the Free World, and Angola and Mozambique are left-oriented states, these attacks are played down and are not called terrorist. Since 1959 Cuba has been subjected to many more terrorist acts than any western democracy, very possibly more than all of them put together, including many assassination attempts directed at the head of state. Sterling and Laqueur can pretend that Communist powers are terror-free only because of the patriotic bias of the propaganda system of which they are a part. With Cuba having been officially declared bad, and the enemy, acts that would be designated terroristic if taken against Free World states like Paraguay or Indonesia lose that character in the propaganda system when taken against Cuba. Furthermore, the manager and sponsor of this terroristic assault on Cuba has been the United States, the leader of the Free World in its struggle against "terrorism."

It is the ultimate double standard, and a tremendous testimonial to the biases and power of the Free Press, that the United States could hire members of the mafia, and other assassins, in an *admitted* eight attempts on the life of Castro, and carry out a secret war of sabotage, murder and political blackmail of quite considerable scope, and come out of this as Uncle-Sam-The-Clean, Fighter-Against-Terrorism. I ask two rhetorical questions: If Colonel Kaddafi had admitted to eight attempts on the life of the President of the United States, what would be the world reaction? Why are small crimes by Kaddafi proof of evil and larger crimes by the United States proof of nothing? I offer a rule applicable within the west: for a given state crime, criminality is inversely related to GNP, firepower, and strength of western affiliation. On this rule it is clear why discovery of a cache of arms from Castro in Venezuela (possibly planted by the CIA), is far more sinister than extended plotting with civil and military leaders for the overthrow of constitutional governments (Brazil, Chile), or the organization and management of literal invasions (Guatemala, Cuba) by the United States. . . .

US Terrorists

In sharp contrast with Castro, our own progeny and assorted other friendly state terrorists are allowed to get away with direct, cross-border murder and numerous other interventions, stretching even to the United States, most of which fail to generate serious publicity or indignation. General Park's South Korea was able to engage in extensive bribery of U.S. politicians without causing significant damage to itself—certainly nothing was done so severe as closing its U.S. Embassy, let alone any major act of hostility. South Africa, also, has been able to expend large sums buying and bribing U.S. newspapers and funding U.S. politicians without significant adverse repercussions. Currently, South Africa is openly propagandizing in the United States on Namibia and campaigning against hostile U.S. politicians through hired law and PR firms and alleged "trade councils," again without real exposure or apparent impediment. . . . South Africa can invade its neighbors and murder their civilians at will without arousing Free Press attention or indignation. Sudanese president Jafar el Numeiry can arrest 12,000 at a crack or announce that he is training several hundred men to infiltrate into Libya on suicide missions aimed at removing key figures in Col. Kaddafi's government, again without notice or comment in the west. The principle of "whose ox is being gored" controls news and indignation both.

7

"The . . . Afghan mujaheddin—'holy warriors'— [are] fighting an Islamic holy war against the Soviet invaders of their country."

Afghan Rebels Are Freedom Fighters

Jack Wheeler

In 1979, the Soviet Union, at the alleged invitation of the Afghan government, entered Afghanistan with tanks and soldiers in order to suppress "reactionary" elements in that country. Numerous human rights organizations have reported the terrible tactics used by the Soviets to subdue the Afghan resistance, including the use of chemical weapons, "toy" bombs, rape, and agricultural destruction. In the following viewpoint, Jack Wheeler discusses some of the terrible atrocities the Soviets have committed against the Afghan people, and explains that the mujaheddin are holy warriors, fighting to repel an evil, heartless regime. Jack Wheeler holds a Ph.D. in philosophy.

As you read, consider the following questions:

1. How does the author describe the morale of the Soviet soldiers who are in Afghanistan? What reasons does the author give for this?
2. What do the Soviets want in Afghanistan, according to the author?

I am drinking tea in a flower garden. Veiled women carrying jars of water on their heads glide silently by. Turbaned men are tending their fields and irrigation ditches. Among the walnut and apple trees and in the marijuana patches, children are laughing and playing. Flowers are planted everywhere, even in the windowsill of a nearby home, one wall of which has a huge hole in it fashioned by a Soviet artillery shell. Beautiful white puffy clouds are building over the mountains, and a gorgeous sunset is developing. A caravan of camels plods insouciantly along, bound for the Pakistan border, each burdened with a load of rough-hewn timbers.

The village I am in is nestled in the foothills of the valley of Jaji (george-gee), Afghanistan, and in the center of the valley floor below me is a fortress under siege, with 1,200 Soviet and Afghan communist soldiers inside. I am drinking tea in a flower garden, watching a war.

In the mountains above and around me, the incessant bursts of DShK ("Dashaka") machine-gun fire and thuds of mortar rounds are in eerie contrast with the laughter of the playing children, who have become inured and oblivious to the sounds of warfare. Small clouds of dust appear whenever a mortar round lands near the Soviet garrison. Tracer bullets from the Dashakas make fluorescent pink arcs across the sky and are answered by returning Dashaka fire from the fortress. Periodically, a Soviet howitzer cuts loose from within the beleaguered fort, and the shell lands with an earshattering blast that makes the entire valley rumble and shudder.

Earlier in the day, I had been in the mountains, at one of the Dashaka positions firing upon the fort. Just five minutes after I left, a howitzer shell scored a direct hit on the position, and everyone was killed.

In the mountains on either side of the valley there are 30 Dashaka emplacements. Such a concentration of precious firepower is directed at the garrison, because it lies directly athwart the main arms-smuggling trail from the Pakistan border to the capital city of Kabul and all of northern Afghanistan. A dense mine field surrounding the fort prevents its being overrun, but a countermine field along all access roads prevents its being supplied or rescued by ground. The water supply to the fort has been poisoned. Inside the fort, food and ammunition are running low, and the only way the Soviets can resupply their desperate countrymen is by helicopter.

The Holy Warriors

But the Dashakas in the mountains prevent the helicopters from landing: the choppers must fly very high and attempt to drop the supplies to the fort. More often than not, they miss. I watch as a load carrying dozens of loaves of bread and 300 mortar shells lands in a gully beyond the minefield perimeter. A small band of turbaned and pajamaed men quickly scurry up to retrieve it.

These scurrying men, the men operating the Dashakas in the mountains, the men with whom I am drinking tea in the garden, are Afghan *mujaheddin*—"holy warriors" fighting a *jihad*, an Islamic holy war, against the Soviet invaders of their country. Often barefoot or in sandals, armed mostly with single-shot bolt-action carbines and a handful of larger weapons, they are the only people in the world who are fighting the Soviet Union face on. Straight up against the awesome might of the Red Army, the Afghan mujaheddin have fought the invading Soviets to a standstill.

Agony in Afghanistan

Afghanistan is being turned into a charnel house.

It is not only that the Soviets and their Afghan puppets have executed or tortured to death thousands of political prisoners. It is not only that they attack civilian targets—wedding parties, farmers in their fields, villagers in the bazaars—or that they single out medical facilities for destruction. It is not only that they pursue, rocket and strafe the slow, plodding caravans of refugees—women and children, mostly—fleeing to sanctuary in Pakistan and Iran. And it is not only that they burn crops, destroy granaries, and kill flocks and herds, or that they smash irrigation systems, pushing rural Afghanistan ever closer to the edge of famine.

These are not the sporadic actions of uncontrolled troups gone berserk. This is the deliberate, calculated Soviet policy of sending Soviet forces into the villages of Afghanistan to rape, to loot, to burn, and to murder most horribly, leaving the mutilated dead as a warning and an omen to survivors. The message of this systematic campaign of butchery is clear: submit, get out, or die hideously.

Jean-Francois Revel and Rosanne Klass, *Reader's Digest*, March 1986.

But the cost of such a fight to the Afghan people and freedom fighters is reaching genocidal proportions. Since the Soviet invasion of Afghanistan in December 1979, at least 50,000, and perhaps 100,000, mujaheddin have died in combat. Some 800,000 Afghan civilians—mostly women and children—have been killed, reports Freedom House, the human-rights-monitoring organization. Aerial attacks by Soviet MI-24 HIND helicopter gunships and MiG jet fighters are responsible for the great majority of these deaths. While the villages of Jaji are somewhat protected from air attack by all the Dashakas, most other Afghan villages are not nearly so fortunate.

(Many statistics regarding the Soviets' war on Afghanistan vary widely from source to source, and because of the obvious problems of verification, most are simply estimates. Those that I report throughout this writing seem most credible to me, after having weighed them against my own observations from two trips inside Afghanistan in August 1983 and conversations and interviews with other journalists, up-close observers, contacts within the intelligence communities of several nations, and many mujaheddin.)

According to present estimates, out of a total Afghan population of 15 million, some 3.5 million are refugees in Pakistan; 1.5 million, in Iran. And because the Soviets have bombed virtually all Afghan villages—some 14,000—incinerating their fields and harvest with napalm, probably another one to two million "internal refugees" have been forced to flee their villages to larger cities, particularly to Kabul, the capital. Thus, close to half of the country's people are refugees.

Widespread Starvation

Starvation is becoming widespread as the Soviets pursue their policy of what Princeton University's Louis Dupree, the premier scholar on Afghanistan, has called "migratory genocide." Under this policy, the Soviet invaders go after civilians, not the guerrillas, and thereby prevent the latter from "swimming like fish in the sea" of the rural population—Mao Tse Tung's prerequisite for the survival of a guerrilla army.

Moscow, it is often said, cares nothing for Afghans, only for Afghanistan, the physical territory itself—250,000 mountainous and arid square miles (about the size of Texas) landlocked between Iran, Pakistan, and the USSR. Today, Soviet administrators are wholly in charge of every department of the "Afghan government." In fact, Moscow is well on its way toward incorporating Afghanistan within the USSR itself. (Moscow has already evacuated the Wakhan Corridor, in northeast Afghanistan, having turned it into a huge military base.) And the Soviets seem fully willing to slaughter every single man, woman, and child in the entire country, if necessary, in order to do so.

But in trying to subdue Afghanistan, the Soviets may well be playing a game of Russian roulette. Almost 20 years ago, Louis Dupree predicted, "If you want to kill the Soviet Union, get it to try to eat Afghanistan." After going inside the country twice with the mujaheddin, and personally witnessing the spirit and courage of the Afghan people, I think there is a chance he may be proven right. . . .

The second time I went inside I was with a group of mujaheddin from the Harakat and Jamiat organizations. Again there was the jeep ride past the infuriating Pak check points. But this time we went up the Kurram Valley to the Pakistani border town of Tara Mangal, the principal point from which arms are smuggled to mujaheddin in central and northern Afghanistan.

(I learned from mujahed sources that Arab and Pakistani connections in China purchase matériel at or near cost, mostly Chinese copies of Soviet weapons. [The Chinese government also donates some arms to the mujaheddin.] Chinese trucks take the arms over the China-Pakistan border, via the Karakorum Highway, down to the city of Lahore. There the wares are transferred to Pak trucks and hauled up to Tara Mangal, where they are distributed. At Tara Mangal I saw three huge truckloads of arms uncrated and put on the backs of mules and donkeys for the trip into Afghanistan.). . .

Pak/Afghan Border

The Pak-Afghan border, laid down by the British in 1893 as the famous "Durand Line," cuts arbitrarily across Pathan and other tribal areas and has always been a sieve. The Pakistan government exercises only nominal control in the whole border area, the Soviet-Afghan "government" none at all on "their" side. At only two points along the entire border do and can the Soviets maintain a presence: where the Quetta-Kandahar road crosses the border at Spin Buldak, in southeast Afghanistan, and at the Khyber Pass itself.

Afghanistan is not flat. The 9,000-foot border pass was only the beginning. We hiked up one crag and down into a gorge or valley, then up again, down again, over and over again. There were five

© 1984, Washington Post Writers Group, reprinted with permission.

of us: Hossein, a mujahed who acted as my interpreter; Commander Sangeen; Sangeen's two lieutenants, Gul-jan and Rahin-jan; and myself. We were on a main trail from Kabul and points north, and groups of refugees were continually going by us, fleeing into Pakistan. At every *chaisana*, there were mujaheddin from various guerrilla groups, drinking tea and eating *nan* amidst the swarms of flies, on their way to their respective battle fronts.

Throughout this trek, one experience was depressingly repeated. Upon coming to the top of a pass, a beautiful valley would appear beneath us: green terraces of corn, orchards and shade trees, picturesque villages—a picture post card. That was at a distance. Close up, we would discover instead a ghost valley: everything shattered and destroyed by the *Shuravi* (the mujaheddin's word for the Soviet invaders); skeletons of homes and villages bombed out; fields turning to weeds; untended orchards of mulberry, apple, and apricot trees. The villages were abandoned and uninhabited save for a few remaining families, especially old people, and an occasional tea house. . . .

Finally we reached the encampment of a famous commander in the Kabul area, Wali Khan. Wali Khan, who is with the Mohaz and Harakat mujaheddin, had managed to acquire an official blue Afghan government truck. After an extension of traditional Afghan hospitality with tea and *nan*, Wali Khan asked me, "How would you like to see Kabul?" Soon I was bouncing along the dusty Sorubi power-dam road that leads to the capital, with a contingent of Wali Khan's men dressed in captured Afghan army uniforms.

We entered Kabul Valley and stopped on the road so that I could view a Soviet garrison not far away. Then we drove to the outskirts of Kabul and parked on a slight rise overlooking the most infamous place in Afghanistan, Pol-i-Charky prison, holding some 22,000 political prisoners. Before the curfew checkpoints started appearing we hot-footed it back to the safety of Wali Khan's camp.

Wali Khan had gotten word from his spies in Kabul that the Soviets were planning an offensive in his area, so I spent the next week with him traveling by truck, foot, and horseback, as he coordinated the preparations at a number of mujahed camps and positions. . . .

A Soviet Spy

We hiked up to the area of Jigdalik and spent a day talking to Hassan Khan, a commander with the Harakat mujaheddin, and Anwar, the leader of all mujaheddin in Logar province, to the south and east of Kabul. From high up on a rocky ledge overlooking the valley, I took in the beautiful sight below—pretty villages and green trees and fields. Before the 1979 invasion, more than 2,000 families lived here. Now, there were less than 50.

Hassan Khan and Anwar had just captured an agent of the Karmal government posing as a mujahed named Nasrullah. The

164

Soviets had paid him several thousand dollars (in Afghani rupees) to spy on the guerrillas.

There were several hundred Karmal agents, I was told, among the mujaheddin. (Of course, there are many more mujahed spies among the Karmal army and government.) The Soviets pay these spies well to join the *Khad* (Karmal secret police), my mujahed hosts informed me. But in addition to those spies who do it for the money, there might, I suggested, be educated or semieducated Afghan youths taken in by Marxist rhetoric or enamored of the power of the Soviet Union and its willingness to use it. They see the Soviet Union as the wave of the future, the mujaheddin as ignorant reactionaries resisting the Soviet attempt to move Afghanistan out of the past, trying to impose a parochial religious tyranny dominated by illiterate fanatic mullahs. Such youths could easily close their eyes to the Soviet barbarism and genocide perpetrated upon their fellow citizens, as many Germans did with the Nazis.

The Greatest Terrorism

The White House and Congress should not be content with voting merely $215 million in military and humanitarian aid for Afghanistan. They should provide these heroic Afghan resistance fighters with whatever they need to continue their fight against the Soviets. And they should make sure the Mujahedeen get all of the weapons and supplies purchased, rather than have a great percentage of them intercepted on the way through Pakistan. . . .

The greatest terrorism taking place in the world today is occurring in Afghanistan. We, the free people of the United States and the world, cannot sit silently by while the brigades of Mikhail Gorbachev butcher innocent men, women and children at will. To do so when we have the power to help is to share the blame.

Oliver Starr Jr., *Amercan Legion Magazine*, January 1986.

Yes, my mujahed hosts agreed. The Russians are not stupid. They have their propaganda, and Quislings can be found in any society. Thousands of Afghan students are being educated in the Soviet Union—but much of this propagandistic effort is backfiring because of overt Great Russian racism toward Central Asians. . . .

It is morning now, sunrise at Jaji. I am peering over a shallow protective trench on top of a hill overlooking the valley, the rising sun at my back. It is a cloudless day, and the sun is spreading over the crazy quilt of field patches on the valley floor. Men are going out to work their fields, and some sheep are grazing nearby.

The entire valley is reverberating from the sounds of two MiGs and a "Frogfoot" fighter as they fly in from the northwest to make their runs on the mujaheddin positions. The Dashakas are pumping at them from a half-dozen of the 30 emplacements on both valley walls. But the jets are too fast and too high. The valley shudders, the hill I am on with it. Napalm bombs fall with enormous thuds, and the mountains to my left bursting into spurting balls of fire.

The jets fly off to the north, and it is quiet again. A pall of smoke rises over the mountains, and a stream of Dashaka fire rains down on the garrison. I walk with Gulab-jan, subcommander under Adam Khel, overall commander and tribal chief of the valley, down to and across the valley floor to the tiny village of Mir Khel, perched on the edge of the mine field surrounding the garrison. Inside an adobe castle-like home I meet a small group of mujaheddin who are planning a rocket attack on the garrison for that night.

Soviet Atrocities

Outside, children are racing around playing hide and seek in the village enclosure. I think of a child, an 8-year-old boy I met at the Red Cross hospital in Peshawar. His name was Nabib, and he told me he had been playing at his village in Afghanistan when a Soviet helicopter flew over and dropped some brightly colored things. He and his playmates rushed over to see what they were. They looked like painted toys—pens, red wagons, birds. Nabib picked one up, and it blew off his hands.

There are few moral issues in this often-confusing world as sharp and clear-cut as Afghanistan. The Afghans—exceptions like Gulbiddin notwithstanding—are not Moslem fanatics. They are a devout people, believing deeply in their religion and the Islamic way of life. They have attacked nobody and are a threat to nobody. They simply want to be left alone. Yet they are being systematically exterminated for the cause of Soviet imperialism. . . .

Despite the mujaheddin's limited resources, the events in Afghanistan provoke this question: if a bunch of guys in bolt-action rifles and sandals can fight off the Soviet Union, must anyone fear the Red boogeyman any longer? If the Soviets can't defeat the Afghans, could they probably take on, say, 250 million Western Europeans?

Why the Afghans are struggling to turn back the Soviet invaders is made painfully clear by the picture of the little boy with stumps at the end of his arms. It was a Soviet-made butterfly bomb that did this. You don't make bombs that look like toys unless you want this to happen. Murdering and terrorizing as many innocent men, women, and children as possible into becoming refugees is the Kremlin's consciously pursued policy in Afghanistan. As you look at this picture, you cannot escape this conclusion: *the Soviets wanted this to happen.* That is the nature of the enemy Afghanistan's holy warriors face.

166

"The counterrevolutionary leaders regard sabotage and terror as one of the principle means of struggle against the people's government."

Afghan Rebels Are Terrorists

G. Ustinov

The Soviet Union defends its occupation of Afghanistan as being a humanitarian mission. The government the Soviets helped overthrow was corrupt and unpopular, they claim. For this reason, the Soviets refuse to refer to the resistance fighters as *mujaheddin* or holy warriors, and prefer to call them counterrevolutionaries. In the following viewpoint, Mr. Ustinov, writing in the Soviet newsmagazine *New Times*, describes how Afghan counterrevolutionaries terrorize the civilian population in an attempt to regain control of the government.

As you read, consider the following questions:

1. Does the author believe the Afghan resistance is a popular movement?
2. What tactics does the author say the counterrevolutionaries use to terrorize the Afghan people?
3. Who supports the counterrevolutionaries, according to the author?

G. Ustinov, "Wholesale Terrorism," *New Times*, January 20, 1986.

On the sunny morning of December 8 [1985] about 100 passengers at Kabul airport were preparing to board a plane bound for Kandahar. Some were already going on board, and the loading of luggage had begun. Suddenly there was a violent explosion on the luggage platform. Six people were killed and more than 70 injured. Three of them died later in [the] hospital.

The investigation revealed that a suitcase with an explosive device had been secreted among the trunks and bags of the passengers. The home-made bomb could not seriously damage airport facilities: stuffed with nails, sharp-edged bits of metal and bullets, it was intended to hit as many people as possible.

Another bomb exploded the next day in Kabul Polytechnic Institute at 12:30, when hundreds of students and lecturers were in the classrooms. Ten people were injured by glass splinters. By a mere chance no one was killed, because the bomb had been planted in the entrance hall which was empty at the time of the explosion.

The institute's pro-rector Naier showed me round the laboratory building where the time bomb had been laid in an inconspicuous spot.

"Had the bomb exploded half an hour later, when the classes end and the flocks of students pass through the entrance hall into the street, the consequences would have been much more tragic," he said.

Terrorist acts of this kind show that the killers are well trained and equipped with modern weapons of murder.

Training Terrorists

At the "farewell" party in the Varsak camp in Pakistan, where saboteurs and terrorists are trained for operations on Afghan territory, Shodihan and Lal Muhammad sat side by side, sipping fragrant green tea from the same teapot. In Kabul they were together again, this time in the investigation cell of a prison. The terrorists were captured at their safe houses, where they had been waiting for a parcel from Pakistan. The parcel was to contain small cylinders filled with a psychotropic substance in the form of aerosol. A gas jet spurted into a man's face can knock him unconscious for several hours, while several jets are enough to send him to kingdom come. The American instructors in the camp told future saboteurs and terrorists that these cylinders would help them remove sentries and neutralize military or police posts with little trouble.

The Varsak camp, near Peshawar, is one of the 100-plus centres set up in Pakistan to train combatants, saboteurs and terrorists for the Afghan counterrevolution. The training period lasts from several weeks to several months, depending on the "specialization."

The training course at the Varsak camp was intensive, 10 to 12 hours a day, with two hours assigned to "theory," Shodihan and Lal Muhammad said. Monstrous lies about the policy and goals of the Afghan people's government were drummed into the recruits. They were also told about the "persecution" of Moslems in the Soviet Union and about the "noble and unstinting aid" given the Afghan "defenders of the faith" by their American, Pakistani and other "friends" abroad. At the camp's training range the recruits were taught how to shoot, plant and defuse mines, use toxic agents, camouflage themselves and cross gorges and rivers.

Poisoners

Lal Muhammad and Shodihan were not the first Varsak camp trainees to have been captured by security bodies of the democratic republic. In 1984 a certain Gulam Haidar, a would-be physician, was caught red-handed 20 km away from Kabul. The nervous behaviour of a young intelligent-looking man caught the attention of the officer in charge of a check point in the town of Pul-i-Charhi. His papers seemed to be in order, but when his knapsack was examined it was found to contain a cellophane bag filled with white powder.

The police thought it was heroin. Gulam Haidar was detained and the bag was sent to the chemical laboratory. The result of the test was completely unexpected. "The smell of bitter almonds, the positive reaction towards Prussian blue, and the appearance of crimson colour in an indicator tube suggest that the substance belongs to the group of cyanic compounds," it said.

Afghan-USSR Friendship

The entire 60-year-long history of relations between the Soviet Union and Afghanistan shows the natural gravitation of the Afghan people towards the northern neighbor which always came to the country's assistance in hard times. It is no surprise, therefore, that in 1979, the Afghan government asked the Soviet Union for military help.

The main reason for the request was the CIA's subversive activity against the progressive movement in Afghanistan and against the gains of the April 1978 revolution.

Ahmed Waziri, *Daily World*.

The bag contained about half a kilo of the white powder ("readily soluble in water," as the chemists pointed out), enough to poison thousands of people.

I was allowed to talk to Gulam Haidar. He told me that he had agreed to deliver the powder to a clandestine band in Kabul for a generous reward. "I wanted to go to Western Europe or the

United States, complete my medical education there, and find work in a reputable hospital," he added.

He was ready to kill in order to cure! Incredible. How had Gulam become so cynical? At 28, he is too far removed in time and space to remember the camps in which nazi butchers in white smocks carried out their monstrous "medical experiments." Or perhaps the three years spent abroad were for him a school of brutality? Who then are his teachers and what morals do they preach?

Gulam Haidar fled his native land seduced by promises of carefree and prosperous life he heard over the "free world" radio. But in Pakistan he found himself forced to do any unskilled job he could find in order to earn a bare living. He ran into debt and could no longer think of continuing his education. Finally, in despair, he came to the Varsak camp, where people like him were given food and shelter, and paid a decent "grant" besides.

In February 1984 Gulam Haidar was invited to the camp office for a talk with his instructor Azad, a tall, long-armed Pakistani, a representative of one of the Afghan counterrevolutionary parties based in Pakistan, and a European looking man whom the Afghan called "our American friend."

A Lethal Assignment

"We have studied your backround and believe it inexpedient to use you as an ordinary mujahiddin (defender of the faith)," Gulam was told. "To live in constant fear of being killed—that is not for you, a literate man soon to become a doctor. We ask you to carry out only one assignment. There is practically no risk, but your future will be ensured."

In addition to the lethal parcel, Haidar received in Peshawar false papers, money for travel to Kabul and back, and verbal instructions for the chief of a Kabul band. The white powder was to be used for poisoning drinking water in the 8th district of the capital, where large government offices and two girls' schools are located.

"This last is particularly important," the Afghan stressed. "Under the new regime our sisters are getting completely out of hand, forgetting their place and the laws of the Sharia. Not long ago I was in Kabul on our business and I saw many of them walking about the street without veils. There are many young girls in the schools and whenever there is a demonstration of some kind they are always in the front ranks. It's time to put the fear of God into them."

Sabotage

The counterrevolutionary leaders regard sabotage and terror as one of the principal means of struggle against the people's government. Their main objective is to frighten the population and provoke unrest. Terrorist acts are carried out by groups specially

170

trained for the purpose by experts from the secret services of the U.S., Pakistan and a number of West European countries. They kill or kidnap party and government officials and servicemen, conduct acts of sabotage in public places, at airports, fuel storages, pump houses, electric power stations, and on transport, and shell housing estates from mobile guns, mortars and other weapons.

Not long ago the Afghan news agency Bakhtar held a press conference to demonstrate the handbooks prepared by the CIA for the sabotage training centres in Pakistan and for the bands and terrorist groups operating in Afghanistan.

Afghan Children Like USSR

There are indeed little Afghans in the Soviet Union—not "legions," but just over a thousand boys and girls. They go to four schools in Tashkent and one in Slavyansk (Krasnodar Territory). The government of Afghanistan, against which international reactionary forces have been fighting a criminal war for six years, killing its citizens and ravaging its economy, is not yet always in a position to provide its children with enough toys, books, schools and kindergartens. Hundreds of Afghan children are able to avail themselves of these facilities in the Soviet Union. They come here of their own accord and with their parents' consent, or that of their relatives if the parents are dead.

Lev Yelin, *New Times*, March 31, 1986.

Among them was a pocket-size booklet, "Lessons of Guerrilla Warfare," distributed by the counterrevolutionary Islamic Party of Afghanistan. Its table of contents includes the following chapters: "How to Use Small Arms," "Types of Weapons," "Chemical Agents and Their Practical Use," "Use of Anti-Tank and Anti-Personnel Mines," "Anti-Aircraft and Rocket Weapons," "Ambushing," "Camouflage," "How to Hide in Mountains and Flat Country," "Destruction of Roads, Bridges and Communication Means," "Combat with Superior Enemy Forces," "How to Behave When Arrested," "Ciphering and Smuggling Letters out of Prison."

Manual for the Underground

Another manual, "War in the Enemy Rear," is intended for the fifth column, for the counterrevolutionary underground. It contains instructions of an entirely different kind: how to become legalized, how to win people's confidence, to engage in subversion at the place of residence and work, how to set managers against their subordinates and tradesmen against buyers, sow panicky rumours, where and how [to] keep arms, manufacture toxic agents and explosives. . . .

Readers probably remember what an uproar was caused some time ago by reports about the manuals issued by the CIA for the contras fighting against revolutionary Nicaragua and how vehemently the CIA denied its complicity in the preparation and distribution of literature of this kind.

At the above-mentioned press conference the Bakhtar news agency also demonstrated by way of comparison the manuals put out for the Somozist bands in Nicaragua. It seems that the authors of manuals for the Afghan bands were not very imaginative—the same general outlines, the same recommendations, and even similar illustrations, but with a slight Moslem tint.

In their war against democratic Afghanistan the U.S. secret services closely cooperate with Pakistani intelligence. This was confirmed once again by a letter captured by Afghan public order forces and published in the Kabul newspaper Hakikate Enkilabe Thawr (Truth of the April Revolution). Here is the translation of this document:

> Top secret.
> From deputy head of the intelligence service of the Northwest Frontier Province, Peshawar.
> To director of the Central Intelligence Service of Pakistan, Islamabad.
> February 6, 1985.
> In keeping with the decision on creating an atmosphere of chaos in Afghanistan and especially in Kabul, by March 21, 1985 [the Moslem New Year] we had infiltrated five of our highly active and experienced men in the groups of mujahiddins and sent them to Afghanistan. Each had been provided with Afghan papers.
> Only group commanders know that we infiltrated these men.
> Secrecy must be observed at all stages of fulfilment of the plan.
> Muhammad Ahmed Khan, deputy head of Northwest Frontier intelligence.
> Copies sent to:
> The war office of the President of Pakistan.
> The Chairman of the Afghan Refugee Committee.

US Involvement

It is easy to guess what decision the author of the letter had in mind. For several years now March 21 has been declared in the U.S. Afghanistan Day. On that day American TV reporters and highly-placed officials pour invective on the people's government of Afghanistan, prate about "solidarity with the courageous defenders of the faith," promise them aid of every kind and, simultaneously, urge them to continue the "holy war" against the revolutionary government without any scruples as to the means and methods used.

The instructors from U.S. secret services incite the counter-revolutionary bands to carry out particularly brutal acts of

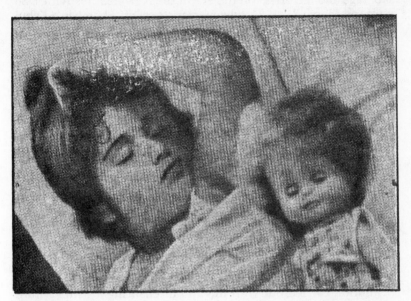

This little Afghan girl now goes to school in the USSR—and she plays with dolls.

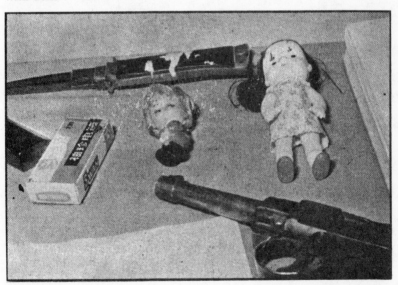

... And these are dolls and other toys with which "teachers" from Washington wanted to kill her and other girls her age in Afghanistan.

sabotage and terrorism on the eve of the New Year festivities. So it was on March 21, 1984, when terrorists set off a bomb in a Kabul mosque during the service there. Four people were killed and 21 injured in the explosion. So it was on March 20, 1985, when an explosive device went off in the rush hour on the crowded market square of the capital. Thirty people were taken to [the] hospital. The lives of some of them could not be saved.

Terrorist acts and sabotage are often timed to coincide with revolutionary and national holidays, festivities and other important dates. The aim is to spoil the holiday and mar the joy, and also to show that the counterrevolutionary forces are still active.

The citizens of Kabul and the entire country condemn terrorist acts against innocent people. Whomever I talked with after the December explosions—victims and doctors, relatives of the dead, and public order officials—all spoke with anger and contempt of those who masterminded and committed these vile crimes. "Venal mercenaries of the CIA. Cowardly murderers. Vain are their hopes," they said. "They will be punished by revolutionary justice. They will never succeed in undermining our determination and militant spirit. They will not check the steady advance of the revolution carried out with the aim of ensuring a better future of the people."

"As the great powers take their own terrorism for granted, they should not be surprised when desperate fanatics . . . emulate their betters."

Both Superpowers Encourage Terrorism

Henry Steele Commager

Henry Steele Commager, a historian, is emeritus professor at Amherst College. In the following viewpoint, Mr. Commager argues that while terrorism may not be morally justified, it is certainly understandable. Throughout history, major countries have resorted to terror tactics. Today's terrorists are merely participating in a longstanding tradition.

As you read, consider the following questions:

1. What is Mr. Commager's definition of terrorism?
2. Mr. Commager uses many examples of what he believes to be terrorist acts committed by major countries. What do these examples have in common? Do you agree that they are terrorist?
3. How do these terrorist acts "breed contempt for the law," according to the author? Does this argument seem plausible?

Nothing can justify the terrorism practiced by the Shiites, the Iranians, the Palestinians and other desperate groups who wage war on innocent victims. But then what can justify terrorism as introduced and practiced by most of the great powers whenever it served their ends over the past century or so?

For what is terrorism but resort to deadly violence against random and innocent victims, and shattering the fabric of society with dynamite and fire!

What is most sobering is that all the Old World nations practiced intermittent terrorism throughout the 19th century; the British in India, the Belgians in the Congo, the Russians and Poles against their own Jews, the Turks against Armenians.

America's History of Terrorism

Americans, too, must confess their own history of terrorism against those they feared or hated or regarded as "lesser breeds." Thus, the extermination of the Pequot Indians as early as 1637; the Sand Creek massacre of some 500 Cheyenne women and children in 1864—and this after the tribe had surrendered; the lurid atrocities against Filipinos struggling for independence at the beginning of this century; Lieut. William L. Calley's massacre of 450 Vietnamese women, children and old men at Mylai in 1969.

Superpowers Bless Terrorism

If we are condemning terrorism on the level of individuals or secret groups and organizations, then we must condemn with even greater severity the stances of the superpowers who bless terrorism when it suits them and condemn it when it does not, as is the case with the United States under the leadership of Ronald Reagan. And if we condemn terrorism and believe that it is counterproductive, then we must condemn even more severely the attempts exerted in the West to link terrorism with a people's right to self-determination, or to equate terrorism with mass, armed struggle to which people resort against imperialism, outside aggression, and occasionally against dictatorial regimes.

Bilal al-Hasan, *al-Yawm al-Sabi*, January 6, 1986.

The formal rationalization—we might almost say legitimization—of terrorism came with World War II when all the major participants abandoned "precision" bombing, directed against the military, for saturation bombing directed against civilians. It was a policy that eventually took the lives of millions of women and children in London, Coventry, Hamburg, Berlin, Dresden, Warsaw, Moscow, Tokyo and scores of other "open cities." The climax of all this was the Holocaust in Germany and, in 1945, the fateful use of the atomic bomb at Hiroshima and

Nagasaki.

By the Vietnam War, terrorism was so taken for granted that it almost ceased to excite comment. The Vietnamese practiced it in the traditional form of jungle warfare. Americans practiced it more systematically by pouring seven million tons of bombs on Vietnam, Cambodia and Laos (with none of which we were technically at war)—three times the tonnage dropped on Germany and Japan during World War II.

As the great powers take their own terrorism for granted, they should not be surprised when desperate fanatics, unable to wage traditional or "legitimate" warfare, emulate their betters.

Observing the Law

What Justice Louis D. Brandeis said a half century ago is now more relevant to the global than to the domestic scene: "In a government of laws the existence of the government will be imperiled if it fails to observe the law scrupulously. Our government is the potent, the omnipotent teacher. For good or ill it teaches the whole people by its example. If government becomes a lawbreaker it breeds contempt for law: it invites every man to become a law unto himself. It invites anarchy."

What confronts us now is international anarchy.

Recognizing Statements That Are Provable

From various sources of information we are constantly confronted with statements and generalizations about social and moral problems. In order to think clearly about these problems, it is useful if one can make a basic distinction between statements for which evidence can be found and other statements which cannot be verified or proved because evidence is not available, or the issue is so controversial that it cannot be definitely proved.

Readers should constantly be aware that magazines, newspapers and other sources often contain statements of a controversial nature. The following activity is designed to allow experimentation with statements that are provable and those that are not.

The following statements are taken from the viewpoints in the fourth chapter of this book. Consider each statement carefully. *Mark P for any statement you believe is provable. Mark U for any statement you feel is unprovable because of the lack of evidence. Mark C for any statements you think are too controversial to be proved to everyone's satisfaction.*

If you are doing this activity as a member of a class or group, compare your answers with those of other class or group members. Be able to defend your answers. You may discover that others will come to different conclusions than you. Listening to the reasons others present for their answers may give you valuable insights in recognizing statements that are provable.

If you are reading this book alone, ask others if they agree with your answers. You too will find this interaction very valuable.

P = provable
U = unprovable
C = too controversial

1. The struggle in Nicaragua has left more than 12,000 dead since 1982.
2. No political movement is above reproach.
3. Aldo Moro was killed by Italian terrorists.
4. US military personnel and CIA officers are now training "antiterrorist" commandos in about a dozen countries.
5. There is no clean way for the US to fight its enemies.
6. The Pak-Afghan border was laid down by the British in 1893 as the "Durand Line."
7. Terrorism is a war in which innocent civilians are targets.
8. Almost every government, Eastern and Western, has committed or encouraged atrocities such as death squads, army massacres and indiscriminate bombings.
9. The primary challenge facing the United States comes from terrorism abroad, not at home.
10. Certain political groups are at war with the Western world.
11. Violent deeds conducted by surrogates are preferable to direct US involvement and the use of American firepower.
12. The CIA has hired mercenaries to help in their covert war against the Sandinistas.
13. The Sandinistan government receives aid and support from Cuba via the Soviet Union.
14. Terrorism is sometimes spontaneous and sometimes a mere response to perceived grievances.
15. The Soviets do not limit their support to groups that are pro-Soviet in their ideologies and aims.
16. The Afghan rebels are fighting the Soviet Union.
17. Starvation is becoming widespread in Afghanistan as the Soviet Union burns crops to terrorize the population.
18. Explosive toys have been used in Afghanistan to terrorize the population.
19. Libya is more independent of the Soviet Union than Cuba.
20. It is the ultimate double standard that the United States could hire members of the mafia in eight attempts on the life of Castro and come out as Uncle Sam the Clean, Fighter Against Terrorism.

Periodical Bibliography

The following list of periodical articles deals with the subject matter of this chapter.

America	"Held Hostage By Terrorism," July 27, 1985.
John Barron	"From Russia with Hate," *Reader's Digest*, November 1985.
Lou Cannon and Bob Woodward	"Using Force: The White House Debate Is Over," *The Washington Post National Weekly Edition*, April 28, 1986.
Leo Cherne	"U.S. Intelligence Requirements for the Late 1980's," *Vital Speeches of the Day*, April 1, 1986.
Noam Chomsky	"Crimes By Victims Are Called Terrorism," *In These Times*, July 24-August 6, 1985.
Brian Crozier	"Terror, New Style," *National Review*, August 9, 1985.
Heinz Dieterich	"Global U.S. Terrorism: An Interview With Noam Chomsky," *Crime and Social Justice*, No. 24.
James J. Drummey	"Communist Threat in the Philippines," *The New American*, June 16, 1986.
Samuel T. Francis	"Terrorist Network a Serious Threat to Security," *Human Events*, August 10, 1985.
Richard Goodwin	"Let the Great Rivals Join Against Terror," *Los Angeles Times*, January 3, 1986.
Yuri Gvozdev	"Terrorism, Washington Style," *Daily World*, February 1, 1986.
Craig M. Karp	"The War in Afghanistan," *Foreign Affairs*, Summer 1986.
Geoffrey Kemp	"Politics, Not Morality, Rules the War Against Terrorism," *Los Angeles Times*, January 6, 1986.
Kirk Kidwell	"Qaddafi and His Soviet Patron," *The New American*, February 3, 1986.
Jeane J. Kirkpatrick	"Afghanistan: Five Years of Tragedy," *Department of State Bulletin*, January 1985.
Robert Leiken	"Reform the Contras," *The New Republic*, March 31, 1986.

The New Republic	"The Case for the Contras," March 24, 1986.
The New Republic	"The Dictatorship of the Double Standard," January 27, 1986.
David Atlee Phillips	"Terrorism Still Searching for the Smoking Gun: Are 'Outlaw States' Simply Surrogates?" *Los Angeles Times*, July 14, 1986.
Joe Pichirallo and Edward Cody	"America's Secret War on Terrorism—In Other Countries," *The Washington Post National Weekly Edition*, April 8, 1986.
William Pomeroy	"Reagan 'Terror' Speech Shocks British Writers," *Daily World*, July 20, 1985.
Ronald Reagan	"The New Network of Terrorist States," *Department of State Bulletin*, August 1985.
Jean-Francois Revel	"The Awful Logic of Genocide," *National Review*, October 4, 1986.
Victor Riesel	"Nationwide Terrorist Network Threatens," *Human Events*, March 16, 1985.
Dmitri K. Simes	"Soviets Face Terrorism, but Handle It . . . Differently," *Los Angeles Times*, July 3, 1985.
John K. Singlaub	"State-Sponsored Terrorism: It Can Happen Here," *Human Events*, January 25, 1986.
John K. Singlaub	"U.S. Should Aid the Contras," *The New American*, March 24, 1986.
Oliver Starr Jr.	"Genocide Continues in Afghanistan," *American Legion Magazine,* January 1986.
Daniel Treisman	"Terror Error," *The New Republic*, October 14, 1985.
Dmitry Volsky	"The Root Cause," *New Times*, October 1985.
Dmitry Volsky and Pavel Davydov	"A Threat Not Only to the Arabs— That's To Be Seen From Damascus," *New Times*, February 3, 1986.
W. Bruce Weinrod	"Thirty Myths About Nicaragua," *Vital Speeches of the Day*, May 15, 1986.
Vasily Yefremov	"Terrorism in the USA's Global Strategy," *Soviet Military Review*, May 1986.

5 CHAPTER

Can Terrorism
Be Eliminated?

TERRORISM

"Terrorism can be easily stopped."

Terrorism Can Be Eliminated

Benjamin Netanyahu

Benjamin Netanyahu was born in Israel in 1949. He served for five years in the special forces of the Israeli Defense Forces. In 1982, he became his country's deputy ambassador of the United States and is presently the permanent representative of Israel to the United Nations. In the following viewpoint, Mr. Netanyahu denies that terrorism is an inevitable part of living in the modern world. By following Israel's example to allow terrorism no leniency, the United States can eradicate incidents directed against itself.

As you read, consider the following questions:

1. According to the author, the terrorist must be able to do one thing to continue his attacks. What is this?
2. What does the author believe is the primary reason for international terrorism?
3. How will terrorism be defeated, according to Mr. Netanyahu? How does his opinion differ from that of Mr. Jenkins, the author of the following viewpoint?

Why should the West concern itself with terrorism? Its victims are few, its physical damage limited, its violence sporadic. In comparison with outright war, it poses a relatively minor threat to the lives and property of the citizens of free societies. Yet terrorism cannot be dismissed so easily. For one thing, it is escalating. The number and scope of attacks is steadily increasing. Aircraft are commandeered, passenger ships seized, politicians assassinated. Anyone is a potential victim. And while the number of those actually involved may be small, the entire world is set on edge—or rather, the democratic world, the West, the principal target of terrorism. . . .

The overriding consideration of all terrorist acts is to humiliate governments and expose their impotence. And this impotence is dramatized with special force and acuity when a handful of people are able to strike at anyone, anywhere, anytime.

The result is a loss of confidence on the part of the ordinary citizen in the resolve and competence of his government. . . .

Having induced in the public a sense of the government's impotence and of his own invincibility, the terrorist now reaps the real reward. For the stage is now set for the second critical phase in the terrorist strategy—the consideration of his demands. I do not mean only the immediate ones (safe passage, money, publicity, release of jailed terrorists, etc.), but the larger *political* claims that he professes to represent. The citizens or, to be more precise, the media, now press the authorities to consider the terrorist claims. The citizens in effect turn to the government and say: You have failed to stop the terrorist. He is not going to go away. Listen to him, negotiate with him, give him what he wants to make him stop.

Nothing to Lose

This is a no-lose proposition for the terrorist. If the government does not give in, the terrorist promises (and often delivers) further terrorism. This induces further criticism of the government and more, increasingly desperate calls to heed the terrorist demands. If the government succumbs, the terrorist scores an obvious victory; even if the terrorist agrees to a temporary hiatus (which he seldom does), the citizen knows that his government has caved in and betrayed his trust yet again. Like a child clamoring for forbidden toys, the public expects the government simultaneously to give in and to hold fast. And once the line of concession is crossed, more atrocities and more demands are sure to follow, with the inexorable logic of blackmail in the face of weakness. The more outrageous the attack, the more outlandish the target, the better. To call terrorist murders "senseless," then, is to miss the point. They are anything but that.

The terrorist's strategy is premised on the ability to deliver future blows, no matter what. The fear and intimidation that terrorism thrives on is totally dependent on the ability to live up to this threat. It is essentially the same kind of terror that every person experiences during childhood in the face of the neighborhood bully. As in the case of the bully, the necessary response is twofold: the conscious refusal to be intimidated and the willingness to fight back. Virtually always, this resolve has to be demonstrated in action. The same is true of the terrorist. Through repeated blows, he must be taught that his victim will not only resist his assaults but fight back vigorously.

Sustaining the Pressure

The terrorist objective, of course, is not negotiation but capitulation. As long as he can sustain the pressure, as long as he can launch attacks with increasing frequency and audacity, he will advance toward his goal. The primary task, then, in fighting terrorism is to weaken and ultimately destroy the terrorist's ability to consistently launch attacks. This is often presented as a difficult or even impossible task. It is asserted that the clandestine nature of terrorism and the openness of Western societies make terrorism against the West nearly impossible to root out. I would argue that exact opposite. Terrorism can be easily stopped. The minute you weaken its ability to deliver repeated blows, you have broken its back. And it is well within the means of the West to achieve this. . . .

We Must Protect US Citizens

Nations that practice terrorism or actively support it will not do so without consequence. If there is evidence that a nation is mounting or intends to conduct an act of terrorism against this country, the United States will take measures to protect its citizens, property and interests. U.S. military counter-terrorist forces are well-equipped, superbly trained and highly capable of responding.

George Bush, *American Legion Magazine*, June 1986.

Whether it is hit-and-run killings or random bombings, the terrorist *always* considers, and fears, a forceful response from his victims. To the extent that he believes that he will be tracked down and punished for his actions, he will curb them. Deterrence works on terrorists just as it does on anyone else.

The cycle-of-violence argument is not only morally wrong; it flies in the face of actual experience. The terrorists may at first respond to a government's policy of firmness with an acceleration of terrorism, but they usually cannot withstand a sustained and resolute policy of resistance and active pursuit. Retaliation and preemption against terrorism are thus acts of self-defense.

Denying the necessity for such self-defense, and blurring the moral basis for it, is dangerous. It undermines a basic principle on which government authority is based. When a government shows weakness toward terrorists, citizens will demand action. If the government does not provide it, segments of the public might well turn to vigilantism and political extremism. Again, a government's first obligation is to protect its citizens. Confusion or vacillation, offered either glibly or high-mindedly, fool no one, least of all the terrorists.

But no policy, however clearly defined, will be worth much without the means and the resolve to carry it out. . . . One point emerges as central: International terrorism as we know it would simply not be possible without the collaboration of governments which have used terrorism to wage hidden war against their adversaries, especially the West. . . .

Actions That Must Be Taken

Once this is understood, the democracies can begin to act effectively in three broad areas against offending states.

First, there are political pressures that can be brought to bear. These could range from international condemnation to cutting off diplomatic relations (as the United States and Britain did in the case of Libya). Political pressures are important for several reasons. They signal to the terrorist state that the victim is not only unwilling to be compliant but is prepared to fully expose the offender to the light of public opinion. This could force other states to take a position against the offender, or at least curb their support for it. Since many states sponsoring terrorism depend on the ability to deny complicity in terrorist crimes, this is not a minor threat. In the case of a severance of diplomatic relations there is an added penalty, the shutting down of embassies. The critical role of embassies, and the abuse of diplomatic privileges and immunities in general, in facilitating international terrorism has not been adequately appreciated. Terrorists simply cannot sustain a concerted campaign of attacks in most Western countries without sanctuary or inviolable means of passing funds, arms, and intelligence. Without embassies, the effectiveness of terrorism in the West would be sharply diminished. . . .

When irrefutable proof links particular embassies to terrorism, they should be shut down. Offending states will be denied their fortresses of terror in our midst.

Economic Pressure

The second broad area in which the West can work against states which engage in terrorism is economic pressure. Most of these countries desperately need Western goods, weapons, or credit. There are certain sophisticated products, including advanced weapons, that only the West can supply. The combined purchasing power of the democracies is enormous. If the West used but a fraction of its formidable economic clout, it could cause regimes supporting terrorism to rethink some of their activities. Economic pressure could be a combination of boycott and embargo. For example, in the case of Libya, a prime offender, an effective policy would be: Don't buy and don't sell. Don't buy Libya's oil, don't sell it Western technology. Even a partial boycott and embargo has the effect, because of the need to go through intermediaries

An American Dream

Reprinted with permission.

and brokers, of raising costs significantly. Of course, this often also has an effect on the countries which undertake these measures, and they must be prepared to shoulder such a burden. The United States, for example, has willingly forfeited hundreds of millions of dollars of trade with Libya in order to send an unmistakable message to that regime. Unlike the more difficult task of taking on a cartel, however, this kind of economic pressure isolates individual governments.

In addition to trade measures, there is another potent sanction that can be readily applied. It, too, has the virtue of not exacting a significant price from the West—the denial of landing rights to the commercial planes of terrorist states. Such states do not care if their planes can land in Moscow. What really counts is that their planes have the right to land in London, Paris, and New York. But if they use those planes to ferry terrorists (or their embassies to shield them, or their intelligence services to assist them), these states must know that their planes will not be able to land in the principal capitals of the West. The same could apply to docking rights for the ships of offending states. . . .

Military Action

The third area of response by the West is, necessarily, military action. This cannot be ruled out, nor should we be bashful about discussing it. When we talk about using military force, we must first consider it in a unilateral context, that is, *one* state taking action against terrorists or a state that shelters them. Obviously, if a terrorist action occurs on a government's own soil, it will take action to foil the terrorists, whether during an actual incident (such as a hostage-taking) or on an ongoing basis. There is no question that a state has the right to act; the only question that is raised and regrettably it is raised only in the West, is the problem of protecting civil liberties. Yet the experiences of Britain, West Germany Israel, and Italy show that it is perfectly possible to combat terrorism effectively without any significant infringements on individual rights. The police, the security services, and the courts have done so by and large using existing legal procedures. The authorities have on occasion asked their legislatures to enact special, usually temporary and limited, legal measures. They have also created specialized military units to track down terrorists, though, as I have noted, these stress the minimal application of force. On the domestic level the approach to fighting terrorism in the democracies is the policeman's, not the soldier's; terrorism is basically treated as a variant of organized crime; the political trappings of terrorism are irrelevant.

But what about a terrorist attack on a country's citizens or installations abroad such as embassies, businesses, or airlines? Here the authorities face a stiffer problem. For the terrorists, by definition, are always under the jurisdiction of another government.

That is so even in the case of piracy on the high seas or in the brief periods when a hijacked aircraft is aloft (a ship's or a plane's registry is, in the legal sense, its national identification outside national jurisdictions). I propose a simple way to resolve the question of conflicting jurisdictions: In the case of hijacking, piracy, or other hostage-taking, the responsibility of securing the release of the hostages is the government's on whose soil (or ship, or plane) the incident takes place. One would hope such governments would adopt a firm policy against the terrorists, i.e., a refusal to yield and a readiness to apply force. Such governments should be held to this standard, at least to the first part, the refusal to yield. It is well within the means of the leading countries of the West to powerfully censure a government for failing to do so. . . .

A Rapid Defeat

The West can win the war against terrorism, and fairly rapidly. It can expose its duplicity and punish its perpetrators and sponsors. But it must first win the war against its own inner weakness. That will require courage. We shall need at least three types of it.

First, statesmen and government leaders must have the political courage to present the truth, however unpleasant, to their people. They must be prepared to make difficult decisions, to take measures that may involve great risks, that may even end in failure and subject them to public criticism.

Second, the soldiers who may actually be called upon to combat terrorists will need to show military courage. They are usually members of special units created precisely for such tasks. It will be up to them to decide whether they can or cannot undertake a particular operation a government is considering. In the special units of the Israeli army, for example, no one has ever been simply *told* by the political leadership that he would have to accept a perilous assignment. The commanders of the unit were always *asked*: Is it possible? Do you think you can do it? And if they had expressed doubts, that would have been the end of the matter. The political leaders would have called the mission off. This was the case in Entebbe and in countless other actions that dealt stunning defeats to international terrorism.

All People Are at War

But there is also a third kind of courage: the civic valor that must be shown by an entire people. All citizens in a democracy threatened by terrorism must see themselves, in a certain sense, as soldiers in a common battle. They must not pressure their government to capitulate or to surrender to terrorism. This is especially true of public pressure on government by families of hostages. Such pressure can only be called a dereliction of civic duty. If we seriously want to win the war against terrorism, people must be prepared to endure sacrifice and even, should there be the loss

189

of loved ones, immeasurable pain.

Terrorism is a phenomenon which tries to evoke one feeling: fear. It is understandable that the one virtue most necessary to defeat terrorism is therefore the antithesis of fear: courage.

Courage, said the Romans, is not the only virtue, but it is the single virtue without which all the others are meaningless.

The terrorist challenge must be answered. The choice is between a free society based on law and compassion and a rampant barbarism in the service of brute force and tyranny. Confusion and vacillation facilitated the rise of terrorism. Clarity and courage will ensure its defeat.

"We cannot expect to eradicate terrorism, any more than we expect to end murder."

Terrorism Cannot Be Eliminated

Brian Michael Jenkins

Brian Michael Jenkins, a respected authority on terrorism, is director of the Rand Corporation's research on political violence. In the following viewpoint, Mr. Jenkins argues that terrorism is as pervasive as poverty, prejudice, and crime and cannot be eliminated.

As you read, consider the following questions:

1. Has terrorist activity diminished, according to the author? Why or why not?
2. Why does the author believe that terrorists persist?
3. What is the most "insidious" consequence of terrorism, according to Mr. Jenkins? Do you agree?

Brian Michael Jenkins, "Terror Becomes a Fact of Modern Life," *Los Angeles Times,* December 15, 1985. Reprinted by permission of the author.

Where will it all end? When will it stop? Our political leaders speak of terrorism as if it were a scourge, a plague or an epidemic. They talk about what must be done to "stop the spread" as if terrorism were a kind of political AIDS. The depressing answer is that it won't stop.

Developments over the past several years suggest that terrorism, like poverty, prejudice and crime, is becoming another of society's chronic afflictions. More and more, the use of terrorist tactics by groups and governments is being institutionalized and tolerated, and to a certain degree, even legitimized as a means of political expression—an accepted mode of conflict among nations. And we may be able to do nothing about it. Why not?

There are several reasons: the sheer persistence of terrorism despite efforts by governments to crush it; the demonstrated utility of terrorist tactics by national governments; the concurrent tendency in other states to tolerate, even appease, state sponsors of terrorism; the continuing wrangles over definition; the tendency toward vigilante responses that are indistinguishable from, or border on, terrorism itself—and, perhaps the most insidious development of all, a growing banality of the whole phenomenon.

Governments have become tougher and more proficient at combatting terrorists. Some groups, like Italy's Red Brigades, have been virtually destroyed.

Terrorism Has Not Diminished

Yet the volume of terrorist activity worldwide has not diminished. Since the late 1970s, the number of terrorist incidents resulting in fatalities has increased each year. A more alarming trend in the 1980s is the growing number of large-scale, indiscriminate attacks—car bombs, bombings in public places like airport terminals, bombs planted aboard trains—all calculated to kill in quantity.

We once relied on terrorists' self-imposed constraints to limit violence. Most terrorists used the minimum force necessary to achieve their goals. They regarded indiscriminate violence as politically counterproductive. In the epoch of the car bomb, constraints seem to be eroding.

This is not to say that terrorists have been ultimately successful. They have attracted publicity, caused alarm, provoked international crises; they have compelled governments to divert vast resources to protection against attacks. But they have not translated these achievements into concrete political gains; in that sense, terrorism has failed.

Why, then, do they persist? In part because, cut off from normal contacts, talking only to each other, they come to believe their own propaganda: Government authority is in its death throes, the revolution is about to begin, victory is inevitable and imminent.

Part of the terrorists' ability to survive may lie in the infrastructure that has grown up to support them. Increased cooperation among terrorists makes them more difficult to combat. There is today a semipermanent subculture of terrorism. Individual terrorists can be arrested, terrorist groups can be "defeated," but governments find it extremely difficult to identify and destroy the resilient web of personal relationships, clandestine contacts, alliances with other groups, suppliers of material and services that sustain the terrorist underground.

In the process of long-term survival, some terrorist groups are changing their character. It costs money to maintain a terrorist group, and those who do not receive support from foreign patrons must get money through bank robberies, ransom kidnapings, extortion, smuggling or participation in the narcotics traffic. Gradually, the activities become ends in themselves and terrorist groups begin to resemble ordinary criminal organizations with a thin political veneer.

In an essay written more than 10 years ago, I suggested that "terrorism, though now rejected as a legitimate mode of warfare by most conventional military establishments, could become an ac-

Ben Sargent, *The Austin-American Statesman*, reprinted with permission.

cepted form of warfare in the future." It was a concern, not an endorsement.

A growing number of governments are now using terrorist tactics themselves or employing terrorist groups as a mode of surrogate warfare. These governments see in terrorism a useful capability, a "weapons system," a cheap means of waging war against another nation. Growing state sponsorship of terrorism puts more resources in the hands of the terrorists, including money and sophisticated munitions. It also provides a sanctuary where they can retreat, recuperate and rearm.

State-sponsored terrorism is far more difficult to suppress than independent groups. Going after it may require going after the state sponsor rather than the terrorists themselves. But it is usually difficult to prove connections between terrorist perpetrator and sponsor.

Because Libya and Iran sit atop vital oil and gas resources, many nations are seriously constrained in contemplating anti-terrorist actions against them. Military options are few and risky and their effectiveness is debatable. Finally, governments that retaliate against state sponsors of terrorism may find themselves the targets of terrorist retaliation.

The paucity of options to combat state-sponsored terrorism pushes governments in the opposite direction. Like hardened passengers in a big-city subway, governments turn the other way, trying hard not to notice. They avoid involvement, evade confrontation, mute their criticisms, issue joint communiques. In a new kind of appeasement, governments afford legitimacy to state sponsors—and indirectly, to terrorism itself, in return for a tacit promise of peace.

Defining Terrorism

Efforts to cope with terrorism are complicated by widespread disagreement over how to define it. The United States and its allies view terrorism as a precisely defined list of criminal acts outside the accepted rules of diplomacy and war. But many nations see it as simply another form of armed conflict, no more and no less reprehensible than guerrilla war. These nations do not see moral distinctions between ramming a truck filled with explosives into an embassy and dropping high explosives on a city from a military aircraft. Even some of our allies have difficulty perceiving the difference between state-sponsored terrorism in the Middle East and U.S. support for the *contras* in Nicaragua.

Many Third World governments see American anti-terrorist efforts as part of a broader campaign aimed at outlawing irregular methods of warfare developed during anti-colonial struggles. Not a few Third World leaders were once called terrorists themselves.

Governments may also find themselves compelled to excuse terrorism in an effort to gain peace. After suffering more than two decades of guerrilla warfare, Colombia passed a law that offers unconditional amnesty for all acts of rebellion and all crimes connected with the rebellion including assassination and kidnapings.

The government tacitly recognized that the assassinations of government officals have been part of the guerrillas' efforts to take power and may therefore be considered part of the rebellion. Kidnapings by guerrillas were also deemed to be political acts because the guerrillas used the ransoms to finance weapon purchases.

Assassinations and Kidnapings

Treating assassinations and kidnapings committed as political acts rather than as crimes will inevitably lend a gloss of legitimacy to such tactics.

Meanwhile, some governments have resorted to a kind of vigilantism to combat terrorism. Outraged by the Palestinian attack on Israeli athletes at the 1972 Munich Olympics and the unwillingness of European governments to take forceful measures against Palestinian terrorists operating in Europe, Israel launched its own campaign of assassination against Palestinian leaders; nine people were shot down or blown up before an innocent person was mistakenly killed in Norway—that ended the operation.

Terrorism Is a Fact of Life

Far from being the work of a few beastly men, terrorism is a natural product of modern life. Like air pollution, family breakdown, excessively casual sexual promiscuity, traffic paralysis and the exaltation of greed, terrorism is one of the many embarrassing byproducts of our blessings.

Russell Baker, *The New York Times*, July 10, 1985.

Beneath the dramatic manifestation of terrorism, a more insidious trend is developing—one that will make terrorism increasingly difficult to combat in the future: With the exception of a few particularly dramatic incidents, terrorism is becoming an accepted fact of contemporary life. The monotony of another hijacking, another assassination, another bombing reported matter-of-factly along with the budget deficit and stock quotes dulls our senses. Except for specific acts, such as hijacking, and particularly atrocious acts, such as mass murder, neither world opinion nor world action are aroused by terrorism. We have come to "expect" diplomats to be kidnaped or murdered; in the future only volunteers may be asked to serve in dangerous areas.

The extraordinary security measures taken against terrorism, like terrorism itself, have become a permanent part of the landscape, of our life style. We no longer protest about every airline passenger having to feed luggage through X-ray machines, pass through metal detectors and submit to searches in front of armed guards before boarding. We no longer resent the precautions taken to screen people entering federal buildings, courthouses, even corporate headquarters.

For these many reasons, terrorism will persist. What then are we to do? We must continue to make every effort to combat terrorism without resorting to terrorist tactics ourselves. We must persuade state sponsors of terrorism that such behavior will not be without costs and that responses may include the use of military force.

Continued terrorism need not dull moral outrage. Outrage remains an appropriate response. At the same time, we must realize that we cannot expect to eradicate terrorism, any more than we expect to end murder. We may be well advised to avoid rhetoric that implies final victories. The bad news is we may have to live with terrorism. The good news is that we probably can.

"We should understand that terrorism is aggression and, like all aggression, must be forcefully resisted."

The US Must Retaliate Against Terrorist States

George P. Shultz

George P. Shultz, secretary of state for the Reagan administration, holds a Ph.D. from the Massachusetts Institute of Technology. During the Nixon administration he served as the secretary of labor, director of the Office of Management and Budget, and secretary of the treasury. In the following viewpoint, Mr. Shultz argues that Americans engage in far too much self-flagellating over terrorist claims of political and social injustice. Terrorists are murderers and lawbreakers, Mr. Shultz claims, and the United States should take forceful and organized action against them.

As you read, consider the following questions:

1. What is the goal of all terrorists, according to the author? Do you agree with his assessment?
2. Does Mr. Shultz believe that terrorist grievances are legitimate?
3. Why does the author believe the United States should follow Israel's example in fighting terrorism?

George P. Shultz, address before the Park Avenue Synagogue on October 25, 1984.

We have learned that terrorism is, above all, a form of political violence. It is neither random nor without purpose. Today, we are confronted with a wide assortment of terrorist groups which, alone or in concert, orchestrate acts of violence to achieve distinctly political ends. Their stated objectives may range from separatist causes to revenge for ethnic grievances to social and political revolution. Their methods may be just as diverse: from planting homemade explosives in public places to suicide car bombings to kidnapings and political assassinations. But the overarching goal of all terrorists is the same: they are trying to impose their will by force—a special kind of force designed to create an atmosphere of fear. The horrors they inflict are not simply a new manifestation of traditional social conflict; they are depraved opponents of civilization itself, aided by the technology of modern weaponry. The terrorists want people to feel helpless and defenseless; they want people to lose faith in their government's capacity to protect them and thereby to undermine the legitimacy of the government itself, or its policies, or both.

The terrorists profit from the anarchy caused by their violence. They succeed when governments change their policies out of intimidation. But the terrorist can even be satisfied if a government responds to terror by clamping down on individual rights and freedoms. Governments that overreact, even in self-defense, may only undermine their own legitimacy, as they unwittingly serve the terrorists' goals. The terrorist succeeds if a government responds to violence with repressive, polarizing behavior that alienates the government from the people. . . .

Meeting the Challenge

The magnitude of the threat posed by terrorism is so great that we cannot afford to confront it with half-hearted and poorly organized measures. Terrorism is a contagious disease that will inevitably spread if it goes untreated. We need a strategy to cope with terrorism in all of its varied manifestations. We need to summon the necessary resources and determination to fight it and, with international cooperation, eventually stamp it out. And we have to recognize that the burden falls on us, the democracies— no one else will cure the disease for us.

Yet clearly we face obstacles, some of which arise precisely because we are democracies. The nature of the terrorists' assault is, in many ways, alien to us. Democracies like to act on the basis of known facts and shared knowledge. Terrorism is clandestine and mysterious by nature. Terrorists rely on secrecy, and, therefore, it is hard to know for certain who has committed an atrocity.

Democracies also rely on reason and persuasive logic to make decisions. It is hard for us to understand the fanaticism and apparent irrationality of many terrorists, especially those who kill and commit suicide in the belief that they will be rewarded in the afterlife. The psychopathic ruthlessness and brutality of terrorism is an aberration in our culture and alien to our heritage.

And it is an unfortunate irony that the very qualities that make democracies so hateful to the terrorists—our respect for the rights and freedoms of the individual—also make us particularly vulnerable. Precisely because we maintain the most open societies terrorists have unparalleled opportunity to strike at us. Terrorists seek to make democracies embattled and afraid, to break down democratic accountability, due process, and order; they hope we will turn toward repression or succumb to chaos.

These are the challenges we must live with. We will certainly not alter the democratic values that we so cherish in order to fight terrorism. We will have to find ways to fight back without undermining everything we stand for.

Combatting Moral Confusion

There is another obstacle that we have created for ourselves that we should overcome—that we must overcome—if we are to fight terrorism effectively. The obstacle I am referring to is confusion.

We cannot begin to address this monumental challenge to decent, civilized society until we clear our heads of the confusion about terrorism, in many ways the *moral* confusion, that still seems to plague us. Confusion can lead to paralysis, and it is a luxury that we simply cannot afford. . . .

Is Retaliation Effective?

The purpose of retaliation is to punish the criminals who have committed terrorist attacks and retreated to safe havens. As these terrorists are beyond the reach of conventional police forces, military force must be used if retaliation is to be conducted at all. The primary example of this kind of retaliation is that of Israel against the Palestine Liberation Organization and its various factions.

Stephen V. Cole, *Conservative Digest*, April 1986.

The grievances that terrorists supposedly seek to redress through acts of violence may or may not be legitimate. The terrorist acts themselves, however, can never be legitimate. And legitimate causes can never justify or excuse terrorism. Terrorist means discredit their ends.

We have all heard the insidious claim that "one man's terrorist is another man's freedom fighter." When I spoke on the subject of terrorism this past June, I quoted the powerful rebuttal to this kind of moral relativism made by the late Senator Henry Jackson. His statement bears repeating today: "The idea that one person's 'terrorist' is another's 'freedom fighter,'" he said, "cannot be sanctioned. Freedom fighters or revolutionaries don't blow up buses containing non-combatants; terrorist murderers do. Freedom fighters don't set out to capture and slaughter school children; terrorist murderers do. Freedom fighters don't assassinate innocent businessmen, or hijack and hold hostage innocent men, women, and children; terrorists murderers do. It is a disgrace that democracies would allow the treasured word 'freedom' to be associated with acts of terrorists." So spoke Scoop Jackson.

We cannot afford to let an Orwellian corruption of language obscure our understanding of terrorism. We know the difference between terrorists and freedom fighters, and as we look around the world, we have no trouble telling one from the other.

How tragic it would be if democratic societies so lost confidence in their own moral legitimacy that they lost sight of the obvious: that violence directed against democracy or the hopes for democracy lacks fundamental justification. Democracy offers the opportunity for peaceful change, legitimate political competition, and redress of grievances. We must oppose terrorists no matter what banner they may fly. For terrorism in *any* cause is the enemy of freedom.

And we must not fall into the deadly trap of giving justification to the unacceptable acts of terrorists by acknowledging the worthy-sounding motives they may claim. Organizations such as the Provisional IRA, for instance, play on popular grievances, and political and religious emotions, to disguise their deadly purpose. They find ways to work through local political and religious leaders to enlist support for their brutal actions. As a result, we even find Americans contributing, we hope unwittingly, to an organization which has killed—in cold blood and without the slightest remorse—hundreds of innocent men, women, and children in Great Britain and Ireland; an organization which has assassinated senior officials and tried to assassinate the British Prime Minister and her entire cabinet; a professed Marxist organization which also gets support from Libya's Qadhafi and has close links with other international terrorists. The Government of the United States stands firmly with the Government of the United Kingdom and the Government of Ireland in opposing any action that lends aid or support to the Provisional IRA. . . .

The Middle East

The terrorist's principal goal in the Middle East is to destroy any progress toward a negotiated peace. And the more our policies succeed, the closer we come toward achieving our goals in the Middle East, the harder terrorists will try to stop us. The simple fact is, the terrorists are more upset about *progress* in the Middle East than they are about any alleged failures to achieve progress. Let us not forget that President Sadat was murdered because he

200

made peace, and that threats continue to be issued daily in that region because of the fear—yes, fear—that others might favor a negotiated path toward peace.

Whom would we serve by changing our policies in the Middle East in the face of the terrorist threat? Not Israel, not the moderate Arabs, not the Palestinian people, and certainly not the cause for peace. Indeed, the worst thing we could do is change our principled policies under the threat of violence. What we *must* do is support our friends and remain firm in our goals.

© Liederman/Rothco

We have to rid ourselves of this moral confusion which lays the blame for terrorist actions on us or on our policies. We are attacked not because of what we are doing wrong but because of what we are doing right. We are right to support the security of Israel, and there is no terrorist act or threat that will change that firm determination. We are attacked not because of some mistake we are making but because of who we are and what we believe in. We must not abandon our principles, or our role in the world, or our responsibilities as the champion of freedom and peace.

Response to Terrorism

While terrorism threatens many countries, the United States has a special responsibility. It is time for this country to make a broad national commitment to treat the challenge of terrorism with the sense of urgency and priority it deserves.

The essence of our response is simple to state: violence and aggression must be met by firm resistance. This principle holds true whether we are responding to full-scale military attacks or to the kinds of low-level conflicts that are more common in the modern world.

We are on the way to being well prepared to deter an all-out war or a Soviet attack on our principal allies; that is why these are the least likely contingencies. It is not self-evident that we are as well prepared and organized to deter and counter the "gray area" of intermediate challenges that we are more likely to face— the low-intensity conflict of which terrorism is a part.

We have worked hard to deter large-scale aggression by strengthening our strategic and conventional defenses, by restoring the pride and confidence of the men and women in our military and by displaying the kind of national resolve to confront aggression that can deter potential adversaries. We have been more successful than in the past in dealing with many forms of low-level aggression. We have checked communist aggression and subversion in Central America and the Caribbean and opened the way for peaceful, democratic processes in that region. And we successfully liberated Grenada from Marxist control and returned that tiny island to freedom and self-determination.

But terrorism, which is also a form of low-level aggression, has so far posed an even more difficult challenge, for the technology of security has been outstripped by the technology of murder. And, of course, the United States is not the only nation that faces difficulties in responding to terrorism. . . . Even Israel has not rid itself of the terrorist threat, despite its brave and prodigious efforts.

But no nation had more experience with terrorism than Israel, and no nation has made a greater contribution to our understanding of the problem and the best ways to confront it. By supporting organizations like the Jonathan Institute, named after the brave Israeli soldier who led and died at Entebbe, the Israeli people have helped raise international awareness of the global scope of the terrorist threat. . . .

The United States Is Not Guilty

Part of our problem here in the United States has been our seeming inability to understand terrorism clearly. Each successive terrorist incident has brought too much self-condemnation and dismay, accompanied by calls for a change in our policies or our principles or calls for withdrawal and retreat. We *should* be alarmed. We *should* be outraged. We *should* investigate and strive to improve. But widespread public anguish and self-condemnation only convince the terrorists that they are on the right track. It only encourages them to commit more acts of barbarism in the hope that American resolve will weaken. . . .

If our reaction to terrorist acts is to turn on ourselves instead of against the perpetrators, we give them redoubled incentive to do it again and to try to influence our political processes.

We have to be stronger, steadier, determined, and united in the face of the terrorist threat. We must not reward the terrorists by changing our policies or questioning our own principles or wallowing in self-flagellation or self-doubt. Instead, we should understand that terrorism is aggression and, like all aggression, must be forcefully resisted. . . .

We must confront the terrorist threat with the same resolve and determination that this nation has shown time and again throughout our history. There is no room for guilt or self-doubt about our right to defend a way of life, that offers *all* nations hope for peace, progress, and human dignity. The sage Hillel expressed it well: "If I am not for myself, who will be? If I am for myself alone, who am I?"

Three Reasons for Retaliation

First, I am totally convinced that our failure to strike back will encourage more and more attacks on us.

Second, the U.S. owes its citizens—here or in any other parts of the world—protection to the degree it can give it. Retaliation would make it clear to everybody that Americans traveling abroad are nobody's free targets.

Third, we have an obligation to punish murder of American citizens in places where courts of law cannot reach.

My conviction is that we will save a lot more lives in the long run by being tough and steady.

Lawrence Eagleburger, *U.S. News & World Report*, July 1, 1985.

As we fight this battle against terrorism, we must always keep in mind the values and way of life we are trying to protect. Clearly, we will not allow ourselves to descend to the level of barbarism that terrorism represents. We will not abandon our democratic traditions, our respect for individual rights, and freedom, for these are precisely what we are struggling to preserve and promote. Our values and our principles will give us the strength and the confidence to meet the great challenge posed by terrorism. If we show the courage and the will to protect our freedom and our way of life, we will prove ourselves again worthy of these blessings.

"Our prime objective should clearly be to correct . . . the fundamental grievances that nourish terrorism rather than engage in . . . retaliatory killing of those affected by such grievances."

Retaliatory Attacks Will Not Eliminate Terrorism

George Ball

George Ball was under secretary of state in the Kennedy and Johnson administrations and a former US ambassador to the United Nations. In the following viewpoint, Mr. Ball challenges Mr. Shultz's solution to terrorism. He argues that retaliatory attacks can only escalate the violence and result in the deaths of hundreds of innocent people.

As you read, consider the following questions:

1. Why does the author believe the US should not follow Israel's example on fighting terrorism? How do his conclusions differ from those of the author in the previous viewpoint?
2. What two types of terrorism does the author outline? Which type does the author believe the US should be most wary of?
3. Why would striking back at terrorists hurt US principles, according to the author?

George Ball, "Shultz is Wrong on Terrorism," *The New York Times*, December 16, 1984. Copyright © 1984 by The New York Times.

Secretary of State George P. Shultz has permitted his obsession with terrorism to distort his normally judicious view of the world. Not only should America, he insists, retaliate with force against terrorist violence; it should not hold back from launching pre-emptive strikes to thwart threatened terrorist attacks merely because such strikes might entail some innocent civilian casualties. For guidance, he recommends that we look to Israel as "a model of how a nation should approach the dilemma of trying to balance law and justice with self-preservation."

That last comment is singularly revealing because Israel exemplifies not balance but excess. Since it is a small, insecure, beleaguered country surrounded by enemies, self-preservation is its dominant imperative. So it is hardly surprising that one reads almost weekly of a bombing attack on some Arab village aimed at destroying a "P.L.O. headquarters" or a "terrorist base."

No doubt such attacks have had some deterrent effect, but they have also, as statistics clearly show, killed hundreds of men, women, and children guilty of no offense other than living in a target area. In 1981, for example, when Israel bombed a Beirut apartment house thought to contain a Palestine Liberation Organization headquarters, it is reported to have killed as many as 300 civilians only to discover the P.L.O. leaders had already left.

America a Secure Country

Because America is, by contrast, a huge nation living in secure borders and obligated by its leadership role to uphold international standards, our problems are sharply different in nature and dimension. Thus, if we need a model, we might more appropriately turn to Britain, which, while suffering terrorist afflictions, has kept faith with humane principles and practices that are our common heritage. Had the British followed the Israeli pattern, they might have answered the Irish Republican Army's bombing of the Grand Hotel in Brighton by blowing up a part of the Roman Catholic section of Belfast. Or, in the pattern of Israel's performance in Lebanon, they might have attacked Dublin because some I.R.A. members were thought to be hiding there.

If we are to cope effectively with terror, we must understand its complexities. Apart from the anarchist madness practiced by the Baader-Meinhof gang and the Red Brigades, which only marginally touched America, two types of terrorism should principally concern us.

The first, directed toward achieving a political aim, is sometimes effective. Four decades ago, the Irgun and Stern Gang successfully used terror to help persuade Britain to relinquish its Palestine Mandate, thus hastening the creation of Israel. But the P.L.O. has accomplished nothing by terrorism. In spite of all its violence, the 900,000 Palestinians dispersed throughout the Arab world have regained not one acre of the land from which they were displaced.

Instead, even though the P.L.O. continues its activities despite Israeli counterattacks, its outrages and doctrinal rigidity have critically damaged the Palestinian cause and strengthened opponents of negotiation.

Retaliation Ineffective

Not that P.L.O. violence poses any direct threat to America: it is sharply focused on Israel. Our own casualties have almost all resulted from a second, different kind of terror fueled by religious fanaticism—a fervor that drives Shiite zealots to strike out blindly against modern Western values symbolized by America—and, in their lunatic fervor, they have so far killed more than 350 Americans. Yet since our logic is missing from their calculus, reprisals have little value; in fact, killing fanatics only inflames their brethren to seek similar martyrdom.

Such passion is hard for Westerners to understand, yet proper diagnosis is essential. Our casualties have not resulted, as Mr. Shultz suggests, because "the technology of security has been outstripped by the technology of murder." The planting of car bombs and the suicidal use of explosive-laden trucks shows little advance over the exploding horse-drawn carriage used in an anarchist attack in Wall Street 60 years ago.

We also confuse the issue when we think of today's political and religious terrorism as phenomena peculiar to our age. In the 19th century, anarchists mowed down princes and potentates all over Europe wih bombs and gunfire. Not only the 12th century assassins but other fanatics have practiced murder in the name of religion. What distinctly colors our predicament is the complicity of renegade governments such as Libya's and Iran's. That radically affects our approach to the problem, for, although America cannot use military force against an offending government without committing an act of war, we should be able, through collective action with like-minded nations, to use economic and political pressures unavailable in dealing with freewheeling terrorists.

Organizing Our Allies

What the situation urgently demands is that Mr. Shultz and his colleagues concentrate on organizing concerted measures with our closest allies. Acting collectively, we would threaten—and if necessary apply—economic sanctions against countries giving aid and comfort to terrorists. All members of such a concert of nations might even agree to break diplomatic relations with—and thus impose political isolation on—any government that violated the embassies or interfered with diplomatic personnel of any participating nation, or condoned such violations.

Obviously such measures would entail political and economic costs that some allies would almost certainly resist; any experienced diplomat knows it is far easier to call for collective action than to achieve it. Still, persuasion is the essence of leadership and the case for action is compelling. State-sponsored terrorism menaces the whole international order, and if we are to maintain even minimum world stability we must ostracize any nation condoning it.

Don't Embrace Counter-Terror

Meanwhile, let us take care that we are not led, through panic and anger, to embrace counter-terror and international lynch law and thus reduce our nation's conduct to the squalid level of the terrorists. Our prime objective should clearly be to correct, or at least mitigate, the fundamental grievances that nourish terrorism rather than engage in pre-emptive and retaliatory killing of those affected by such grievances.

So let us be guided by our own time-tested traditions and not, as Mr. Shultz suggests, adopt as national policy the Talmudic injunction, "If one comes to kill you, make haste and kill him first." For we would be tragically wrong to abandon those cherished principles of law and humanity that have given our country its special standing among nations. Otherwise, we may find our position confused with that of the warrior bishop during the Albigensian Crusade, who, when asked by a soldier how they could tell the Catholics from the heretics, replied that they should kill them all, since "God will know his own."

"The deliberate brutality of much of today's terror demands the exaction of capital punishment . . . for taking innocent human lives in the course of committing acts of terrorism."

Terrorists Should Be Given Stricter Penalties

Elliot Rothenberg

Elliot Rothenberg is president of the North Star Legal Foundation in Minneapolis, and a former US State Department official. In the following viewpoint, Mr. Rothenberg argues that terrorism, which includes the deliberate killing of innocent human beings, is a heinous crime. Whenever possible, he believes, terrorists should be caught and automatically given the death penalty.

As you read, consider the following questions:

1. How do international terrorists endanger the US, according to the author?
2. Does the author believe the political motives of terrorists should be considered in their trials? Why or why not?
3. Why does the author believe the death penalty would deter terrorists?

Elliot Rothenberg, "Making Punishment Fit the Crime of Terrorism," *Human Events*, November 16, 1985. Reprinted by permission.

The national euphoria over the brilliant skyjacking of the PLO terrorists who murdered American Leon Klinghoffer aboard the *Achille Lauro* is in welcome contrast to the widespread frustration over the previous U.S. failure, in the TWA flight 847 incident with the murder of Robert Stethem and other crises going back to the Carter Administration, to take strong retaliatory action against terrorists and the regimes which harbor and finance them.

One hopes that this successful operation portends consistent and forceful responses to future terrorism abroad. Even assuming this happens, we must raise the costs for terrorists domestically as well.

US Largely Free of Terrorism

With certain exceptions like Kathy Boudin and the Weatherpeople, and the Puerto Rican FALN extremists, the U.S. largely has been free from organized terrorist activity. That may not be the case for much longer.

Shiite and PLO terrorists have threatened, even boasted, of their intention to extend their operations to the U.S. Especially when one takes into account the professional training and organizing of international terrorists and their generous support and leadership from several states and the KGB, the threat must not be considered an idle one. On the contrary, the inability or unwillingness to exact from terrorists a price for their past crimes makes an escalation all the more likely.

It is imperative, then, that terrorists be made to suffer appropriate punishment for their crimes wherever they occur.

In addition to reprisals of a general sort, individual terrorists could be tried in the U.S. not only for their acts within this country but for like offenses abroad if they were seized and brought to the U.S. for justice. The Italian government's ignominious release of PLO terrorist leader Abul Abbas cautions against trusting the resolution of others.

Unfortunately, the past record of our judiciary is not cause for reassurance. Instead, American courts' treatment of those who commit crimes from political or religious fanaticism at home resembles the leniency two administrations have shown to the practitioners of terrorism abroad.

In recent years, various federal and state courts have decided cases under the peculiar principle that persons violating the criminal law and the rights of others in order to advance their political causes, through attendant media coverage and/or by physically harming their opponents (a *modus operandi* of the same character as that of international terrorists), somehow should be exempt from punishment of their crimes. Adding insult to injury, some judges have even praised lawbreakers for acting pursuant to their political beliefs. . . .

In the most egregious decision of all, New York U.S. District Judge John E. Sprizzo, in December 1984, refused to extradite to

Great Britain an IRA terrorist escaped from prison who had been convicted of murdering a British army captain. Judge Sprizzo viewed the killing as "political" and not criminal and ruled that the use of violence was not "in itself dispositive" of whether a crime had been committed. He added, "The court is not persuaded by the fact that the current political administration in the U.S. has strongly denounced terrorist acts." Rather, said the judge, the IRA had the requisite "organization, discipline and command structure" so that "the act of its members can constitute political conduct."

The decision offered nothing to assuage fears that the same tortured reasoning could and would be used to exonerate terrorists tried initially under U.S. law.

Severe Penalties Are Necessary

Thus, a comprehensive defense against terrorism must include legislation which will not only assure the expeditious imposition of deservedly severe penalties upon terrorist criminals but will limit the authority of the judiciary to use and abuse discretion to allow terrorists to evade the consequences of their crimes.

Make Terrorists Hostages

Terrorists should be given a swift death penalty as an act not of vengeance but of prevention—to avert another incident demanding their release. By the same token, the world's nations should round up their convicted terrorists, hold them under international auspices, and let it be known that terrorists acts to secure their release will result in their immediate execution. Make the terrorists themselves hostages against terrorism.

Raymond Price, *The Washington Times*, October 17, 1985.

Several reforms are essential to accomplish these objectives. The deliberate brutality of much of today's terror demands the exaction of capital punishment, on a mandatory and not discretionary basis, for taking innocent human lives in the course of committing acts of terrorism.

To insure the speedy administration of justice and to reflect the gravity of the offense, trials of alleged terrorists should be given priority on court calendars over other criminal or civil matters. Persons convicted of terrorist murders should be allowed a single appeal, which should also be given expedited consideration, to higher courts.

Testimony on political ideologies of accused terrorist murderers should be declared inadmissible as having no bearing on whether they committed a crime, and defendants should no longer be permitted to turn their trials into political circuses. On the other hand, all relevant evidence should be admitted, and the exclusionary rule . . . should be made inapplicable to terrorist trials.

Overwhelming Support for Death Penalty

There is growing public sentiment for the death penalty for committing murder. Notwithstanding the opposition of academic and media elites, every recent poll demonstrates support of capital punishment by overwhelming margins rarely seen for any controversial issue. The reasons for adopting the ultimate sanction for terrorist murders are particularly compelling.

First, there is the deterrence aspect of a penalty commensurate with the crime. Liberal professors and editorial writers have devoted reams to articles and books seeking to disprove the commonsense notion—which is the basis of our criminal jurisprudence—that a reasonable certainty of severe punishment will deter at least some from committing crimes.

Today's terrorists predominantly are highly skilled and rational practitioners of crime, rather than crazed maniacs, who presumably are capable of weighing the price of terrorism against its supposed benefits.

Capital Punishment Would Deter Terrorists

Some terrorists, to be sure, may feel that their death in a suicide bombing or their execution will speed their ascent to Allah, but it can hardly be denied that there are potential murderers who would be daunted. Even if only a few would be so deterred, that alone would justify capital punishment for terrorists.

Yet, there are other, equally important, reasons for mandating the death penalty for those convicted of killing others in terrorist acts.

A policy of certain capital punishment is the only assured means of protecting the public from future crimes resulting from a return of those convicted to their profession of terrorism.

A mere prison term, even under an ostensible life sentence, will not guarantee the incapacitation of terrorists. Life sentences for murder often are reduced sharply by parole, time off for good behavior, or executive clemency. Convicted terrorists under present law would enjoy the same privileges. Moreover, as with the TWA hijacking, international terrorists are following the practice of taking hostages to force release of their fellows, wherever imprisoned.

Even when targeted governments are complacent, these hostages may be savagely murdered, like Stethem and diplomat William Buckley, or held in extended captivity, like the unreleased Americans in Beirut. Executing terrorist murderers, besides preventing repetitive crimes by the same offenders, would eliminate any cause or pretext to endanger innocent persons to obtain their release.

Finally, enactment of the death penalty for terrorist murderers would be a fitting expression of national outrage over the indiscriminate and random killing of innocent and defenseless persons, like the paralyzed Klinghoffer, to further some political agenda.

The sanctity of human life is dishonored by allowing terrorists license to make any of us their victims with impunity. The fashionable set is fond of deriding public anger demanding retribution for crimes. But the bedrock of a fair system of justice, consonant with morality and worthy of public faith, is the promise of a punishment proportionate to the abhorrence of the crime.

A Credible Threat Needed

The threat of capital punishment will curb terrorism only if it is a credible one. That is the reason for making it mandatory (which also disposes of the claim of selectivity of enforcement of the death penalty in some states) and, further, disallowing use of the subterfuges which have made actual administration of the penalty exceedingly remote even for the most heinous crimes in those states which allow capital punishment.

Start a Terrorist Tribunal

Anyone tempted to join the terrorist underground should be put on notice that enlistment is his own death warrant, exercisable whenever and wherever he is caught.

Individual terrorists must be made to hurt. Their organizations and their causes must be made to hurt. Countries that give them support and sanctuary must be made to hurt.

If doing so makes other countries unhappy with us, that's tough. We worry too much about their opinion of us, without making them worry enough about our opinion of them.

Raymond Price, *Los Angeles Times*, October 10, 1985.

Capital cases, if they reach final resolution at all, are indefinitely prolonged through seemingly unlimited numbers of motions, appeals, and habeas corpus proceedings. There is no evidence that innocent persons have been saved from execution by the use of these post-conviction procedures. Instead their availability for the most frivolous of reasons has interminably delayed or prevented the dispensing of penalties in many cases and has made a mockery of our system of criminal justice. The entitlement to one appeal would be sufficient to protect the constitutional rights of accused terrorists.

The exclusionary rule barring the introduction of relevant or even decisive evidence because of some alleged technical infirmity of police conduct is a phenomenon unique to American trials. Application of this court-crafted requirement has enabled otherwise guilty persons to escape conviction and commit more crimes. Without clarification of its status, the potential remains of its use to exonerate defendants in terrorist cases.

Despite the popularity with the general public of the proposals outlined above, their introduction in Congress or state legislatures would set off howls of protest from the law professoriate, the American Civil Liberties Union, and like-minded interests with formidable financial resources and political influence. Even if the opponents were unsuccessful with elected bodies, there would be predictable efforts before liberal federal or state judges to invalidate enacted legislation on various claims of unconstitutionality.

President's Task

It is a task, therefore, for the President to vindicate his own pledges to strike against terror and to mobilize the public's horror over violent international terrorism by pushing for laws to insure adequate punishment of terrorists and for a complementary constitutional amendment to preempt any moves to judicially eviscerate the legislation. The issue is sufficiently fundamental to our national wellbeing to justify the constitutional approach.

Appeasement of terrorists abroad has failed to end or even reduce international terrorism; it has had the opposite effect as the movement has fed upon its successes. Similar treatment of those tried at home will not lead to their "rehabilitation" but will release them for more crimes, mocking their past and future victims and the U.S.

"Merely arresting and executing [terrorists] will do little to stop terrorism as long as the communities that they come from see themselves as under attack with no way out."

Stricter Penalties Will Not Eliminate Terrorism

William O. Beeman

William O. Beeman, an anthropologist specializing in the Middle East at Brown University, has lectured on terrorism at the Naval War College. In the following viewpoint, Mr. Beeman argues that terrorism is a response by beleaguered communities to political and social injustice. Using more severe punishments for individual terrorists will not reduce terrorism. He believes instead that attempts must be made to correct the conditions under which these people live.

As you read, consider the following questions:

1. Does the author believe that there is an effective way to deal with terrorists?
2. Where does the author believe terrorism originates? Why is this significant?
3. What minor measures can be taken internationally to prevent terrorism, according to the author?

William O. Beeman, "A Long-Term Approach to Terrorism," *Los Angeles Times*, January 9, 1986. Reprinted by permission of the author.

Terrorist activity is increasing at 12% to 15% a year, a new report from the Rand Corp. concludes, and soon may become a normal feature of life on Earth if measures are not taken to curtail it.

Even more disturbing is the fact that governments have no effective way to deal with terrorists. Despite retaliation threats from Washington and other world capitals, terrorism continues unabated. The Rand report itself was noticeably lacking in suggestions of what to do.

If the world really wants to reduce terrorism, the worst thing that we can do is persist in seeing it as a phenomenon of isolated, conspiratorial groups supported by certain governments. An alternative view can be drawn from anthropological research on disaffected communities. While it offers no quick-fix solutions, it suggests a more effective long-term approach.

Community-Based

The most important insight about terrorism is that it is community-based—an outgrowth of the social dynamics of particular communities where individuals feel themselves to be beleaguered and ignored both at home and by the international community. When they feel themselves under siege, community members begin to tolerate more extreme behavior in the name of community causes. The surest sign of imminent terrorist activity is unwillingness of community leaders to condemn their own extreme elements for fear of losing overall support.

Such communities can be described as terrorist-generating. The Sikh community in India, Catholics in Northern Ireland, Shia Muslims in Lebanon and Palestinians throughout the Middle East are good examples. These communities feel, rightly or wrongly, that they have exhausted every channel in getting their needs heard and addressed. They feel that no one cares about them and thus that violent force will give a sense of movement to their cause, galvanizing internal support and attracting international attention.

Terrorist-generating communities are not a new phenomenon, nor are they restricted to the developing world. The Central Intelligence Agency has used the "Sons of Liberty" from the American Revolution as a case study of a terrorist organization.

Terrorist Acts Virtuous

Because community members see their causes as righteous, indeed even sacred, the terrorist acts in their name are often perceived as virtuous. And because these acts are based in the community, attacking individual terrorists is a futile control device. Individuals who are arrested or executed become martyrs to the community cause and are quickly replaced by others inspired by their terrorism.

Thus virtually every terrorist act in 1985 involved individuals completely prepared to sacrifice their lives for the sake of their mission. Today, no matter what the Israeli and U.S. governments do to try to weaken Palestinian extremist leadership, new cells of terrorist resistance crop up everywhere, so nebulous in origin that they can't be pinpointed at all. Witness the international attempts to try to apprehend terrorist leader Abu Nidal.

Some Action Possible

But some measures can be taken.

To forestall terrorist attacks against their citizens, the United States and other nations should avoid making public statements in support of actions and groups that terrorists feel are oppressing them.

Destroy or Help

If terrorism in the Middle East is to recede—it will never disappear there or elsewhere—the Palestinians must either be destroyed as a people or provided with a homeland. That is the reality. The first solution is beyond Israel's power and unacceptable to world opinion and most Jews. So the second solution must be found, however painful the process for all sides.

Charles William Maynes, *Los Angeles Times*, May 4, 1986.

Avoiding emotionalism in reporting these acts would do a great deal to make them seem less cosmic in their importance.

Finally, we need to find ways to address the real grievances of the communities from which terrorism is arising. These communities feel trapped and at the end of their resources, to the point where young people are willing to trade their lives for 20 minutes of television time. The media, religious organizations and governments should work to establish platforms where communities that feel themselves under siege can air their grievances before the world without having to throw bombs to be heard. At present there is no such official platform anywhere.

Of course, individual terrorists should be pursued and convicted. But it must also be recognized that their crimes are crimes of conscience, not undertaken for personal gain. Merely arresting and executing them will do little to stop terrorism as long as the communities that they come from see themselves as under attack with no way out.

"The moralistic complaints against secrecy, or against the unpleasant necessities of counterterrorism . . . are nothing more than excuses for abandoning any serious attempt . . . to fight back."

Covert Operations Can Fight Terrorism

Michael Ledeen

Michael Ledeen is a senior fellow at Georgetown University's Center for Strategic and International Studies and the author of *Grave New World*. In the following viewpoint, Mr. Ledeen argues that Americans feel unjustifiably squeamish toward the use of secret military operations. This feeling must be overcome, he believes, if the US is to successfully strike back against terrorism. Methods such as counterterrorism and selective assassinations are necessary in repelling communist-inspired terrorism.

As you read, consider the following questions:

1. Why can't the United States use direct military power, according to the author?
2. Why, according to Mr. Ledeen, do Americans find covert activity distasteful? Should they, in his opinion, feel this way?
3. When does the author support assassination?

The direct use of massive American military power, even in situations where it might be the most effective response, is so politically controversial that no President can be expected to order it unless it is clearly proportionate to the provocation; and even then he is unlikely to do so unless he believes that the struggle will be quite short and a successful outcome a virtual certainty. He might send American armed forces to fight in Grenada against a few Cubans and local militiamen, but he is not going to send American soldiers to fight Cubans in Angola or Sandinistas in El Salvador, Honduras, or Nicaragua itself. After all, when 55 American military advisers were sent to El Salvador, there was a vociferous cry of "another Vietnam," followed by congressional insistence that our Salvadoran allies be certified as morally upright every 90 days. One can then imagine the uproar over the deployment of American fighting men against proxy forces. Clearly, in many of these cases, we need to find a different response.

Aiding Anti-Communist Forces

One obvious and traditional method is to help anti-Soviet or anti-Communist local forces. This has several advantages over the commitment of our armed personnel: our involvement is limited to providing assistance, and therefore is not likely to draw the United States into direct conflict; we are clearly helping people who themselves are committed to the cause, because it is they who risk their lives and fight the actual battles; and, finally, it is a symmetrical response, a measured "punishment" that seems to fit the crime committed by the hostile proxies in the first place. If the Soviets can recruit the likes of Castro, Arafat, and Ortega to do their work for them, if the Ayatollah Khomeini can organize suicide squads through his Shiite followers all over the Middle East, and if Qaddafi can send hired gunmen against Western targets and his own emigres, why should the United States be barred from supporting others who wish to fight for our common objectives? . . .

Covert Activity Is Sinister

Such indirect use of American power necessarily involves a certain degree of secret or covert activity, and there is a deep-seated conviction among Americans that covert activity is in itself sinister, and that any secret effort by the United States to challenge our enemies is bound to be morally demeaning.

The view of the world behind this conviction reached its apogee at the time of Watergate, when the late Senator Frank Church and former Congressman Otis Pike headed congressional commissions that investigated the past sins of the CIA. That period—and the chilling Carter years that reaped the Watergate harvest—provided the basic elements in the still ongoing national debate over both covert action and a more vigorous policy generally. . . .

In the important field of counterterrorism, assassination—even of known killers of Americans—remains unacceptable, and the slightest hint that the United States might secretly support foreign groups who want to strike back at those who have murdered our people is greeted with the same cries of scandal and outrage that were heard in the 70's. Thus, when it was discovered that the CIA had worked with a Lebanese intelligence organization that in turn had been responsible for bombing the headquarters of Hezbollah—the radical Shiite terrorist group that appears to have been a prime mover in the murders of hundreds of Americans in Lebanon over the past few years and in the holding of hostages from TWA Flight 847—even this remote involvement of the American government was roundly condemned by members of Congress, by much of the media, and by former officials of the Carter administration.

Need for Secrecy

It is often difficult to tell if the critics object to our efforts to fight back, or only to the methods that are employed.

Occasionally, for example, one hears it said that if we must support groups like the Afghan resistance or the *contras* we ought at least or do it openly. But this misses the essential point about such assistance. Secrecy is often required, not because we have anything to be ashamed of, but because those who are actually doing the fighting wish for reasons of their own to keep our relationship secret. . . .

Covert Action Prevents Terrorism

We can't shoot a terrorist with an MX missile. We can't even discourage terrorists with the 16-inch guns of the battleship New Jersey. Large-scale military measures are not the answer.

The real answer is the defensive use of small-scale, covert action to detect terrorists and nip their plans in the bud. . . .

If our intelligence is good, and we know we can hit terrorists who are going to hit us, then pre-emptive action is justifiable self-defense. It is never illegal or immoral to engage in self-defense.

Ray Cline, *USA Today*, April 23, 1984.

In Central America, every country feels mortally threatened by the Sandinistas, and in their hearts all Central American leaders would like to see the Managua regime either removed or rendered significantly less threatening than it is today. Not only do the Sandinistas now boast an army that is larger than the sum total of all the other armies in the region, they support and control guerrilla movements in El Salvador, Honduras, and Guatemala.

Quite logically, the government of Honduras is willing to permit its territory to be used by the *contras*. But equally logically, the Hondurans are loath to see these activities—and our support for them—become public knowledge. Insofar as they do become public knowledge, the chances of Sandinista incursions into Honduran territory are increased, and ammunition is lent to domestic opponents of the current government. Finally, given our record of abandoning allies under siege, the Hondurans (and who can blame them?) desperately wish to retain the option of coming to terms with the Sandinistas if we bail out of Central America. They may need to deny their own active involvement at some later date, and to condemn us for secretly operating in their country.

High Standards Provoke Failure

Just as the critics of secrecy in effect leave us with no possibility of effective action, so those who attack our attempts to recruit allies in the war against terrorism erect standards that in practice lead either to paralysis or to failure.

To fight back against terrorists, we need first-class information about their intentions, and this information can only come from people who are on intimate terms with the terrorists. For the most part, this means that we either have to infiltrate the terrorist groups (which can only be done if the infiltrators commit terrorist acts themselves) or recruit active terrorists directly. In short, we have no choice but to work with some unsavory types, even if our objective is limited to gathering information. (Here, incidentally, is another area in which secrecy is an absolute requirement of success, since the survival of our informants is at stake.)

Nor will it "solve" the problem to say, as Senator [Patrick] Leahy does, that we should use our own people, rather than proxies, to strike at the terrorists. In the first place, to repeat, taking action directly entails the risk of an all-out war—and while under certain circumstances a reprisal against, say, Syria or Iran might be worth the risk, under other circumstances the risk might be better avoided.

In the second place, if Americans are going to operate against terrorists in the Middle East, the requirements for detailed information become even greater than before, thus putting us once again in the hands of terrorists who are willing to collaborate with us. Furthermore, there are times when it is simply impossible for Americans to enter places with reasonable safety, while locals have a much better chance.

Objections to Assassination

Many of the same considerations apply to the highly-charged subject of assassination. There was great outrage when it was discovered that the CIA-financed "manual" that was apparently being used to train some of the *contras* suggested the possibility of "neutralizing" selected political and military commissars of the Sandinistas. The implication of the uproar was that it might be all right to train men in warfare, but not to kill specific individuals. This is of a piece with the confusions surrounding the use of proxies in counterterrorism, and the necessity of secrecy. For the blanket rejection of assassination risks actions, either by Americans or by proxies, that will lead to greater violence, and more death, especially of innocent bystanders.

To take the Nicaraguan case first: selectively targeting the leaders of the Sandinista armed forces, or their Cuban, East German, Libyan, and Palestinian advisers, is certainly preferable to the obvious alternative, which is large-scale assaults against the conscripted armed forces of Nicaragua, with inevitable harm to the civilian population. And where Afghanistan is concerned, ruling out any American involvement with assassination would mean encouraging the Afghan resistance to engage in all-out assaults against the Red Army, rather than selectively going after the Soviet commanders and "advisers.". . .

Moralistic Complaints

One is left with the suspicion that the moralistic complaints against secrecy, or against the unpleasant necessities of counterterrorism and of the war against Soviet-sponsored proxies in Central America, are nothing more than excuses for abandoning any serious attempt by the United States to fight back. If the critics both in and out of Congress are not prepared to support armed struggle against enemy proxies, whether in Central America or in the shadowy realm of the terrorist war, so be it. But they should not be permitted to hide sanctimoniously behind the current rationalizations for refusing to do anything effective against a dangerous challenge to the interests and security of the United States.

"Counterterrorism [is] U.S. doublespeak for official state terrorism in the service of U.S. interests."

Covert Operations Are Terrorism

Revolutionary Worker

The following viewpoint is taken from a report in The *Revolutionary Worker*, the weekly newspaper of the Revolutionary Communist Party, USA. In it, the author chronicles US counterterrorist efforts in Central America and the Middle East and argues that the use of such tactics is immoral. The US, he writes, has a long history of covert operations in other countries and each time it has used them to quell needed revolutions.

As you read, consider the following questions:

1. How was US counterterrorism used in Vietnam, according to the author?
2. Describe some of the methods the author claims are used by the CIA.
3. After reading this viewpoint and the previous viewpoint, do you believe the US should pursue counterterrorism? Why or why not?

Excerpted from, "A Special Type of Soldier," in the February 3, 1986 issue of *Revolutionary Worker*. Reprinted with permission.

Among the war cries developed amid the Great American Terrorist Mania have been renewed calls for more and greater U.S. "counterterrorism." Projected here is increased use of the beefed-up "Special Forces"—or, as *Time* magazine called them in a recent article, "a warrior elite for the dirty jobs." *Time* noted that "unorthodox struggles require a special type of soldier: bold and resourceful, often trained in the black arts of stealth and sabotage, suitable for an elite unit that can vanish into alien terrority or strike anywhere with speed and surprise." Training others in the "black arts" required for "dirty jobs" is also a part of the story here. *Time* states: "To train friendly forces in the art of guerrilla warfare, the army has sent hundreds of teams to 60 nations in the past six years—more than twice as many as it sent overseas during a comparable period in the 1970s." The administration is also seeking, under the Central American Counterterrorism Act (which the Senate Foreign Relations Committee passed last year by a 15-1 vote), funds, training, and equipment for the notorious political police agencies in Central America, which have long been known as the official homes of the region's "death squads" and torture chambers. This is "counterterrorism"—U.S. doublespeak for official state terrorism in the service of U.S. interests.

Vietnam

This is not new. U.S. "counterterrorism" has a sordid and bloody history, dating back to the 1960s. There is one well-documented case (revealed in 1971 Congressional hearings) where the term "counterterror" was officially used—Vietnam. U.S. Army Special Forces troops, under the operational direction of the CIA and its "Special Operations Division," used "assassinations, abuses, kidnappings, and intimidation," according to one former foreign service officer. . . .

The "counterterror" operation worked like this: a "blacklist" (often called a "greenlist") was drawn up, with three accusations from any sources sufficient to target an individual as either "VCI (Viet Cong Infrastructure) cadre" or "VCI suspect." Then, the "CT teams" (referred to as "Provincial Reconaissance Units") were put into operation. In some cases, these teams were deployed in the countryside to attack the target, often executing her or him on the spot. In other cases, a "cordon and search" operation was carried out, where all the inhabitants of a village would be rounded up and their identities checked against the list. Those discovered were either executed on the spot or returned to the base compound for a number of torture sessions designed to extract information, after which they would be executed. According to the Congressional testimony of former U.S. officers, the "counterterror" operation also installed a body quota system, with prize money awarded for live or dead "VCI" brought into headquarters. Many of those killed or captured were women and children, since these were the easiest "targets" for the teams to hit. According to the South Vietnamese government, this U.S. "counterterror" program killed almost 41,000 civilians in a little over three years, although the actual number of people assassinated and executed through this operation will probably never be known. [Former CIA director William] Colby described the "counterterror" operation as necessary "to protect the Vietnamese people against terrorism."

Central America

While official documents revealing other specific instances where such U.S. "counterterror teams" were put into operation remain classified, there is no doubt that the doctrine and methods of "counterterrorism"—or U.S.-sponsored terrorism in the guise of "combating terrorism"—has been an integral part of the U.S. arsenal since the early 1960s. One area where U.S. "counterterrorism" has been applied for over twenty years is Central America, particularly Guatemala and El Salvador. . . .

The Price of Intervention

Our government is pursuing an interventionist foreign policy that involves the United States in disputes across the globe. We are flouting the very international institutions and laws that once gave our involvement legitimacy. As citizens we are thus put at risk, personally vulnerable to the abhorrent weapons of the weak—terror, kidnaping, suicidal assault. We have been blessed that such terror has not yet come to our shores. No technological fix, no retaliatory strikes can protect us. We must bear the price or change the policy.

Robert Borosage, *Los Angeles Times*, July 4, 1985.

"Counterterror" was one of the main planks in the U.S. program of "counterinsurgency" initiated in the early 1960s in a desperate effort to stem the tide of national liberation struggles. Generally accompanied by a program of imperialist development, such as the Alliance for Progress in Latin America, "counterinsurgency" sought to prop up the U.S.'s neocolonial regimes against real and potential uprisings from the oppressed masses. To that end, Military Assistance Programs and Public Safety programs funneled weaponry, training, advice (and direct orders), and U.S. Special Forces troops, policemen and agents in large numbers to the armies and police agencies of the U.S.'s neocolonies. The point of all this was to defeat existing revolutions and intimidate and terrorize any who might harbor thoughts of joining or starting one.

"Counterterrorism" was part of the plan from the very beginning. Indeed, the infamous "death squads" had their origins in U.S. "counterterrorism." For example, declassified documents show that in 1962, a U.S. Special Forces Mobile Training Team, headed by General William Yarborough, was sent to Colombia to determine the "counterinsurgency" needs of the government there. In a "Secret Supplement" to the team's report to the Joint Chiefs of Staff, Yarborough wrote:

> It is the considered opinion of the survey team that a concerted country team effort should be made now to select civilian and military personnel for clandestine training. . . . This should be done with a view toward development of a civil and military structure for exploitation in the event the Colombian internal security system deteriorates further. This Structure should be used to . . . as necessary execute paramilitary, sabotage, and/or terrorist activities against known Communist proponents.

Practice of Counterterrorism

Together with the theory of U.S. "counterterrorism" came the *practice*. In El Salvador, it was initiated with the formation of the official paramilitary network ORDEN (democratic nationalist organization) whose *orejas* ("ears"), mostly military reservists, spied on the population in nearly every town and village in the country. By the late 1960s ORDEN was conducting armed attacks on opposition party meetings, demonstrations, and strikes—as well as foreshadowing later "death squad" activity; in one incident, ORDEN "disappeared" two leaders of the national teachers union; their mutilated bodies were found later. By the mid-'70s, "death squad" activity was rampant in El Salvador. The FALANGE (Anti-Communist Liberation Armed Forces) took credit for a series of assassinations, mutilations, and "disappearances" of political and union activists, while the UGB (White Warriors' Union) specialized in committing the same atrocities against liberal and radical activists, within church groups. The communiques of both groups reflected not only their obvious close links with the Salvadoran security forces, but also the U.S.'s doctrine of "counterterror." For example, one FALANGE communique stated, "The public must understand that this organization will act outside the limits of the law for the good of the population itself, and for its freedom. . . .

In Guatemala, the big leap in U.S. "counterterrorism" occurred in the mid-'60s, with a pattern of "disappearances" and murders throughout the country, "death lists" circulated widely, mass graves, and numerous photographs of multilated bodies in the press complete with descriptions of police efforts to identify the bodies, not to find the murderers. This is because it was well known that the atrocities were carried out under the direction and control of the state repressive apparatus. U.S. specialists in such matters certainly knew it. For example, a Rand Corp. expert attributed the Guatemalan government's "success" in "counterinsurgency" to, in large part, "the utilization of paramilitary civilian groups" and the "psychological impact of terror tactics."

The direct connection between U.S. military aid to these countries and the spread of state terrorism remains hidden in the vaults containing the many documents that the U.S. still refuses to declassify. Nevertheless, the involvement is readily apparent. In El Salvador, the U.S. military mission was actually headquartered in El Salvador's military headquarters and dispensed training and "advice" essentially *within* the military. In addition, Mobil Training Teams were shuttled in and out on a regular basis for specialized training. It is also no coincidence that a big leap in the murder and mutilation of civilians as well as the deployment of regular Salvadoran army units as assassination squads (in addition to the previously used "irregular" and police forces) occurred after 1980, at the same time that the U.S. vastly increased its military aid and military "advisors" to El Salvador. . . .

A Mask for CIA Terrorism

One of the themes of the current calls for more U.S. "counterterrorism" stresses the importance of improving intelligence. This also has a certain history in Central America. While the documents pertaining to U.S. Army Intelligence remain classified, the involvement of the CIA and the Agency for International Development (AID) through the Office of Public Safety and police intelligence has been amply demonstrated. In both El Salvador and Guatemala, such activity involved the creation or special presidential intelligence agencies, the coordination of these agencies with other police agencies in the country, and the coordination of such intelligence between the various countries through the U.S. military headquarters in Panama. In Guatemala, the central agency set up by U.S. advisors was eventually moved into an annex within the Presidential Palace and became the nerve center for "counterterror" assassination activities generally attributed to "death squads" or "vigilantes." In El Salvador, U.S. advisors developed intelligence networks based on the work of the paramilitary ORDEN and set up the agency that eventually became ANSESAL (the Salvadoran National Security Agency). ANSESAL, the former home of the notorious Roberto D'Aubuisson, has been accused of being the nerve center for the activity of the Salvadoran "death squads" by various former Salvadoran and U.S. officials. U.S. Public Safety advisors also worked on the intelligence networks and lists of the Treasury Police, National Police, National Guard, and Immigration Police—all of whom have earned worldwide notoriety for "death-squad" atrocities. Certainly, the importance of intelligence in developing hit lists for the "death squads" cannot be underestimated. In 1981, the Press Council for the Armed Forces released such a list of "subversives" and "terrorist bandits"; it was identical, including in the random order of the names, to a list that had circulated in El Salvador the year before attributed to the "death squads."

227

Another key aspect of CIA involvement in previous U.S. "counterterrorism" in Central America took the form of providing training to internal security/political police agencies, with the training taking place in either the U.S., their own, or another country. "Interrogation" was one of the subjects—and it is undoubtedly no coincidence that, according to Edward S. Herman in *The Real Terror Network*, human torture came into widespread and *institutionalized* use in the period of the '60s and '70s, having previously been essentially an aberration. Indeed, by the mid-1970s, 80 percent of Amnesty International's "urgent cases" of torture were coming from nineteen Western hemisphere countries and twelve others also in the U.S. "sphere of influence."

Building and Making Bombs

There were other CIA-taught subjects that are also relevant to this discussion. For example, at the Border Patrol Academy in Los Fresnos, Texas, the CIA taught something called the "Technical Investigations Course" to cops from Central and South America. The course included work with "Terrorist Devices; Fabrication and Functioning of Devices; Improvised Triggering Devices; and Incendiaries," and another session on "Assassination Weapons: A discussion of various weapons that may be used by the assassins." Practical training was given in how to build and use various explosive devices. And the AID, under whose auspices the course was delivered, admitted that the purpose of the course had nothing to do with *defusing* the bombs, but rather how to build and make use of them. More extensive CIA training in these and other "counterterror" matters was delivered within the various countries.

This discussion of previous U.S. "counterterrorism" in Central America should, of course, in no way be considered an exhaustive report. There are numerous specific instances that have been documented, and there is undoubtedly still a wealth of documentation of more horrible U.S. atrocities still locked up in the vaults. Furthermore, such other vital aspects of U.S. "counterinsurgency" as peasant massacres, massive aerial bombardment, opening fire on demonstrators, etc.—all of which are certainly just as terroristic as the crime the U.S. officially designates as "counterterrorism"—have not been covered. Still, from this very partial report of U.S. "counterterror" activity in a couple of countries, it can be clearly seen that any U.S. efforts to "combat terrorism" can only mean that even more of the U.S.'s blood-drenched terrorism will be brought down on the masses.

Distinguishing Between Fact and Opinion

This activity is designed to help develop the basic reading and thinking skill of distinguishing between fact and opinion. Consider the following statement as an example: Terrorism cannot be eliminated easily. This is a fact with which few people would disagree. Terrorism's persistence is evidence of this. However, consider another statement: Swift, sure retaliation against terrorist states can easily wipe out terrorism. Such a statement is clearly an expressed opinion.

When investigating controversial issues it is important to be able to distinguish between statements of fact and statements of opinion.

The following statements are taken from the viewpoints in this chapter. Consider each statement carefully. *Mark O for any statement you believe is an opinion or interpretation of facts. Mark F for any statement you believe is a fact. Mark I for any statement you believe is impossible to judge.*

If you are doing this activity as a member of a class or group, compare your answers with those of other class or group members. Be able to defend your answers. You may discover that others will come to different conclusions than you. Listening to the reasons others present for their answers may give you valuable insights in distinguishing between fact and opinion.

If you are reading this book alone, ask others if they agree with your answers. You too will find this interaction very valuable.

O = *opinion*
F = *fact*
I = *impossible to judge*

1. Some governments will undoubtedly use CIA intelligence to stifle dissent.

2. If the US is going to be serious about dealing with the terrorist threat to its national interests, it has to realize that there is no clean way to fight its enemies.

3. Most politically-motivated murders of US citizens in recent years have come as a result of terrorism abroad, not at home.

4. Some people argue that terrorism can involve the regular armed forces of sovereign states.

5. Violent deeds conducted by surrogates are preferable to direct US involvement.

6. The only legitimate source of power is the free electoral process.

7. Guatemala by itself is more of a terrorist problem than the entire Soviet network.

8. A Soviet satellite is a government, country, or organization that, while ostensibly independent, is in truth firmly controlled by the Soviet government.

9. The main objective of the leaders of the resistance in Afghanistan is to frighten the population and provoke unrest.

10. Reagan's approach, intensifying the US presence around the globe, will just intensify the problem of anti-US terrorism.

11. The Sandinistas overthrew the US-allied Somoza government.

12. Many statistics regarding the Soviets' war on Afghanistan vary widely from source to source and most are simply estimates.

13. Moscow cares nothing for Afghans, only for the physical territory of Afghanistan.

14. The Afghan resistance often commits major acts of sabotage to coincide with revolutionary and national holidays, festivities, and other important dates.

15. The contras in no way represent a democratic influence on Nicaraguan politics.

16. Qaddafi was not installed in power with significant or decisive assists from the United States.

Periodical Bibliography

The following list of periodical articles deals with the subject matter of this chapter.

Jerome Greer Chandler	"Terror in the Sky," *American Legion Magazine*, October 1985.
William L. Chaze	"Reagan's Hostage Crisis," *U.S. News & World Report*, July 1, 1985.
William L. Chaze	"Time for Weighing the Lessons," *U.S. News & World Report*, July 15, 1985.
Charles Colson	"Terrorism's 'Catch-22,'" *Christianity Today*, January 17, 1986.
Conservative Digest	"Improved Intelligence Is the Key," February 1984.
Anthony H. Cordesman	"Who Glorifies Terrorism? We Do," *Los Angeles Times*, March 28, 1986.
Brian Crozier	"How NATO Became Important," *American Legion Magazine*, June 1986.
Brian Crozier	"The Protracted Conflict: Response to Terrorism," *National Review*, February 14, 1986.
Samuel T. Francis	"Dealing With Terrorists: A Stronger U.S. Policy is Needed," *Conservative Digest*, November/December 1984.
David Gergen	"The Brave in the New World," *U.S. News & World Report*, July 1, 1985.
Robert E. Hunter	"Blundering Militarily From One Dilemma to Another," *Los Angeles Times*, April 16, 1986.
Robert E. Hunter	"Terrorism: Fighting Fire with Fire," *Los Angeles Times*, May 14, 1985.
Geoffrey Kemp	"Policies to Deter Terrorism," *Los Angeles Times*, July 7, 1985.
Robert H. Kupperman and David Williamson Jr.	"Fighting Terrorism With Violence Isn't a Solution—It's an Invitation," *The Washington Post National Weekly Edition*, December 17, 1984.
Lewis H. Lapham	"Imperial Masquerade," *Harper's*, July 1986.

Walter Laqueur	"The Future of Intelligence," *Society*, November/December 1985.
Walter Laqueur	"A Decisive Tool of Foreign Policy," *Society*, November/December 1985.
Flora Lewis	"The Big Bark," *The New York Times*, July 7, 1985.
Martin E. Marty	"Vengeance and the Roots of Retribution," *Los Angeles Times*, June 7, 1985.
Charles William Maynes	"Neither Conciliation Nor Toughness Is the Answer to Terror," *Los Angeles Times*, June 30, 1985.
Robert D. McFadden	"Terror in 1985: Brutal Attacks, Tough Response," *The New York Times*, December 30, 1985.
Daniel Patrick Moynihan	"Nurturing Terrorism," *Harper's*, March 1984.
The Nation	"High Cost of 'Firm Action,'" December 7, 1985.
The New Republic	"Terror Firma," November 19, 1986.
Newsweek	"Getting Even," October 21, 1985.
Kevin Phillips	"From Force, A Question of Consequences," *The New York Times*, April 20, 1986.
Norman Podhoretz	"Reagan—a Pitifully Crippled Hawk," *Los Angeles Times*, June 26, 1986.
Robert M. Sayre	"International Terrorism: A Long Twilight Struggle," *Department of State Bulletin*, October 1984.
George Shultz	"Terrorism: The Problem and the Challenge," *Department of State Bulletin*, August 1984.
Abraham D. Sofaer	"Terrorism and the Law," *Foreign Affairs*, Summer 1986.
Joel S. Sorkin	"The Piratical Ensigns of Mahomet," *National Review*, March 28, 1986.
Mark Whitaker, et al.	"Ten Ways to Fight Terrorism," *Newsweek*, July 11, 1986.

Book Bibliography

Paul Bew and Henry Patterson	*The British State & the Ulster Crisis: From Wilson to Thatcher.* Norfolk, Great Britain: The Thelford Press, 1985.
Zbigniew Brzezinski and Robert Kupperman	*The International Implications of the Papal Assassination Attempt: A Case of State Sponsored Terrorism.* Booklet available from The Center for Strategic and International Studies, 1800 K Street NW, Washington, DC 20006.
Zev Chafetz	*Double Vision: How the Press Distorts America's View of the Middle East.* New York: William Morrow and Company, 1985.
Ray S. Cline and Yonah Alexander	*Terrorism: The Soviet Connection.* New York: Crane, Russak & Company, 1985.
Ray S. Cline and Yonah Alexander	*Terrorism as State-Sponsored Covert Warfare.* Fairfax, VA: Hero Books, 1986.
Helena Cobbar	*The Palestine Liberation Organization.* New York: Cambridge University Press, 1984.
John K. Cooley	*Libyan Sandstorm: The Complete Account of Qaddafi's Revolution.* New York: Rinehart & Winston, 1982.
Martha Crenshaw, ed.	*Terrorism, Legitimacy, and Power: The Consequence of Political Violence.* Middletown, CT: Wesleyan University Press, 1983.
Mike Davidow	*Afghan Diary.* Moscow: Novosti Press Agency Publishing House, 1984.
Christopher Dickey	*With the Contras: A Reporter in the Wilds of Nicaragua.* New York: Simon & Schuster, 1986.
James Downey	*Them & US: Britain-Ireland and the Northern Question.* Dublin: Ward River Press, 1983.
Ernest Evans	*Calling a Truce to Terror.* Westport, CT: Greenwood Press, 1979.
Facts on File, Inc.	*Counterattack: The West's Battle Against the Terrorists.* New York: 1982.
William Regis Farrell	*The U.S. Government Response to Terrorism.* Boulder, CO: Westview Press, 1982.

Elizabeth Warnock Fernea and Robert A. Fernea	*The Arab World: Personal Encounters.* New York: Doubleday, 1985.
Franklin L. Ford	*Political Murder: From Tyrannicide to Terrorism.* Cambridge, MA: Harvard University Press, 1985.
John F. Galliher and Jerry DeGregory	*Violence in Northern Ireland: Understanding Protestant Perspectives.* New York: Holmes and Meier, 1985.
Roberta Goren	*The Soviet Union and Terrorism.* Boston: George Allen and Unwin, 1984.
Jonathan Harris	*The New Terrorism: Politics of Violence.* New York: Julian Messner, 1983.
Helsinki Watch and Asia Watch	*To Die in Afghanistan.* Available from Helsinki Watch, 36 W. 44th St. New York, NY 10036 or Asia Watch, 739 8th St. SE Washington, DC 20003, December 1985.
Kevin Kelley	*The Longest War: Northern Ireland & the IRA.* Westport, CT: Lawrence Hill & Co., 1982.
Robert Kupperman and Darrell Trent	*Terrorism, Threat, Reality, Response.* Stanford, CA: Hoover Institution Press, 1979.
John Langone	*Violence: Our Fastest Growing Health Problem.* Boston: Little, Brown, & Co., 1984.
Neil C. Livingstone and Terrell E. Arnold	*Fighting Back: Winning the War Against Terrorism.* Lexington, MA: Lexington Books, 1986.
Carlos Marighella	*The Terrorist Classic: Manual of the Urban Guerrilla.* Chapel Hill, NC: Documentary Publications, 1985.
James B. Motley	*US Strategy to Counter Domestic Political Terrorism.* Washington, DC: National Defense University Press, 1983.
Conor Cruise O'Brien	*The Siege: The Saga of Israel and Zionism.* New York: Simon & Schuster, 1986.
Stefan T. Possony and L. Francis Bovency	*International Terrorism: The Communist Connection.* Washington, DC: American Council for World Freedom, 1978.
Steve Psinakis	*Two Terrorists Meet.* San Francisco: Alchemy Books, 1981.
Uri Ra'anan, ed., et al.	*Hydra of Carnage: The International Linkages of Terrorism and Other Low-*

Intensity Operations. The Witnesses Speak.
Lexington, MA: Lexington Books, 1985.

David C. Rapoport
and Yonah Alexander

The Morality of Terrorism: Religious and
Secular Justification. New York: The
Pergamon Press, 1982.

Gayle Rivers

The Specialist: Revelations of a
Counterterrorist. New York: Stein and Day,
1985.

Alex P. Schmid and
Janny de Graaf

Violence as Communicator: Insurgent
Terrorism and the Western News Media.
London: Sage Publications, 1982.

Michael Sheane

Ulster & the British Connection. Stockport,
Great Britain: Highfield Press, 1979.

Soviet Press Reports

Terrorism: An Instrument of US Foreign
Policy. Moscow: Novosti Press Agency
Publishing House, 1983.

Claire Sterling

The Terrorist Network. New York: Holt,
Rinehart & Winston, 1981.

Robin Wright

Sacred Rage: The Wrath of Militant Islam.
New York: Simon & Schuster, 1985.

Index

Achille Lauro hijack, 48, 210
  as unjustified, 120
Afghanistan
  and Soviet occupation
    as desired by Afghans, 169
    as terrorism, 159-166
    need for US intervention, 134,
      164
    number of casualties in,
      161-162
  rebels
    as freedom fighters,
      159-166
    as terrorists, 167-174
    violence justified, 23
African National Congress, 23
Ahmad, Eqbal, 58
al-Hasan, Bilal, 176
Anderson, Bill, 62
Arafat, Yassir,
  as manipulated by the West,
    115-116
  as Soviet surrogate, 150

Baker, Russell, 195
Ball, George, 204
Beeman, William O., 215
Bernstein, Dennis, 139
Blitt, Connie, 139
Borosage, Robert, 225
Bradford, Nora, 105
Brandeis, Louis D., 177
Bush, George, 131, 185

Calero, Adolfo, 142
Callejas, Alfonso Robelo, 142
Central Intelligence Agency
  (CIA), 216
  as terrorist, 130-131, 227-228
  in Afghanistan, 169-173
  in Nicaragua
    as terrorist, 138-139, 140
  tactics
    as necessary, 221-222
    public repugnance to,
      219-220
Chamorro, Edgar, 137
Cline, Ray, 220
Cole, Stephen V., 28, 199

Commager, Henry Steele, 175
contras
  as freedom fighters,
    142-144
  as murderers, 139
  as terrorists, 137-141
  respect human rights, 143-144
  US should support, 220-221
Cruz, Arturo José, 142
Cuba, 153
  as Soviet surrogate, 148-149
  involvement in Angola,
    153-154

Dean, Morton, 77
democracy
  as vulnerable to terrorism,
    198-199
  as false, 185
dictators
  as terrorists, 29
DiScala, Spencer, 115
Dostoevsky, Feodor, 57
Dupree, Louis, 162

Eagleburger, Lawrence, 203

Feehan, John M., 96
Francis, Samuel T., 145

Gorbachev, Mikhail, 165
government oppression
  as cause of terrorism, 87-
    88, 97, 99-101, 114, 117,
    129
  as false, 53, 54, 55
Graham, Katharine, 75
guerrillas
  as terrorists, 194-195
    as false, 93, 94
Gvozdev, Yuri, 156

Haidar, Gulam, 169-170
Hearst, Patty, 64
Herman, Edward S., 152, 228
Hitler, Adolf, 93
  as terrorist, 29
Hubbard, David G., 26, 30
Hunter, Robert E., 24

Ireland
    as two nations, 109-110
        fallacy of, 99-100
    Northern, *see* Northern Ireland
Irish Republican Army (IRA), 19
    and media publicity, 72
    and terrorism
        as justified, 96-104
        as unjustified, 106-112, 200
        as freedom fighters, 23, 97-98
        as supported by the people,
            104
        as murderers, 106
    drug connections, 108-109,
        112
    PLO connections, 110
    Soviet connections, 109
    US support of, 200
        as immoral, 107-109, 110,
            111, 112
    see also Northern Ireland
Islamic fundamentalism, 31-32
Israel
    actions against terrorism,
        195
        as correct, 189, 202
        as wrong, 205
    US support of
        as right, 201
    violence against Palestine, 199

Jackson, Henry, 94, 199-200
Jansen, G.H., 117
Jenkins, Brian Michael, 191
Johnson, Paul, 11
just war tradition
    terrorism violates, 92-93

Kemp, Geoffrey, 133
Kennedy, John F., 50
Kidwell, Kirk, 149
Kirk, Richard M., 63, 66
Kirkpatrick, Jeane J., 119
Klass, Rosanne, 161
Krauthammer, Charles, 39, 73
Kupperman, Robert H., 33

Laqueur, Walter, 157
Latin America, 19
Ledeen, Michael, 218
Libya
    as independent of the Soviet

Union, 154-155
    as terrorist state, 19, 37
    bombing of
        and Western allies, 23

Maynes, Charles William, 217
McGurn, William, 57, 90
media
    and need to expose terrorist
        grievances, 212
    and need to report terrorism,
        75-87
    as cause of terrorism, 69-74
        as false, 77
    as democratic necessity, 81
    as manipulated by CIA,
        138-139
    in Northern Ireland
        as censored, 99, 104
        manipulation by terrorists,
            79-80
    publicity of terrorism
        negative, 32, 35
Michaels, David, 132
Middle East
    Soviet role in, 150
    terrorism, 19, 49
        need to resolve, 217
    US policy in
        as taking sides, 24
Mossad (Israeli Secret Service),
    115, 116

Netanyahu, Benjamin, 183
Netanyahu, Benzion, 51
Nicaragua
    Cuban involvement in, 149
    US involvement as terrorism,
        132
Nidal, Abu, 113, 120, 217
NORAID (Irish Northern Aid
    Committee), 110, 112
Northern Ireland
    British occupation of
        as inciting terrorism,
            97-104
        as wanted, 106-110
    percentage of deaths by ter-
        rorism, 106
    religious struggle, 99-100

O'Brien, Conor Cruise, 74

O'Sullivan, John, 69
Oppenheimer, Martin, 86

Paisley, Ian, 105
Pakistan
    as training Afghan rebels,
        168-169
    skimming of Afghan aid, 163
Palestine Liberation Organization
    (PLO), 54
    as failure, 205-206
    as Soviet surrogate, 149-150
    splinter groups of, 19
Palestinian
    cause, 49
        not justification for ter-
            rorism, 121-122
        hatred of the US, 114
        need to recognize, 217
Price, Raymond, 211, 213

Qaddafi, Muammar, 37, 91, 155

Rand Corporation, 216
Reagan, Ronald, 131
    as inciter of terrorism, 176
    as terrorist target, 114
    position on terrorism is
        wrong, 23-24, 129-132
    support for the contras, 144
Red Brigades, 65
retaliation
    as counterproductive, 28-29,
        59, 194
    as ineffective, 48, 49
    need for, 197-203
Revel, Jean-Francois, 161
Rothenberg, Elliot, 209
Rowan, Carl T., 49

Sadat, Anwar, 200
Sandinistas, 138
    as insincere, 143-144
Sands, Bobby, 98
Sartre, Jean Paul, 40
satellite
    defined, 148
Savimbi, Jonas, 134
Schorr, Daniel, 79
Shi'ites, 19, 50
    as unjustified, 40-41
    cause desperate, 129-130

Shultz, George P., 30, 94, 134,
    197
    position on terrorism, 197-203
    criticized, 205-208
Siemsen, Henry S., 66
Singlaub, John K., 35
Sobran, Joseph, 135
South Africa, 158
    violence justified, 23
Sowell, Thomas, 65, 66
Starr, Oliver Jr., 165
state-sponsored terrorism, 129,
    194
    as cause of terrorism, 59, 186
    US, 132
Sterling, Claire, 67, 155, 157
Stockwell, John, 153
surrogate
    defined, 148

Taylor, John, 105
terrorism
    as attack on civilians, 91-92
    as community based, 216
    as crime, 26-32
    as dispensing fear, 184-185
    as form of warfare, 194
    as inexpensive, 35, 36, 67
    as justified, 86-89
        as never justified, 90-95,
            199
    as political violence, 34, 40,
        198
    as self-defeating, 81
    as serious threat, 17, 34, 38,
        91, 198
    causes of, 17
        as lies, 40-41, 51-57
        as unimportant, 31, 63,
            211-212
        economic, 62-68
        government oppression,
            58-61, 87-88
        media, 69-74
            fallacy of, 75-81
        political, 18
    deaths caused by, 63
        as insignificant, 27
    definition of, 88-89
        as inaccurate, 86
        as murder, 40-42, 53
        as political terrorism, 16-21

238

as too broad, 23
as war, 33-38
eliminating
  as impossible, 191-196
  as possible, 183-190
  need for
    covert operations,
      218-222
      as reprehensible,
        223-228
    military action, 188-189
    retaliation, 185-186,
      197-203
      as ineffective,
        204-208
    stricter penalties,
      209-214
    will not help, 215-217
goals
  as irrelevant, 119-122
  as relevant, 48
historical roots of, 207
international, 34
Middle East
  as justified, 113-122
need for audience, 76, 79
no effective way to eliminate,
  216
political motivation
  as not terrorist, 22-25
superpower involvement in
  as both guilty, 176-177
  US, 128-136
  USSR, 145-158
terrorist
  as a fraud, 53
  as committed, 219
  as criminal, 70
  as freedom fighter, 47-50, 136
    differences in, 23
    myth of, 53-54, 200
  as inept, 30
  as murderer, 73, 120
  as oppressor, 56
  as primitive, 30, 31, 56
  as virtuous, 216-217
  attacks
    logic to, 30-31
    on US, 20
    incidents
      Achille Lauro, 48, 49,
        120, 210

TWA Flight 847, 32
manipulation of the media,
  70-71, 79-80
need for death penalty,
  211-214
  as unnecessary, 215-217
need for power, 65, 66, 67
self-interests of, 63-68
state-sponsored, 18-19
US support of
  as immoral, 128-132
  as unnecessary, 133-136
Thatcher, Margaret, 76
Third World
  population of, 17
totalitarian governments
  as terrorists, 29

US
  actions in Lebanon
    as negative, 23-24
  as supporter of IRA terrorism,
    107-109, 110, 111, 112
  as terrorist, 158, 224-228
  as vulnerable to terrorism, 20,
    36
  courts
    as soft on terrorism, 211
  in a state of war, 136
  intervention in Nicaragua, 226
    as negative, 25, 140-141
    as positive, 142-144
  involvement in terrorism, 176
  need to support Afghanistan,
    164
  need to support covert oper-
    ations, 218-222
  policy on terrorism, 20-21
    as ill-considered, 23, 91
    as right, 201-202
  support of Israel
    as bad, 88
    as right, 201
USSR
  as sponsor of terrorism, 56,
    145-151
    myth of, 38, 152-158
  involvement in Afghanistan
    as terrorist, 159-166
    as wanted, 167-174
  involvement in Nicaragua,
    149

use of surrogates
    as false, 153
    as true, 148-150
Ustinov, G., 167

Vice President's Task Force on
    Combatting Terrorism, 16, 23
Vietnam
    US terrorism in, 224-225
vigilantism, 88
violence
    as legitimate warfare, 102,
      114
    as right, 23, 25
    defined, 97

Walzer, Michael, 95
Waziri, Ahmed, 169
Weir, Benjamin M., 48
Wheeler, Jack, 159
Wright, Robin, 47

Yelin, Lev, 171